# The Pemigewasset Valley

# A History

*Also by Daniel Heyduk*

Huayrapampa

Meredith Chronicles

Stories in the History of New Hampshire's Lakes Region
and Pemigewasset Valley

The Story of Franconia Notch

# The Pemigewasset Valley

## A History

## Daniel Heyduk

ISBN 9781727455588

Kindle Direct Publishing

This book is complete in itself. It also can be read as a companion to
*Stories in the History of New Hampshire's Lakes Region and
Pemigewasset Valley* by the same author.

Front cover illustration: "Plymouth Intervale," by Robert Wilkie,
Courtesy of the Trustees of the Boston Public Library, Louis Prang &
Company Collection

*To the Heyduk and Pola Families*

# Contents

7

# Introduction

In the past, the name "Pemigewasset" carried some powerful emotional associations: danger, adventure, opportunity, power, beauty, escape, wonder, and fragility. Some of these associations still come to mind when one hears mention of the river or its valley, but for the most part, today's Pemigewasset has lost its old identity and meaning. One can travel the Pemigewasset Valley along Interstate 93 and occasionally glimpse the river or see its name posted on signs at high bridges, but the roadway and its exits have replaced the old river landmarks as main points of reference.

The Pemigewasset River, with the Merrimack, forms the central axis of New Hampshire, aligning with a major pass through the White Mountains at Franconia Notch. For thousands of years the river and its tributaries were the means of travel and of sustenance for Native Americans. Then these waterways became the route followed by hostile raiders of the "Indian Wars," and by hunters and trappers who risked their lives in the "no-man's land" between warring French and English America. Even during those hostilities, the river carried surveyors who marked boundaries of newly-granted towns along the river bank and in the seemingly endless forest.

Settlers followed the river to cut openings in the forest and establish farm homes and water-power mills. Rich alluvial river terrace soil grew their crops as it had the Native Americans' corn, beans and squash. Soon the Pemigewasset and its feeder streams were powering saw and grist mills, but also carrying mills and bridges away in seasonal high water and periodic great floods. Lumbermen used waterways far up the Pemigewasset's watershed to float pine, fir, and spruce logs downstream to their mills. Towns grew where water supplied power for industry, and railroads made use of easy-gradient river valley routes to carry goods and people in and out. Artists and tourists arrived to appreciate the beauty of the river and its surrounding mountains, especially along the upper Pemigewasset and in Franconia Notch. Summer lodgings in the valley and nearby mountains were sought for their health benefits by thousands escaping the big cities.

The river itself was dammed and tapped for electricity. It received the waste of industry, the raw sewage of towns and resort hotels, and the sediment-laden run-off from logged mountain slopes. Public outcry later moderated logging, industry declined and disappeared, and legally-mandated wastewater treatment restored the valley and its river. Canoes and kayaks now run the Pemigewasset's alternating quiet water and rapids, and children swim from sandy riverside beaches. Many stories are to be found in the Pemigewasset Valley's eventful, but often forgotten history, and they are the reason for this account.

## *The Pemigewasset Valley in This Book*

The Pemigewasset River has three sources: at Profile Lake in Franconia Notch, in the vast White Mountain basin drained by its East Branch, and in streams descending the slopes of mounts Moosilauke and Kinsman on the west. The main stream runs south for some seventy miles to meet the Winnipesaukee River, where their combined flows become the Merrimack, and continue to the Atlantic Ocean. The Pemigewasset's main stem touches fourteen towns, which make up its valley, while three more outlying towns are linked closely to the valley historically. It is these seventeen towns that make up the Pemigewasset Valley history in this book. From south to north, they are:

| | |
|---|---|
| Franklin | Campton |
| Sanbornton | Thornton |
| Hill | Waterville Valley |
| New Hampton | Woodstock |
| Bristol | Lincoln |
| Bridgewater | Franconia |
| Ashland | Bethlehem |
| Plymouth | Sugar Hill |
| Holderness | |

Of the towns away from the Pemigewasset's main stem and valley, Waterville Valley lies east on the tributary Mad River. It depended - and still depends - on the Pemigewasset Valley for transportation connections and supplies, thus sharing a common history. Bethlehem and Sugar Hill lie north of the Pemigewasset's drainage, but they have played a major role in the history of Franconia Notch, as will be seen.[1]

## Acknowledgements

In preparing this book, I wanted to draw as fully as possible on the historical contributions of the valley's own people. I am indebted to many historical societies, and historians both past and present, in towns in the Pemigewasset area:

Franklin – Helen LaPlante Duchesne, Albert G. Garneau, Mary A. Proctor, and Moses Thurston Runnels

Sanbornton – Evelyn Corliss Auger, Roberta Yerkes Blanshard, Mildred L. Coombs, Joshua Lane, Moses Thurston Runnels, Millie Shaw, Faith and William Tobin, and the many active members of the Historical Society

Hill – Carol Snow-Asher, Nancy I. Chaddock, George Haig, Lucy Natkiel, Marie Stanley, and the many contributing authors of the Historical Society

New Hampton – Kent Bicknell, Thomas S. Curren, Carole and Robert Curry, Gordon DuBois, John Gowan, Pauline Swain Merrill, Jinga Moore, Kathy Neustadt, Patricia Slesinger, and the dedicated Historical Society

Bristol – Charles E. Greenwood, John McV. Haight, Jr., Lucille Keegan, Richard W. Musgrove, and the Bristol Historical Society

Bridgewater – Thomas S. Curren, Judith Faran, John McV. Haight, Jr., and the town Historical Society

Ashland – David Ruell, the Ashland Historical Society and the Ashland Centennial Committee

---

[1] The towns of Rumney, Wentworth and Warren on the tributary Baker River have been covered in Joseph Bixby Hoyt's book (see bibliography).

Plymouth – Roland Bixby, Cynthia Cutting, Rebecca Enman, Richard Flanders, Katherine Hillier, Joseph Bixby Hoyt, Louise McCormack, Mary Anne Hyde Saul, Eva A. Speare, Ezra S. Stearns, the Museum of the White Mountains at Plymouth State University, and the very active Historical Society

Holderness – Margie Emmons, George Hodges, Margaret Howe, Susan Bacon Keith, Patty Sue Salvador, and the Holderness Historical Society

Campton – Brenda Boisvert, Marjorie Broad, Frank Oliver Carpenter, John Dole, Virginia Stickney Erickson, Alan Hill, Nancy Mardin, Robert Mardin, Patrick O'Bannon, Gray & Pape, and the dedicated Historical Society

Thornton – Marjorie Broad, Richard T. Holmes, Gene E. Likens

Waterville Valley – Grace Hughes Bean, Brenda and Preston Conklin, Arthur L. Goodrich, Nathaniel L. Goodrich

Woodstock – Frank Oliver Carpenter, Mike Dickerman, Ida Sawyer, the Woodstock Bicentennial Committee and the Upper Pemigewasset Historical Society

Lincoln – Mike Dickerman, Bill Gove, James Everell Henry II, Rick Russack, the Upper Pemigewasset Historical Society and WhiteMountainHistory.org

Franconia – Karl P. Abbott, Jeremy K. Davis, Kimberly A. Jarvis, Frances Ann Johnson, Andrew H. McNair, Megan McCarthy McPhaul, Rick Russack, William B. Swett, Sarah N. Welch, and Aria Cutting Roberts.

Bethlehem – Karl P. Abbott, Mike Dickerman, and the Society for the Protection of New Hampshire Forests

Sugar Hill – Arthur A. March, Jr., Esther Tefft Serafini

I also drew on the work of historians Kent Bicknell, Joseph Bixby Hoyt and Bryant Tolles, who covered broader areas. I was fortunate to have access to the extensive collection of the Museum of the White Mountains, and help by Cynthia Cutting and Rebecca Enman, and to resources of the Lamson, Moultonborough, State, Pease, Thornton, and Sanbornton libraries. Guide book authors Thomas Starr King, Moses Sweetser and Frank O. Carpenter described the valley at the time of their writing. Archaeologists Richard Boisvert, Mark Doperalski and David Trubey of the New Hampshire Division of Historical Resources gave me information and images. The New Hampshire State Archive provided records. Patrick O'Bannon of Gray and Pape and James Gage of Powwow River Books shared images from their files. The Mount Kearsarge Indian Museum, Robert S. Peabody Institute of Archaeology, and Shelburne Museum granted permission to use items from their collections. Larry Sullivan shared his research on the region's drinking fountains. Many people kindly gave me their time and advice, loaned me hard-to-get material, shared documents and images, made referrals, and offered meetings.

My wife Beverly traveled with me to exhibits and presentations, patiently bore my schedule of research and writing, and with my son Andrew and daughter Robin, proof-read and critiqued the manuscript.

## A Guide for the Reader

This book is complete in itself, but it also can be read as a companion to *Stories in the History of New Hampshire's Lakes Region and Pemigewasset Valley*. The two books together cover a larger area, while each provides more depth on particular topics.

Readers who are thoroughly familiar with the Pemigewasset River and its watershed may wish to skip Chapter 1. The nature of the river and configuration of the valley were important to historical events, so the first chapter's descriptive tour is intended as both orientation and explanation.

After a picture of Native American life in and around the valley in Chapters 2 and 3, Chapter 4 catalogs the almost simultaneous granting and settlement of the Pemigewasset's towns, and Chapter 5 describes the settlers' challenges and adventures. Chapter 6 and those which follow are a portrayal of the progressive, and sometimes sudden, changes that people of the valley experienced – a story of many twists and turns, with some particular scenes presented as windows to the times.

This is a regional history, drawing on many sources. Those who are interested in more detail on individual towns will find sources of that history in the bibliography, and at very helpful town historical societies.

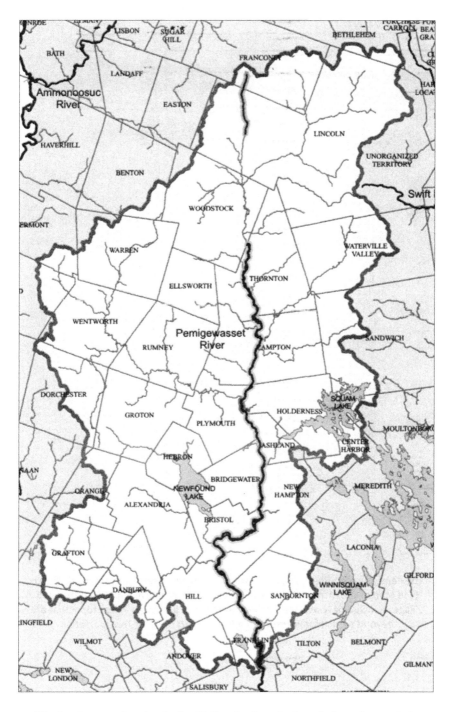

The Pemigewasset watershed, with the river's main stem darkened, except at Woodstock, showing tributaries and towns. *NH Dept. of Env. Services*

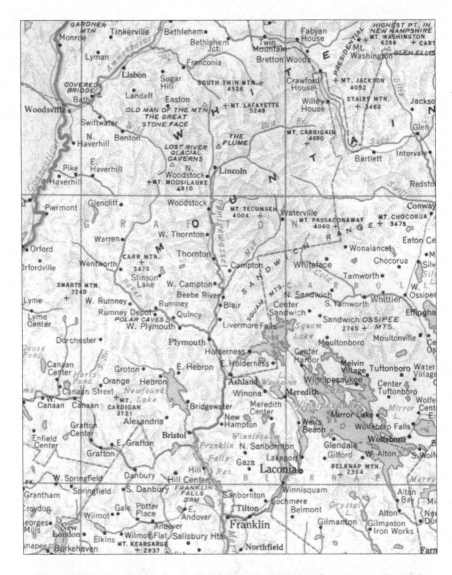

The Pemigewasset River is shown flowing N-S in dark gray, from Franconia Notch (Old Man of the Mtn) in the north to Franklin in the south, with tributaries and villages – including those of Franconia, Bethlehem and Sugar Hill at top – that are beyond the Pemigewasset's headwaters. *NH Dept. of Transportation*

*Chapter 1*

# The Setting

Landforms, drainage, soil and rock, the forest, and other physical factors had much to do with what happened in the Pemigewasset Valley, both for the original Native Americans and for successive waves of occupants. Whether one was hunting, fishing and growing food with stone-age tools, or building a recreational resort, the land had a significant impact on what was done.

The Pemigewasset River has its beginnings in Franconia Notch, a narrow, glacially-carved valley where mountains rise to over 5,000 feet from the 1,500 – 2,000 foot level of the valley floor. Water flows swiftly by many streams down from the mountain ridges, and through numerous cascades and waterfalls. The high point of the Notch floor lies between Echo Lake, which drains to the north, and Profile Lake, which is the source of the south-flowing Pemigewasset.

From Echo Lake, the north-descending floor of the Notch opens to a plateau and rolling hills on the north, where rivers drain west to the Connecticut River valley. While it lies outside the Pemigewasset River drainage, this area provides the northern access to the Notch, the Pemigewasset Valley, and lands to the south.

Flowing south through Franconia Notch, the Pemigewasset River descends from Profile Lake through a series of shoots, pools and potholes, among which are the "Basin" and "Pool" scenic sites. It flows beneath Cannon Cliff, which rises 1,000 vertical feet, and continues below the former location of the "Profile," or stone face of the "Old Man of the Mountain" high on the west side of the Notch. Descending further, the Pemigewasset passes the "Flume," a 20 foot wide, 60 foot high vertical-sided cleft that was eroded by water running off the Franconia Range on the Notch's east side (McNair 1949: 11).

In Franconia Notch the Pemigewasset flows through shoots and pools, and carves potholes in the bedrock. *D. Heyduk*

Leaving the Notch, the Pemigewasset continues south, where it is joined at Woodstock by its even longer East Branch. The East Branch drains an over 70,000 acre basin surrounded by many peaks of the White Mountains (Gove 2012: 61). Water entering from the East Branch more than doubles the volume of the main stem (National Park Service 1996: 4).

Looking south over Echo Lake into Franconia Notch: "Echo Lake, Franconia Mountains, New Hampshire" by Sylvester Phelps Hodgdon. *The Athenaeum*

The forested East Branch is a swift-flowing, high volume river, rocky in summer and ice-choked in winter. *D. Heyduk*

The Pemigewasset's West Branch, or Moosilauke Brook, also joins the main stem at Woodstock. Following glaciations, it was responsible for cutting through the jumbled rock formations of today's "Lost River" scenic site in Kinsman Notch. Draining the high slopes of Moosilauke and Kinsman mountains, it augments the main river even more.

Carved by the West Branch, or Moosilauke Brook, Lost River is a deep gorge of potholes and tumbled rocks. *D. Heyduk*

The Pemigewasset's Franconia Notch main stem and East and West branches have rocky, narrow beds enclosed by forest, but where they join, the gradient moderates and the valley widens. At Woodstock the river follows a winding channel cut through many terraced sand and gravel deposits from the last Ice Age. It erodes its banks in a more level and open landscape, but the valley is still enclosed by mountains on its east and west sides. Before entering Thornton, the river flows narrowly once again though the encroaching mountains. Fed by streams and rivers flowing out of those mountains in Thornton, the Pemigewasset Valley widens once more, but still does not offer ready travel access to the east or west.

Rivers joining the upper Pemigewasset from the east drain considerably more territory than those flowing from the west. Hubbard Brook, which drains a 12 square mile valley on the west, is some 6 to 7 miles long, while the Mad River on the east drains 61 square miles and runs for 18 miles from Waterville Valley down to the Pemigewasset (White Mountain National Forest 1997: III-14). The Beebe River in Campton on the east is almost 17 miles long. All streams feeding into the Pemigewasset carry runoff from high slopes and cause the main stem to rise rapidly following heavy rain, rapid snowmelt, or at times - both together.

After the Pemigewasset passes the Beebe River it begins to downcut more rapidly, and enters a narrow rocky gorge ending in the 50 foot drop at Livermore Falls - the largest waterfall along its length. Below the falls the Pemigewasset resumes its moderate, winding course through Holderness, until it is joined by the Baker River flowing from the west.

The Baker is some 36 miles long, reaching upstream to the west and north as far as Mount Moosilauke, and draining 214 square miles. Its valley is wide and its volume high, so that when it reaches the Pemigewasset north of Plymouth Village, the combined rivers have a wide floodplain. Here there is fertile, though flood-prone land. The Baker valley offers the first easy travel route west from the south-flowing Pemigewasset.

An alluvial plain continues on the Pemigewasset's west side for a few miles south of Plymouth, where it next receives outflow from the Squam River on the east. The Squam, which drops along its course through Ashland, carries the combined outflows of Squam Lake, Little Squam Lake and White Oak Pond. Squam Lake alone occupies over 10 square miles and the discharge into the Pemigewasset is considerable. This is the first point along the Pemigewasset's course from Franconia Notch where convenient travel to the east is available.

The Pemigewasset drops through Livermore Falls at Campton. *D. Heyduk*

Below Sawhegenit Falls the river flows between sandy banks. *D. Heyduk*

At its convergence with the Squam River the Pemigewasset drops some five feet over Sawhegenit Falls, before continuing its course south. The riverside terraces are higher here. For a time after melting of the ice sheet some 14,000 years ago, the Pemigewasset Valley was a lake extending as far north as Plymouth. Terraces along this part of the river contain extensive sand deposits from the old lake bottom (New Hampshire Dept. of Environmental Services 2019).

The Pemigewasset continues its southward run between Bridgewater on the west and New Hampton on the east. Here the valley is wide and the land is hilly east of the river and more mountainous west. For the first time in the Pemigewasset's course, it is blocked in the south by the mass of Hersey Mountain and White Oak Hill, and forced to flow west for some miles between New Hampton on the south and Bristol on the north. Here the banks are steep and there are rapids, which continue intermittently as the river runs west and then turns south again. Just after the southward turn, the Newfound River enters from the west. That river drains the lake of the same name, which at seven square miles in area and over 150 feet in depth, produces a strong flow. The Newfound River is only some three miles in length, but it drops steeply over that course. The Pemigewasset's rapids continue as it passes White Oak Hill to the east.

After passing the outlet of Blake Brook, which drains 2,000 foot-high Hersey Mountain on the east, the Pemigewasset flows around islands and is joined by the Smith River on the west. The Smith is 25 miles long and carries a large volume of water, plunging over 40 foot-high Profile Falls before it joins the Pemigewasset.

As the Pemigewasset continues south, the valley opens and wide terraces appear along its west bank at the Town of Hill. The terrace soil is fertile, but vegetation reflects a history of frequent flooding. Here Needle Shop Brook enters from the west, dropping from higher land above the floodplain. On the east bank the land rises steeply to Hersey Mountain in Sanbornton, drained by Prescott and Knox brooks. The Pemigewasset enters Franklin and drops over Eastman Falls in an area of floodplain, especially on its east side. There the Winnipesaukee River approaching from the east flows through a double oxbow before joining the Pemigewasset. In that complex meeting of waters – from Franconia Notch in the north, and from Lake Winnipesaukee in the east – the Pemigewasset and the Winnipesaukee become the Merrimack and continue to the Atlantic Ocean.

The Pemigewasset's rapids upstream from Blake Brook. *D. Heyduk*

The quiet Pemigewasset south of Blake Brook outlet (at bottom). *D. Heyduk*

The Pemigewasset Valley is a finger of milder climate between the bordering hills and mountains. As such, it has a great variety of vegetation types – from the deciduous forest of ash, butternut, oak, beech, maple and birch typical to the south, to the northern forest of spruce and fir. Even in the southern part of the valley where mountains are 2,000 feet high, as one climbs the slopes, the forest changes from predominantly deciduous to mixed deciduous-coniferous above 1,500 feet elevation. In Franconia Notch, the floor of the valley is at 1,500 feet and the bordering mountains rise to over 5,000 feet, but even here there is deciduous forest at the bottom of the slopes. From 2,500 to 4,000 feet above sea level, spruce and fir dominate; from 4,000 to 4,500 one finds fir, paper birch and mountain ash; above that is the alpine zone of scrub fir and spruce; and finally, tundra (Kostecke 1975: 28).

The Pemigewasset historically had major spawning runs of fish: shad ascended the Merrimack from the ocean, and continued into the Winnipesaukee River. Atlantic salmon and American eel ascended further up the Pemigewasset and its tributaries, successfully passing Livermore Falls. The river contains brook and brown trout, yellow perch, chain pickerel, common shiner and longnose sucker (Federal Energy Regulatory Commission 1990: 3-13).

A great variety of birds use the Pemigewasset Valley and the several forest communities on its slopes. Waterfowl use the Pemigewasset and its related water bodies and wetlands. Turkeys are common. Mammals, from moose and bear to deer, beaver and other fur-bearers are present in good numbers.

The natural features included in this chapter have been described without mention of their role in the Pemigewasset Valley's history. They will appear again at various points in the valley's story where their influence comes to bear. Readers may wish to refer back to this description as needed.

*Chapter 2*

# Paleoindians and the First Farmers

Native Americans treaded lightly on the land and left few signs of their more than 10,000 year occupation. In addition, later arrivals chose the same locations in which to settle, farm, and erect their buildings, disturbing earlier remains in the process. Thus, our knowledge of the first people in the Pemigewasset Valley is not as complete as one would hope.

The first people to visit present-day New Hampshire were nomadic hunters who pursued herds of caribou and other grazing animals on the tundra landscape of some 12,000 years ago. Prior to 14,000 years ago the Pemigewasset Valley had been buried under a slow-moving, mile-high ice sheet that scraped the land. As the glacier melted back to the north, an infant Pemigewasset River carried large quantities of meltwater laden with sand, rock and other debris. This material settled on the bottom of a long lake that occupied the Pemigewasset Valley below Plymouth and on the bottoms of ponds such as today's Quincy Bog in Rumney. Samples of sediment taken from the bog (Doner 2013) and other similar locations show a progression of emerging plant life from lichens to more abundant mosses, herbs, grasses and wildflowers – a tundra environment. The tundra was attractive to herds of grazing mammoth, musk oxen and caribou and to the large prehistoric bears, wolves and cats that preyed on the grazers. Also moving through this landscape were people – called "Paleoindians," who hunted and camped as they followed the migrating herds.

Although the ice sheet had melted from New Hampshire by 13,000 years ago due to warming of the climate, there was a renewed surge of cold from 12,900 to 11,600 years ago known as the "Younger Dryas," which brought the tundra and its animals back south, allowing the newly-arrived

Paleoindians to make their nomadic living.[2] Archaeological sites from southern to northern New Hampshire offer a picture of their lifestyle, which was based on hunting primarily caribou and moving with the herds. The Paleoindians quarried smooth-fracturing chert and rhyolite from which to make their spear points, knives, hide scrapers, awls and other tools for hunting, butchering, turning hides into clothing and tent material, and working bone, antler and wood. They obtained this highly valued stone from as far away as northern Maine, indicating the extent of their travels. Their most emblematic artifact was a long, lance-like spear point, made of fine-grained stone, and expertly chipped to shape – sometimes with a channel running down its middle, to help mount it to a spear shaft. The hunters also would have used an *atlatl*, or spear-thrower: a hand-held stick or bone with a hook at the end that fitted into a socket at the base of the spear. This extended the hunter's arm, giving his throw greater force.

Archaeological sites show where Paleoindians camped briefly in their migrations: on higher ground above rivers, streams, lakes and wetlands – overlooking the likely routes followed by their prey. Indications are that their groups were small, perhaps just a few families. It is likely that people stayed in groups for safety from the other predators that pursued caribou and larger grazers. Sites excavated thus far are south and north of the Pemigewasset Valley, but not in the valley itself (Boisvert 2013). As the hunters followed their migrating prey, a valley migratory route or a route crossing the valley would have been necessary to bring them here. There have not been many archaeological excavations in the valley, and notably not in the appropriate locations, so evidence is simply lacking.

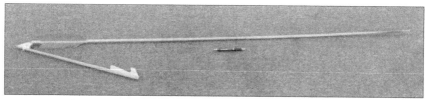

A modern atlatl and light spear. *Robert S. Peabody Institute of Archaeology. D. Heyduk*

---

[2] This is a summary of longer descriptions in Caduto 2003: 51-68, Eusden and Thompson 2013: 1-22, and Heyduk 2017: 11-15

A Paleoindian 5-inch spear point from the Conway valley shows expert chipping and removal of the central channel flake for hafting to a spear shaft. *Richard Boisvert*

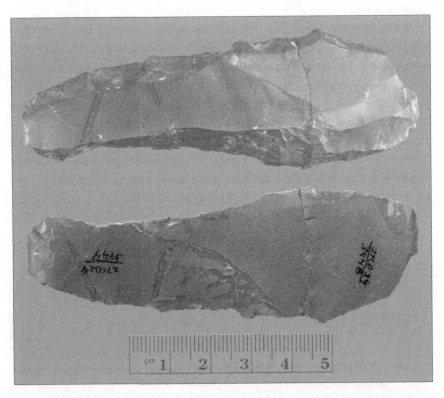

A stone flake that has been chipped for use as a knife or scraper. *Richard Boisvert*

The Younger Dryas climate period ended some 11,600 years ago and temperatures climbed. The tundra environment moved north and its animals followed it, while some became extinct. In the Pemigewasset Valley trees such as spruce, alder, fir, birch, jack and red pine began to grow. After 10,000 years ago oak entered the area, and by 8,000, hemlock, beech and white pine. With the forest came a new lifestyle for people of the valley, one based on hunting forest animals and wildfowl, fishing, and collecting a variety of wild edibles. This period is known archaeologically as the "Archaic."

Archaic people camped in one place for longer periods of time than did the Paleoindians. They moved camp in a seasonal round to take advantage of resources that were available at different times and in different places. Shellfish were an important part of their diet. They hunted moose, deer and smaller animals with different stone points on their spears, and built fish weirs and used nets to catch fish – especially during times when the salmon, eels and shad were running the rivers. They trapped beaver and other fur-bearers for food and pelts. Archaic folk used natural rock basin mortars to grind wild nuts and berries. They used dug-out canoes to travel the area's waters, and at some point they developed the birch bark canoe, which could be carried around rapids and waterfalls and from one water body to another. An advantage of the birchbark canoe was that it could be built and repaired almost anywhere, using bark of white birch, black spruce roots for stitching, bent spruce or white cedar for shaping and sheathing the inside, ash or maple for the thwarts and paddles, spruce for the top rails, and spruce gum for sealing the seams.

The Archaic hunters and gatherers chose campsites near water for the variety of resources available there and for ease of transportation. There is evidence of their camps at the joining of the Winnipesaukee and Pemigewasset rivers, along the Pemigewasset's terraces, at the Smith and Newfound rivers, where the Squam and Baker rivers join the Pemigewasset, at Livermore Falls, and along terraces of the upper river. A well-known canoe portage trail ran from the Pemigewasset at Blake Brook east and then north to rejoin the river along its east-west course in New Hampton. This "long carrying place" allowed travelers to avoid the rapids around Bristol and to follow a shorter north-south route through a valley between White Oak Hill and Hersey Mountain.

A birch-bark canoe, showing internal sheathing and ribs, thwarts, top rails, and outer birch-bark sealed with spruce gum. *Mount Kearsarge Indian Museum*

Archaic folk used a wide variety of natural foods and medicines, but they did not produce any. Hunting, fishing and collecting around their home territory met most of their needs and trade between groups supplied what was lacking. Trade was especially important for the specialized stone used to make tools and weapons, which was available only in certain quarries. Those who could reach a quarry broke the raw rock into "blanks," which were easier to carry and to trade. Then the blanks were fashioned into tools, either by the quarrymen or by those to whom they traded them. Decorative items also were traded. Fish runs, when several groups came together at prime fishing spots such as the Winnipesaukee-Pemigewasset confluence, Sawhegenit Falls and Livermore Falls, were opportunities for socializing and trade. By these and similar get-togethers, goods moved about the region.

Beginning some 3,000 years ago, change came to the Pemigewasset Valley: the growing of food – corn, beans and squash, the making of pottery, and use of the bow and arrow. Also around this time, ground stone tools started to be used and tobacco-smoking pipes appeared (Caduto 2003: 134-142)(Starbuck 2003: 74-90). This period is known by archaeologists as the "Woodland" time, and it was the way the Pemigewasset Valley's historically-known Abenaki people lived for many years prior to European contact. The old patterns of hunting and gathering continued, and innovations were added as appropriate. Agriculture, for example, was less dependable in the upper valley and it may be that people there relied upon it less.

Good land for growing crops was the same land that had been preferred for camps: valley terraces, especially the larger terraces where two rivers met. Woodland farmers did not clear land as Europeans later would, because their stone tools were not very useful for cutting down large trees. Instead, they girdled or burned the trunks of trees as they simultaneously burned the understory. They then planted among the trunks each spring "when oak leaves are the size of a squirrel's ear," putting kernels of their 8-row "Indian Corn" in the sun-warmed ground along with beans and squash. When production began to decline, the process was repeated in a new piece of forest. Ceramic pots went along with farming, being useful for cooking corn and beans, and especially helpful for dry, animal-proof storage of produce. Woodland agriculture disturbed the land very little, limiting erosion and hastening re-growth of the forest. Former Woodland village sites therefore left few signs: just pottery shards, shells, stone tools, hearths and charcoal.

Agriculturally-supported villages were larger and more permanent than Archaic camps had been. People thrived and the population grew. Tribal organization under chiefs emerged. Thus it was until Europeans arrived around 1600.

This stone hearth was excavated in 2019 at Livermore Falls. From fish bone and associated charcoal, it appears that the stones were heated with fire, then covered with sticks, and the fish cooked on top. The charcoal yielded a date of some 2,700 years ago. *Excavation and information: NH Division of Historical Resources. D. Heyduk photo*

31

A pottery fragment. *Richard Boisvert*

PLATE XVI.   The reverse side of the inscribed stones.   Note No. 20 which shows the map of the river at Odell Park and the two points of land.

Inscribed stones found in the oxbow of the Winnipesaukee River in Franklin by Mary Proctor, who called them "amulets." This was an important fishing site, and because of the stones' holes and necks, they may be sinkers for fishing nets. Stone no. 26 shows two shad. *Proctor 1930. Courtesy of Powwow River Books*

Detail of a Woodland Period riverside terrace settlement, with family dwellings and a longhouse. *Shattuck Farm Diorama, © Robert S. Peabody Institute of Archaeology, Phillips Academy, Andover, MA. All Rights Reserved*

Ground stone axes with a channel for hafting to a handle. *Robert S. Peabody Institute of Archaeology, D. Heyduk photo*

*Chapter 3*

# Abenaki and Colonists

In the spring and summer of 1614, Captain John Smith sailed what would become the Maine, New Hampshire and Massachusetts coast in a small fishing boat (a shallop) accompanied by his Native American guide Tisquantum (who would later be the Pilgrim's "Squanto"), and a small crew. They sailed close along the land with the purpose of mapping its landmarks and harbors. At the village of Accomac where they landed to meet Tisquantum's people, there were "fortie or fiftie" men-at-arms of a total population much larger still (Lawson 2015: 129-131). Six years later, in 1620, the Pilgrims landed at the same place – Plymouth - and found it deserted with unburied skeletons on the ground. The first of many plagues had decimated Native Americans who had no immunity to European diseases like smallpox, influenza, measles, diptheria and typhoid. Periodic epidemics swept through New England, reducing the native population – including the Abenaki of the Pemigewasset - to as little as ten percent of its former size (Starbuck 2006: 92).

In the Pemigewasset Valley, Abenaki villages that are known from their archaeological remains were abandoned as survivors gathered together in a few remaining settlements, Penacook (Concord) being one, and Aquadoctan (The Weirs) being another. A village on the Baker River at Plymouth probably continued to be occupied. Those who remained were able to continue their traditional lifestyle and language, while they also traded furs with the English and French, learning those languages as necessary. Beaver pelts were in such high demand that beaver were mostly eliminated from New Hampshire. Goods that the Abenaki obtained via trade included brass and copper items, clay tobacco pipes, knives, hoes, beads, fire-arms, gun flints, lead shot, iron axes, and kettles.

While the Abenaki population had plummeted, English settlements to the south were growing. There were confrontations between English settlers and Abenaki, as there were with other tribes all around the rim of expanding English occupation. In 1675 King Philip's War, named for a Wampanoag chief, erupted along this wide front, and English settlements were attacked and burned. The Abenaki of the upper Merrimack and the Pemigewasset remained neutral, but with defeat of the hostile tribes in 1676, they were under even more English pressure. From this time on, families began to move to Canada, where the French welcomed them.

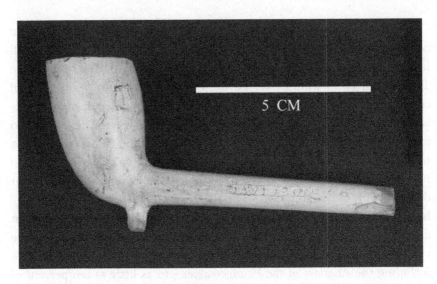

A clay tobacco pipe excavated at Livermore Falls. *Photo by Mark Greenly, Courtesy of NH Div. of Historical Resources*

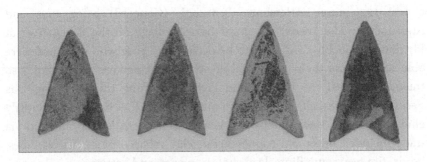

Arrowheads made from European trade brass. *Richard Boisvert*

War also began and continued intermittently between the French in Canada and the English in New England: King William's War (1688-97), Queen Anne's War (1702-13), King George's War (1740-48), and the French and Indian War (1754-63) (Borneman 2006: 6-11). English towns were attacked via the Baker, Pemigewasset and Merrimack rivers, and Abenaki settlement in the Pemigewasset Valley became ever less secure, especially after 1724, when the Massachusetts government offered a bounty of 100 Pounds for every Native American scalp presented to it.

The first record of the Baker-Pemigewasset route being used to take captives north (for ransom) was in 1689 after a raid on Dover. In 1711-12, Lieutenant Thomas Baker, who himself had been carried to Canada as a captive and escaped or was ransomed, led a company of "rangers" up the Connecticut River and down to the Baker Valley via Oliverian Notch. In March, 1712, they descended the Baker until they came upon an Abenaki village where the Baker joins the Pemigewasset. As they did not see many men (who were probably away fishing or hunting), Baker's men fired into the village. The few residents fled and rangers ransacked the settlement, seizing furs and burning the dwellings. When the Abenaki men returned, there was a battle in which their chief, Waternomee, is said to have been killed (Hoyt 1990: 31-37, Speare 1988: 7). Baker's party then retreated hastily down the Pemigewasset, using the long-established Native American trail on its west side. Baker's rangers are reported to have received 20 Pounds bounty in Massachusetts "for two enemy Indians by them slain" (Stearns 1987: 6).

Despite such prior hostilities, an Abenaki named Coaus visited Portsmouth in 1743 to ask that a trading post be established in the Pemigewasset-Merrimack area. He said that at least fifteen Abenaki would trade furs there. Governor Wentworth chose Canterbury, and the provincial assembly voted funds for rum, blankets, cloth for stockings, shirt linen, powder, shot, bullets and flints, pipes and tobacco to stock the post. The project ended when hostilities renewed in 1744 and the Pemigewasset Valley once again became hostile territory.

On a 1751-52 winter trapping trip, John Stark, Amos Eastman, William Stark and David Stinson of today's Manchester area collected many furs during nominal peacetime on land of the Baker Valley. They were ready to return home when they were attacked by a party of Abenaki. Attempting to escape with their furs, Stinson was killed and Amos Eastman and John

Stark were taken as prisoners to Canada. William Stark escaped to report the tragedy (Hoyt 1990: 43-44) (Speare 1988: 7).

In 1754, five members of the Meloon family of today's Franklin were captured, as well as two hunters near Newfound Lake (Hoyt 1990: 46). About that time, Robert Fletcher was surveying the boundaries of the newly-granted town of New Chester (today's Bridgewater, Bristol and Hill) when he came upon a hastily-vacated camp with the campfire ashes still warm. According to proprietors' records, "being frightened by Indians he run the [survey] line no further . . . making ficticious boundaries." The proprietors later finished the survey themselves in peacetime (Curren 1988: 11).

Many military expeditions entered the Pemigewasset Valley, including Captain Peter Powers' foray in June of 1754. He wrote:

> . . . some of the men went in the canoes and the rest on the shore . . . to the crotch [Franklin oxbow] and then up the Pemigewasset about one mile, and camped above the carrying place, which . . . is about one hundred rods long [one third of a mile].

This portage trail ran along the east side of the Pemigewasset from the oxbow, avoiding the rapids at Eastman Falls. Powers' men then ascended the Pemigewasset to Smith River, and camped a bit north at Blake Brook. On June 19 he recorded:

> We marched on our journey and carried across the "long carrying place" on Pemigewasset River two miles north east, which land hath a good soil, beech and maple, with a good quantity of large masts [pines].

Soil was judged by the trees growing on it, and beech and maple indicated good soil. White pines that were straight and tall were reserved to become masts for the Royal Navy, and hence Powers was indicating those trees. He described re-launching canoes into the Pemigewasset where it runs E-W, then paddling east and turning north upriver to Sawhegenit Falls, where they portaged about four rods (less than 100 feet), probably where the Bridgewater town park is today. From the falls, they paddled two miles to "Pemigewasset interval," perhaps the terrace on the west bank, and then four miles more of "extremely crooked" river to camp "on a narrow point of land." The next day:

> *We steered our course one turn with another, which were great turns, west, north-west, about two miles and a half to the crotch or parting of the Pemigewasset river, at Baker's river mouth; thence from the mouth of Baker's river up said river north-west by west, six miles. This river is extraordinary crooked, and good interval* [fertile floodplain]. *Thence up the river about two miles north-west, and there we shot a moose, and the sun about a half an hour high, and there camped* (quoted in Musgrove 1904: 25-26).

Powers continued on, but did not find any Abenaki, who by that time were resident in Canada, and making just brief forays into their old homeland. While the French and Indian War raged, the Pemigewasset Valley was a no-man's land which neither side could occupy securely. In 1760, the English seized Quebec and the French failed to recapture it, finally finishing the war. French control of Canada ended by treaty in 1763. That opened the way for towns to be settled by colonists from the south who were anxious for new land. Many former Abenaki village sites, as at the Winnipesaukee oxbow and the Smith and Newfound rivers, had been abandoned since the plagues of the 1600s and even their last settlements were returning to forest by the time the new settlers arrived. It seemed to the newcomers that they were entering a wild land.

# Chapter 4

# New Towns in the Valley

British control of Canada from 1760 put an end to hostile French and Abenaki incursions into the Pemigewasset Valley, while the many English military expeditions through the area had offered an enticing glimpse of its resources. Even though some towns had been granted before and during hostilities, actual settlement had not progressed beyond Salisbury on the Merrimack. For war-weary English colonists the valley went from being a place of danger to being a place of opportunity. A great many things were about to happen in a very short time.

The economy of the time was agricultural and farm families were large, eight or more children being the rule. Single men and women could not operate farms, so young people married early in order to start farming, and then were anxious to have children. While warfare dominated the first six decades of the 1700s, the rapidly growing population in already-settled towns created a demand for new land that could not be satisfied inside the defensible, but static frontier. New towns were created, such as Sanbornton - 1748, Holderness (including Ashland) – 1751, and New Chester (later Hill, Bridgewater, and Bristol) – 1753, and were even surveyed into lots, but were not settled until after 1760.

There were two sources of land grants: the "Masonian Proprietors," and the Royal Provincial Government of New Hampshire. The former were a group which had acquired a large grant made to John Mason in 1629, to include all land between the Piscataqua and Merrimack rivers and running inland along those rivers for 60 miles. The vague inland boundary between the two rivers was interpreted by the Proprietors to include the lower Pemigewasset Valley, and they then made smaller grants to groups of petitioners who wished to create towns. The grantees were required to settle their land within a certain period of time or forfeit the grant. Once land granted by the Masonian Proprietors was settled, residents could petition the provincial government for a charter and become an official town of the Province of New Hampshire. Sanbornton and New Chester were Masonian land grants which later obtained charters and officially became towns.

At the same time, Royally-appointed Governor Benning Wentworth also was making grants of land in the Province of New Hampshire, presumably beyond the grants made by the Masonian Proprietors. Wentworth's grants also required that settlement be made within a set time, and if those requirements were met, included a town charter. The Town of Holderness was created in this way, as were other non-Masonian towns in the valley.

In order to be settled, towns had to be surveyed into lots which could be sold. Demand for land was strong enough that both the Masonian Proprietors and the governor chose to have lots set aside for themselves in the new towns that they had granted. They were hoping to sell those lots to anxious farmers and thereby earn a profit on the land they had granted. The burden of developing a new town by paying for a land survey and for building the first roads and mills fell upon the group of investors who had obtained the land grant, and who were "proprietors" of the new town. The town proprietors, also hoping to sell land, divided the remaining lots among themselves and assessed themselves for development costs. Thus, the Masonian Proprietors and governor held lots in a town which they could sell, but they passed all development expense to the proprietors of the newly granted town. The lots owned by the Masonian Proprietors and governor also were exempt from taxation.

Despite such strategic financial planning by the Masonians and Governor Wentworth, the return on their real estate investment was realized only slowly. Many empty lands had been granted as new towns outside the Pemigewasset Valley, and in the remainder of the valley too, after 1760: Campton - 1761, Holderness – 1761, Plymouth - 1763, Thornton - 1763, Woodstock - 1763, Franconia - 1764, Lincoln - 1764, and New Hampton - 1765. Town proprietors in all those towns were competing to attract settlers, and actual settlement did not grow as quickly as had been expected. Factors such as the proprietors' religion, and their willingness to work and spend, also affected the speed of settlement.

Settlers coming into an essentially wild and empty land faced many challenges, as individual histories of Pemigewasset Valley towns amply attest.

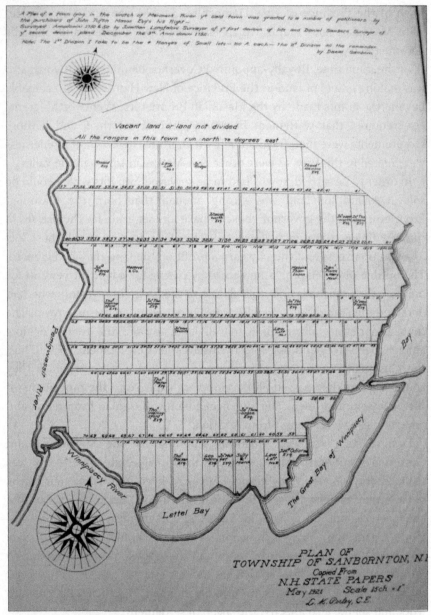

The survey of Sanbornton, showing E-W ranges of lots with "rangeway" roads running between. The Pemigewasset River is on the west and the Winnipesaukee River is on the south. The steep Hersey Mountain area at top was left as common land.
*Sanbornton Historical Society*

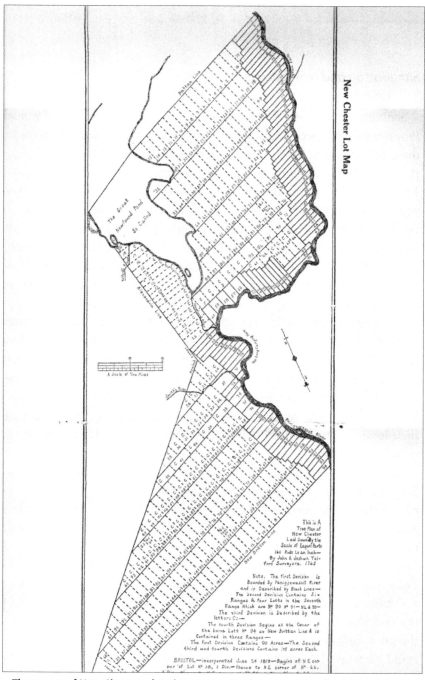

The survey of New Chester, showing narrow Pemigewasset riverfront lots at right.
*E.P.Musgrove in Haight, Jr. 1941: 32-33*

## Sanbornton and New Chester

Sanbornton and New Chester were on land granted by the Masonian
Proprietors, and needed to meet the Proprietor's requirements in order for
the grant to remain valid. In April of 1748, sixty men of Exeter petitioned
the Masonian Proprietors to grant them thirty–six square miles of land.
They planned to begin the town (Sanbornton) "the first year after we have
peace with our French and Indian enemies." The petitioners then paid to
survey a boundary which ran north along the Pemigewasset River from its
confluence with the Winnipeasukee River for some six miles, then northeast and south-east over Hersey Mountain to Great Bay (Lake
Winnisquam), south and south-west along that lake, and then west along
Little Bay and the Winnipesaukee River back to the Pemigewasset.

The grant was made in December, 1748, to be divided into 100 shares,
with one share for the "first Minister of the Gospel who shall be Settled on
the said Land," one share to support the gospel ministry, and one share to
support the school. Six acres were to be set aside for the meeting house,
school house, militia training field, burial ground, and other public uses.
Seventeen shares were to be reserved for the Masonian Proprietors (ie.
their lots), and the remaining 80 shares were to be divided among the 60
grantees, who became proprietors of the town.

In receiving the grant, the proprietors agreed to "make a Regular
Settlement there at their own Charge," and each to build a house
equivalent to eighteen feet long by fourteen feet wide, and clear three
acres "fit for Tillage or mowing within Eight Years." They must also build a
meeting house "fit for the Public worship of God" within ten years and
"maintain the Preaching of the Gospel there Constantly after twelve
Years." Twenty acres were to be set aside on some convenient stream for a
saw mill, the builder of which "Shall Saw the Loggs of the said Owners of
the said Shares & other Inhabitants there to the halves [ie. keeping half of
the sawn lumber as compensation] for the term of ten years." If no person
could be found to build and operate the saw mill, the grantees were to
arrange it at their own expense. Further, the grantees were to agree to be
assessed for any other expenses "necessary to make a Settlement."

The width of roads was stipulated, and an overall plan of lots and roads was to be delivered to the grantors at the grantees' expense. The "Seventeen Reserved Shares [of the grantors]" were to be "Exonerated acquitted and fully Exempted from paying any Charge towards making the said Settlement," and were not to be "Liable to any Tax or Assessment until Improved by the Respective Owners." Finally, "all White Pine Trees fit for his Majesty's use for Masting the Royall Navy [must] be . . . Reserved and . . . granted to his Majesty . . . for that Purpose." (Batchellor 1896: 234-238)

Following issuance of the grant in December, 1748, the town proprietors arranged to have the first 82 lots of 100 acres each surveyed in four E-W ranges by August, 1750, and an additional five ranges of lots surveyed by November, 1752. The Masonian and town proprietors then drew two lots each in February, 1753. The French and Indian War began in 1754 and lasted until the signing of a treaty in 1763, and no settlement took place, nor were any meetings held during those years. The opportunity had come to settle the town in 1763, but the town proprietors were mostly men of substance living comfortably near the coast who did not plan to clear wild forest, build a log cabin and pull stumps. They therefore offered 200 Pounds to each of the first twenty settlers who would clear land, build a house, and begin farming. Settlers arrived in 1764, but in the next year they petitioned the proprietors for aid due to their "inability to support their families by reason of the scarcity of provisions." The proprietors voted to give the petitioners 20 Pounds each.

By 1768, 32 families had settled and the residents of Sanbornton asked the provincial government for a town charter, which was granted in 1770. Thus did a Masonian land grant become a New Hampshire town (Runnels 1882: 34-50).

New Chester followed a similar route from Masonian land grant to town charter, but with some of its own peculiarities. The Masonian grant was made in 1753 to eighty-seven men, mostly of Chester, and was accordingly named New Chester. The terms required owners of lots to clear three acres, build and occupy a house, and contribute to building a meeting house, hiring a minister, and laying out roads. The Masonian Proprietors reserved twenty of 93 shares for themselves, which were to be free of any assessment until improved. Since making the Sanbornton and other grants, the Masonians apparently decided not to participate in a general drawing of lots, which included some lands much better than others, and instead reserved for themselves 500 acres of their own choosing. One inconvenience of the grant was that the town was nineteen miles long and in one place, only one mile wide. An advantage was that it contained much Pemigewasset riverfront on the fertile terraced west bank.

The inducement to the first ten settlers voted by the town proprietors was 120 Pounds each, with 80 Pounds to each of the next ten, and so forth until 40 settlers had arrived. It was at this time that Robert Fletcher was engaged to survey the boundaries, but failed to do so due to "being frightened by Indians" (Chapter 3). As in the case of Sanbornton, the French and Indian War intervened and no roads were created until 1762. Settlement did not begin until 1768, and then was slow to take place. The Masonian Proprietors therefore declared the New Chester grant forfeit in 1771 and sent an agent to evaluate the situation. He found only twenty-one settlers where there should have been forty under the terms of the grant (Musgrove 1904: 29-43). Historian Richard Musgrove looked into this situation and concluded:

> . . . the Masonian Proprietors appear to have taken no further action in regard to the forfeiture of the grant of New Chester. The grantees do not seem to have been at all disturbed, and continued to sell the lands as occasion presented. The settlement of the territory continued even during the time of the controversy . . .
> (Musgrove 1904: 43).

It was not until 1776 that the residents petitioned the New Hampshire provincial government for a charter, and then due to the Revolutionary War, it was not until 1778 that a charter was granted by the State of New Hampshire (Hammond 1883 Vol XII: 196-197). A charter allows for the election of officers and empowers them to act on behalf of the town, so this was a very important step, especially in wartime.

Sanbornton and New Chester show two paths from the seeking of new land to attainment of township status. The human drama in that process was only hinted at, but will emerge in later chapters. Other parts of the Pemigewasset Valley took different routes to becoming towns, routes that involved both grants of land and of town charters directly from the provincial government.

## New Hampton – The Moultonborough Addition

New Hampton lies north of Sanbornton on the east side of the Pemigewasset, but its origins are much further east. The Masonian Proprietors granted land for what would become the Town of Moultonborough in 1763, and the grantees then commissioned a survey which revealed that their grant contained much water of Lake Winnipesaukee and rocky upland of the Ossipee Mountains and Red Hill. They then petitioned the Masonians for more land, and were granted an additional tract running west to the Pemigewasset River. Both this new tract and the original Moultonborough grant were at the northern limit of the Masonian's vague boundary. Following granting of the neighboring Town of Sandwich by provincial Governor Benning Wentworth, the boundary between the two towns came into dispute and Moultonborough lost territory.

Jonathan Moulton, the lead Moultonborough grantee, then hoped to guarantee the Masonian's additional grant by making it a provincial grant as well. He is said to have presented a prize 1,400 pound ox, decorated with flowers and flags and led by two of his slaves, to Governor Wentworth along with the request that the governor make a grant of the additional land. The governor obliged by granting the Moultonborough Addition in 1765, thus assuring the integrity of that territory. The land was surveyed into lots and drawn by the Moultonborough proprietors. By attrition of deceased or inactive proprietors and by purchase, Jonathan Moulton eventually became owner of many of those lots (Merrill 1977: 15-20) (Heyduk 2017: 20-27).

Moultonborough then extended from the Pemigewasset River on the west to the extreme east shore of Lake Winnipesaukee, making a very unwieldy territory to administer. Therefore, when the residents of the Masonian Moultonborough grants applied in 1777 for provincial town status, they applied for two separate charters, one for Moultonborough in the east, and one for the Addition - which was named New Hampton - in the west. New Hampton thus became a town, but was further divided when Center Harbor became a town in its own right in 1797.

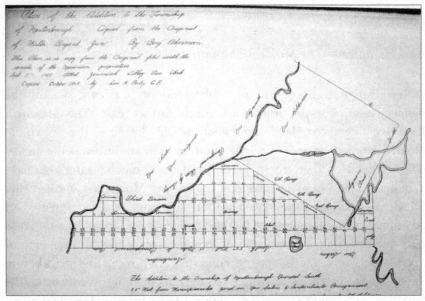

The 1765 survey of lots in the Addition, showing the Pemigewasset River at left and top and the Town of New Holderness at upper right. *Author's collection*

## Plymouth and Holderness

Beyond the boundary of the "Masonian Patent," land belonged to the royal government of the Province of New Hampshire and those wishing to establish towns there needed to petition Royal Governor Benning Wentworth. A group of some 57 men of Hollis and vicinity organized themselves to petition the governor to grant a town in the Pemigewasset Valley. Even before their grant was received, these future proprietors of Plymouth had decided on a plan of lots and on hiring a surveyor to lay out smaller lots of "intervale" (floodplain) and larger lots of upland. Surveyor Matthew Patten, one of the future proprietors, made a trip up the Pemigewasset in March, 1763 with four companions. They spent one night four or five miles north of the oxbow and on the following day passed through the "long carrying place" at New Hampton, camping overnight half way along that trail. The next day, Patten and his companions proceeded upriver and reached the Plymouth intervale, where they set up camp and spent twelve days surveying 60 lots of some five and one-half acres each. On the way home on March 30th, the surveying party were able to spend the night at a logging camp near the oxbow (today's Franklin), indicating yet another activity already underway along the still-wild Pemigewasset. During the remainder of 1763, 120 upland lots of 50 acres each and 60 sixteen-acre intervale lots also were surveyed (Stearns 1987: 34-38).

The Plymouth proprietors were relatively confident regarding the area of their town because the surrounding towns – New Chester, Cockermouth (Hebron), Rumney, Campton and New Holderness - had already been granted. About half way through the survey process, in July of 1763, the grant of the Town of Plymouth was received. Governor Wentworth had reserved 500 acres of land fronting on the Pemigewasset in the northeast corner of the new town. He reserved such tax-free land, known as the "governor's right" or the "governor's farm," in each of the towns he granted, amassing tens of thousands of acres in his own name. In December, 1763 the proprietors met and each drew two 50-acre lots of upland, and one sixteen-acre lot and one five and one-half-acre lot of intervale land. The town was then ready for settlement.

The Plymouth Intervale by Robert Wilkie. *Trustees of the Boston Public Library, Louis Prang & Co. Collection*

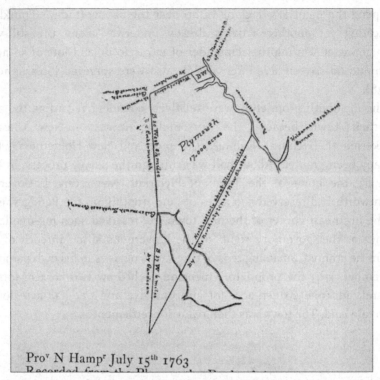

Pro^v N Hamp^r July 15^th 1763

The boundaries of Plymouth in 1763, showing the Pemigewasset River and the
governor's lot marked "BW" at top right, and Newfound Lake at bottom.
*Batchellor1895: 456*

Governor Wentworth was making so many town grants in the early
1760s that a standard form was printed with blank spaces to fill in the
particulars of each town. According to their grant provisions, Plymouth lot
owners were to "plant and cultivate five Acres of Land, within the term of
Five Years, for every fifty Acres contained in his or their Share . . . in said
Township . . . " and, ". . . all white and other Pine Trees within the said
Township, fit for Masting Our Royal Navy, [must]be carefully preserved
for that use." Shares, or lots, also were to be allocated to support
"Propagation of the Gospel in Foreign Parts, . . . a Glebe for the Church of
England, . . . the first Settled Minister of the Gospel, and . . . the Benefit of
a School in Said Town."

The well-organized Plymouth grantees were prepared to comply. They arranged "to send persons to view a place for a road from the mouth of Smith's River to the lower end of the Intervale and when the men return home to open out the small stuff so as horses can travel," whereupon eight men from the group of proprietors promptly did so. Furthermore, of the 60-odd proprietors, some five were among those settlers who arrived in the first year of the grant (The Town Register 1908: 14). While land speculation was an inherent part of every grant, the Plymouth proprietors are notable for their dedication to establish a working town.

In 1761, following the end of hostilities of the French and Indian War, but before the conclusive treaty of 1763, 61 petitioners from Durham and vicinity asked for renewal of the 1751 provincial grant of New Holderness. The earlier grant had lapsed due to the war, but its territory remained the same - six miles square, on the east side of the Pemigewasset River:

> *Begining at a Red Oak Tree at the foot of the Great Falls* [Livermore Falls] *in Pemidgewasset River thence runing east six miles then Turning off at Right Angles and runing South Six Miles then Turning off again & runing Westerly Six Miles to a White Pine Tree Marked Standing on the Bank of the river afore Said then runing up Said River No[r]thely as that runs to the Bounds first Mentioned as Bounds began at . . .* (Batchellor 1895: 129)

This territory lay north of what was to become the Moultonborough Addition, and was on the Pemigewasset's east side, opposite New Chester and future Plymouth. In re-issuing the grant in October, 1761, Governor Wentworth increased his governor's farm from 500 acres in the 1751 grant to 800 acres, also specifying that it be on the most fertile intervale land along the river. As in Plymouth, the grant required the 61 grantees to clear and cultivate five acres for every 50 acres that they held, but gave them only two years, instead of five, in which to do that.

The proprietors hired surveyor John Bachelder to mark out 67 lots of eight acres each on the riverside intervale in 1762, and then lots of 100 acres each were surveyed inland. These lots were drawn in 1765, and the town was ready for settlement. In addition to the Pemigewasset and Squam rivers, the provincially-mandated Province Road provided access from the south. This road was built in the late 1760s through the towns of Meredith and New Hampton before entering New Holderness, and then continued across the Pemigewasset to Plymouth and on to the Connecticut Valley. It was a route that new settlers could follow, but was also intended to carry trade between the seacoast and the interior. In 1771, a second long distance road was ordered by Governor John Wentworth, who succeeded Benning, to run through Moultonborough and then northwest through New Holderness to Plymouth. Despite these two provincial access roads, its Pemigewasset Valley location, good land, and the water power of the Squam River, only nine families settled in New Holderness during its first twelve years (Colby 1881: 177). Historian George Hodges pointed out that: "The town was so poor that the only action that was taken at the first town meeting, after the election of officers, was to vote to raise no money for that year [1771]" (Hodges 1907: 57).

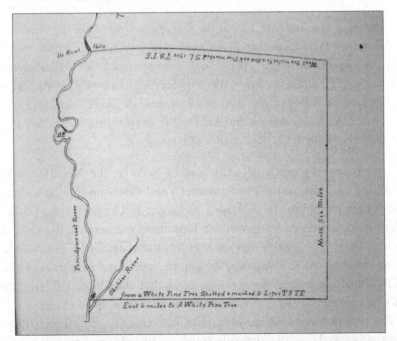

The town boundary survey of New Holderness, with the Pemigewasset River on the left, "BW" marking the governor's land, Livermore Falls at upper left, and the Squam River at lower left. The Squam Lakes are not shown.
*Batchellor 1895: 127*

## Campton and Thornton

Above the confluence of the Baker River, the Pemigewasset was less frequented by visitors. The historic route to Canada had been up the Pemigewasset Valley and then northwest up the Baker River Valley and across the height of land to the Connecticut Valley. Alternately, the Squam River Valley offered a route east for those ascending the Pemigewasset, before the mountains closed in on both sides. So, the new towns that were granted north of Plymouth and Holderness were more remote and more focused on the Pemigewasset's narrow valley. In ascending the Pemigewasset, Campton was the first town to have land on both sides of the river.

A grant of the Town of Campton was first made in 1761 to Jabez Spencer of Connecticut, but after his death the other 57 grantees appear not to have made any progress, so the town was re-granted in 1767 to 61 men, including Spencer's heirs, plus the provincial officials whose names appear on all grants. The territory was six miles square, bounded on the southeast by New Holderness, on the east by Sandwich (granted in 1763), on the north by Thornton (granted in 1763), on the west by Rumney, and on the southwest by Plymouth – with the Pemigewasset dividing Campton into east and west sections. Benning Wentworth took his 500 acre parcel in the southwest corner of the grant, bordering Plymouth and Rumney. The requirement that each grantee "plant and cultivate five Acres of Land within the Term of five Years for every fifty Acres contained in his or their Share" is familiar, as is the restriction on cutting any pine trees fit for use as masts.

Unlike towns to the south, Campton was settled by people from southern Connecticut and from the lower Merrimack Valley in Massachusetts, two Connecticut men being regarded as the first settlers in 1762 or 1765, under the first grant (Willey 1868: 15) (Hammond 1882: 248). The first survey of lots was probably done following award of the 1761 grant, enabling settlers to clear their lots and build homes. Campton was not enumerated in the provincial census of 1767, but in 1773, 139 residents were reported, including 22 married couples, 40 unmarried women, and 53 unmarried men and boys. Only one resident was over 60 years old.

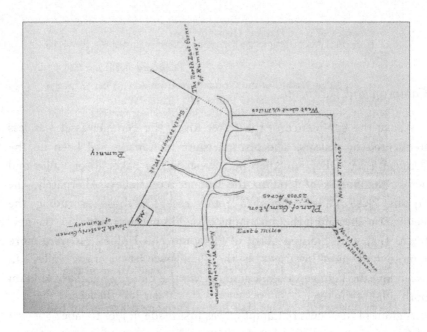

The 1761 boundary survey of Campton, showing the Pemigewasset River dividing the town, with its tributaries, and with the governor's parcel marked "BW" in the southwest corner. *Batchellor 1894: 508*

The Pemigewasset divides Campton, requiring bridges to link the town. *D. Heyduk*

North of Campton, Thornton was granted in 1763 to a group of petitioners led by Matthew Thornton, and named in his honor. As in Campton, the town was laid out on both sides of the Pemigewasset, among the mountains which effectively enclose it on the east and west. Surveyed with difficulty, the new town was widest from east to west in the south, where it ran along both sides of the river. The west boundary then ran northeast, crossing the river, and reached a sharp point twelve miles to the north and well among the mountains. The proprietors were not active and after five years the grant lapsed. In 1768, Matthew Thornton petitioned the new governor, John Wentworth, for a re-grant, saying:

> *And Whereas Sundry, of the Grantees, have not been at Expense or Trouble, neither for Obtaining the Charter, nor for viewing, surveying, or Settling. And the rest have been at great Expense and Trouble, in all the above Respects. And have four men now dwelling on the premises, and a great number ready to make Immediate settlement, and only wait till the Grant is Renewed, and we have lately surveyed said Township, and laid it in a more convenient form . . . Therefore your Petitioners pray your Excellency and Honors, to . . . Regrant said Township as laid down in the last mentioned plan . . .* (Hammond 1884: 566-568)

The governor re-granted the town that year, adding more territory, to bring it from 23,000 acres in the original grant to 40,000 acres, to be divided among some 80 grantees. He apparently heeded Matthew Thornton's observation that: ". . . the great number of uninhabitable Mountains, makes it necessary, that a Large allowance should be made, Otherwise what appears by the plan, Enough for two, will not make one Good parish" (Ibid). John Wentworth removed Benning Wentworth's 500 acre parcel which was included in the 1763 grant, taking no such portion himself, and allowing more land for the actual settlers to utilize. The new grant also required that twelve families be settled by 1770 and 60 families by 1776 (Batchellor 1895: 574-581).

Settlement then proceeded, and in the inventory of the town for 1773 there were eighteen voters (adult men), three horses, six oxen, fifteen cows, and some 35 acres of cleared land. It is unlikely that the stipulated 60 families had settled by 1776, but by that time the Revolutionary War was underway, John Wentworth had fled New Hampshire, and Matthew Thornton was a signer of the Declaration of Independence.

In 1781 the residents of Thornton petitioned the General Assembly for a charter, noting that they could not: "... Assess, levy and Collect Taxes ... [and] that the State Tax already apportioned to the Town of Thornton ... cannot be Collected until the inhabitants thereof are enabled by Authority to do the same ... " (Hammond 1884: 569). The charter was then promptly granted.

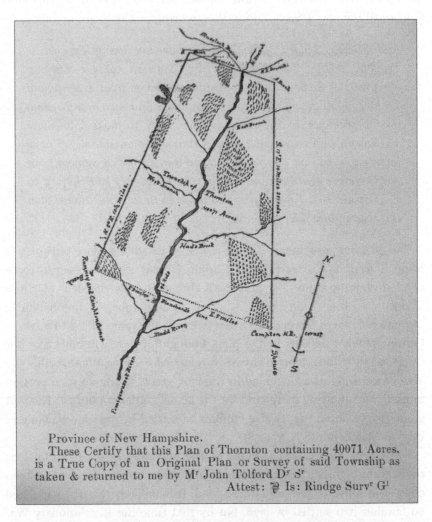

Province of New Hampshire.
These Certify that this Plan of Thornton containing 40071 Acres, is a True Copy of an Original Plan or Survey of said Township as taken & returned to me by Mr John Tolford Dy Sr
Attest: ℈ Is: Rindge Survr Gl

**The 1768 survey of Thornton, showing the Pemigewasset River dividing the town and mountainous areas shaded.** *Batchellor 1895: 581*

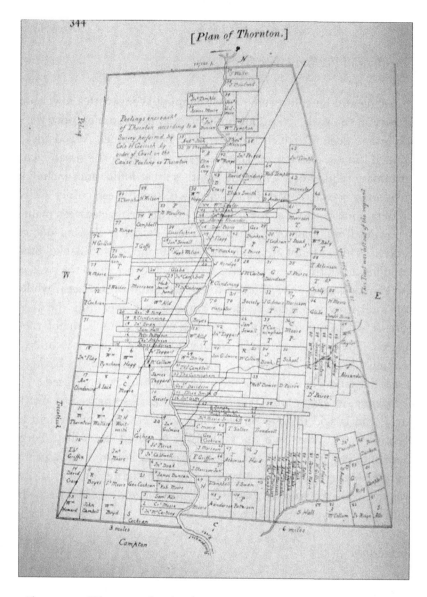

The survey of Thornton, showing the Pemigewasset River dividing the town into east and west portions, with narrow lots along the rivers and larger lots in the upland. *Author's collection*

## Lincoln and Peeling (Woodstock)

Peeling and Lincoln were part of Benning Wentworth's town-granting activity in the early 1760s, but both suffered from coming onto the stage too soon. Peeling, which later would be re-named Woodstock, was granted in 1763, and Lincoln in 1764, each to be six miles square, with the customary requirements that the grantees must fulfill, and including the governor's 500 acre parcel in each town's southwest corner. This was mountainous territory at the confluence of the Pemigewasset's main stem - flowing from Franconia Notch, its East Branch - flowing out of the central White Mountains, and its West Branch (Moosilauke Brook) - tumbling down the steep western slopes. Peeling occupied the west side of the Pemigewasset Valley bordered by Thornton on the east, while Lincoln's territory was more to the north and east, including the southern part of wild Franconia Notch and the equally wild basin of the East Branch. There were no roads. Neither town was a likely location for a farming settlement at that time, with so many other towns having more accessible land. No settlement took place, and both grants lapsed.

In 1771, Governor John Wentworth granted Peeling again, and James McNorton is said to have settled about 1773. He went off to fight in the Revolutionary War, and is said to have died at Valley Forge or Germantown, after which his wife returned to Portsmouth. Lincoln was regranted in 1772, but did not receive a town charter until 1782. Peeling was not surveyed into lots until the 1790s and did not receive a charter until 1799 (Sawyer 2013) (Conrad 1897: 11).

## Franconia

Benning Wentworth's town grant-making included a 1764 grant of the Town of Franconia to a group of petitioners who incurred the now-familiar obligations to clear land and settle within five years. The new town bordered Lincoln on the south for some seven and three-quarter miles, making the northern portion of Franconia Notch and the source of the Pemigewasset River in Profile Lake a part of Franconia's territory. The "Old Man of the Mountain" and other scenic wonders of the Notch were unknown at that time, and Franconia was first notable for a rich iron deposit in the Gale River Valley, which led to mining and smelting, and a foundry. Farmers there grew potatoes from which potato starch was made and sold (Merrill 1817) (March 1997: 21-24). The 1790 census recorded just 72 people.

Franconia's earliest transportation links were with the Connecticut Valley to the west rather than with the new and sparsely populated Pemigewasset Valley settlements to the south. In 1790, the proprietors of Franconia and other towns north of the Notch petitioned the legislature for a road to Thornton: "to accommodate them to go to Portsmouth, Plymouth, and all the towns below with whom we must have Communication for our market and Supplyes of goods, which Road would save us thirty miles travel . . ." They reported that: "they have already at their own Expense look'd out, marked and measured, through to Thornton line . . . [but found] the burden too heavy for new and Infant Settlers to bear the whole Cost themselves" (Hammond 1882 XI: 692-93) (Kostecke 1975: 4). There probably was no road through the Notch and into Thornton until the early 1800s (Welch 1972: 69).

In 1805, Luke Brooks and Francis Whitcomb were working on a survey line in the Notch and stopped at the east side of Profile Lake to dip water. Looking up, Brooks saw the outline of a face on the cliff above the lake and Whitcomb remarked that it looked like Thomas Jefferson (Welch 1972: 161).[3] As the Notch road was improved in the years following, the Old Man of the Mountain and other sights began to draw wider notice and Franconia's fortunes would increasingly be linked to them.

---

[3] This is the most accepted of several versions of the discovery.

The Old Man of the Mountain, or Profile, at the south end of the Cannon Mountain ridge, was 1200 feet above Profile Lake. *John W. and Anne H. Newton Collection, Museum of the White Mountains, Plymouth State University*

# Chapter 5

# The World of the Early Settlers

In the Pemigewasset Valley, no towns had been settled before 1760, the forest was virtually unbroken, and there were no facilities such as roads or bridges, or saw mills, or grist mills. The new settlers who arrived in the valley's wild and empty towns – in a territory stretching some 70 miles along the river - faced many challenges, some of which have been recorded and passed down.

Due to the short time in which towns were created, all the towns of the Pemigewasset Valley were settled simultaneously. The first settlers in Sanbornton and the first to arrive in Thornton were clearing forest at the same time. Some towns grew more quickly, and some were closer to the established facilities of the Merrimack Valley to the south, but all began as wild land in which pioneers had to establish their homes and their livelihoods.

Proprietors were usually prompt in opening a blazed path through the forest that gave access to a town from the outside, allowing horses and oxen to pass through, but in the remainder of a town – 36 square miles of rough territory in many cases – it was up to each settler to reach his property and link it to the world outside. Surveys of lots allowed for "rangeway" roads of standard width – usually 3 rods (50 feet) - to run between them and provide access, but that was simply on paper. On the ground there were streams, ponds and wetlands, cliffs and gullies, and many places where the most convenient route did not follow the right angles of a survey. The survey established rights-of-way, 50 feet in width, but settlers cleared only as much forest as would allow themselves and their animals to pass.

The first concern of a lot owner was to locate the best agricultural land within his lot and the best location for his house. Then he needed to cut down trees, cut them into manageable pieces, and burn them more than once to clear the ground between the stumps for planting. In the process he would build a log cabin to live in and secure firewood for the coming winter. In the first spring after clearing, corn, rye, beans and potatoes would be planted to provide food for the winter. Stumps would be pulled later as time and animal power - usually of oxen - allowed, and then the land could be plowed.

The first years were difficult, as a 1768 petition to Governor John Wentworth from the settlers of Sanbornton reveals:

> We, the Inhabitants of this Town, Promicing our selves your Excellency's Protection, Both in our Public & Private interests, humbly beg ye Liberty of Declaring to your Excellency, ye Present Condition of this infant Town, which is as followeth, viz: We have thirty-two Familys in Town, & a number more we expect will soon move in, & we doubt not But that in a few years we shall if Prospered, be a flourishing Town, able to support our familys, and be a help to ye Publick, But at Present we are under a necessity of going to other Towns for many things to support our selves and our Cattle which are but very few, ye time Being so very short since we moved into Town, there Being no more than seven familys that have Been in Town so long as two years, & they were Poor People that mov'd in for ye sake of Cetching a few fish to support their familys; many of us have Been here But one year & some not so long, our Land is very heavy to clear & after it is clear'd & affords us a considerable Crop of Indian Corn it is next to impossible to Plow the Land for some years by Reason of ye stumps & Roots; there hath Been But a very few acres ever Plow'd in Town, not more than six or seven men that have Plow'd any & on ye whole it is not without a great deal of Difficulty that we Bring ye year about, Being obliged to spend on the Store we had Before we moved up, those that had any & those that had not, to Run in debt many of us or be beholden to friends, which cant we humbly conceive be thought strange considering that this was all a wilderness so very lately.
> . . . our humble Petition is, that your Excellency would Consider our Sircumstnces & Release us from paying any tax for a Little time . . .
> (Bouton 1875: Vol IX: 755)

The petition was signed by thirty-four men, who were probably all the "polls," or taxpayers, in Sanbornton at the time. The seemingly strange mention of catching fish to live on probably refers to the massive runs of shad, salmon and eels, which were as much sought by the settlers as they had been by the Abenaki. The fish and eels were dried or smoked to provide food for a much longer time.

To corroborate the above petition, Sanbornton historian Moses Runnels wrote that: "the three first actual settlers seem to have . . . procured their subsistence . . . chiefly from the river and bays (Runnels 1882: 53-54).

"First Harvest in the Wilderness" by Asher Durand, shows a recently cleared homestead with a log cabin and stumps in the field. This may have been based on the view from Profile Lake to Eagle Cliff in Franconia Notch, with the infant Pemigewasset at bottom. *Brooklyn Museum*

## Wild Resources and Dangers

The oxbow of the Winnipesaukee River where it meets the Pemigewasset was a prime spot to catch shad in nets, while nearby Eastman Falls in the Pemigewasset was equally good for salmon. Salmon ascended the Pemigewasset and its tributaries, and also were taken at Sawhegenit Falls, Livermore Falls, and many other places where they could be speared in resting pools at the base of a fall. Eels were caught in autumn when they moved downstream.

Wild animals could be hunted and trapped and good hunters had an advantage in the early settlement years. Matthew Patten mentioned that his group hunted while surveying the intervale lots at Plymouth, and during a longer eight week surveying trip he wrote: "I got 10 lb of Beaver by catching while I was out" (Stearns 1987: 35, 38). The beaver would have been taken while he was surveying Plymouth's upland lots, at streams and ponds well away from the Baker and Pemigewasset valleys.

Peter Powers' men shot a moose while that large group in several canoes was entering the Baker River in 1754, and Hoyt writes that moose were so plentiful that 100 moose-skin breeches were made in the Baker Valley in 1776 (Hoyt 1990: 23). As of 1786, wolves were still found in the Baker Valley and passenger pigeons appeared in huge flocks during some years, taking days to pass. Deer were heavily hunted, for their meat and hides, and also to protect the settlers' crops (Ibid: 25-26).

When settlers first arrived, turkeys were plentiful in the lower Pemigewasset. Flocks of 30 or more birds ranged the forest, and settlers found them easy to hunt. Turkey meat was an early staple for settlers while their fields were being cleared and their crops were being planted. Later, the birds would come out of the woods in flocks to find grain in the fields, and could be easily killed. Turkey wings were used as brooms, tails became fans, and feathers were used to stuff bedding. Turkeys are ground-nesters, so their eggs could be collected by the settlers as a delicacy or be destroyed by grazing animals. Clearing of the forest destroyed turkey nests and habitat, the cutting of oaks and other nut-bearing trees reduced their food, and the ease of taking them and their eggs led to their eventual disappearance.

Bears were hunted for meat, fat and skins, and also because they ate lambs and pigs, corn and berries. Benjamin Emmons, one of the first settlers of New Chester, cleared his land and planted corn, but needed to go to Boscawen to renew his provisions. While he was away, neighbors came to visit and counted seven bears in Benjamin's corn field (Musgrove 1904: 48). Porcupines, known as "hedgehogs," damaged fruit trees, corn and other crops. The settler hunted these animals to protect his vital crops and livestock as much as for his larder.

## Provisions and Roads

Settlers who were coming to take up their lots needed to bring provisions to supply themselves while they were cutting trees and building cabins. The staples at that time were corn meal and dried beans, to which water was added to make a porridge. Salt, dried herbs, maple sugar, locally procured meat, or found items such as berries varied the otherwise monotonous diet. In winter the porridge was kept frozen and portions were cut off to cook. Tea was the hot drink.

Harvests in the early years were small and subject to depredations by animals, so it sometimes became necessary to get more food from neighbors or outside the town. On one occasion, Stephen Smith's family of the Knox Mountain neighborhood in Sanbornton ran out of food and he went away to get more. When his return was delayed, and with nothing to eat, his anxious wife walked one and a half miles carrying their twin children in her arms to the nearest neighbor's house, where she thankfully met her husband making his return (Runnels 1882: 54).

Jotham Cumming, Jr. of Plymouth reported his mother's story of being an early settler:

> My mother rode from Hollis on horseback, brought a child on her lap, and baggage which contained all her furniture to keep house with. Their sufferings for a few of the first years were most distressing. They had to go to the meadows and pull wild onions and fry them in the fat of bear's meat, to subsist upon, without a morsel of bread. My father, with others, went to Concord on snow-shoes, with hand-sleds, and hauled up three bushels of corn-meal each; and for a number of years – as late as the Revolutionary War – I well remember how good a piece of bread tasted, after being without it for three weeks (Child 1886: 582).

On the rude cleared paths that led to most towns, men often walked, carrying their belongings and supplies in summer or pulling sleds in winter, and women rode a family's single horse, carrying young children and other goods. Careful attention had to be paid to the axe-blazed trees that marked the way, especially with snow cover, when the path underfoot was hidden and spaces between the trees all looked about the same. The next improvement was to clear passage for a yoke of oxen and a cart, which then made more of a real road, but still not nearly the survey's anticipated fifty feet wide.

Building roads took much effort. In New Chester, more than twenty men worked for three weeks in 1766, the first year of settlement. Then the same number spent one week on road work in each of the next three years, and more roads still needed to be built (Musgrove 1904: 37). In 1785, the residents petitioned the legislature for aid, because: "wee have upwards of Fifty Miles of Roads . . . to maintain" (Hammond 1883: 200).

## Mills

Two of the settlers' most urgent needs were a convenient saw mill to cut building lumber for houses, barns, and other frame structures, and a grist mill to grind their grain into flour. Town proprietors took steps to encourage the early establishment of mills, with land given to the miller, rules which allowed millers to keep part of what they produced, and even cash payments to whoever undertook to build and operate a mill. In a petition to the New Hampshire General Court (legislature) in 1797, Col. Matthew Thornton, proprietor of the town named for him, pointed out that: "notwithstanding its being a Fronteer town, and the late [Revolutionary] War at that time raging between Brittain and America, yet as I paid for Building Grist and Saw Mills . . . [it] is now become a fine flourishing Town . . ." (Bouton 1875: 572). Col. Thornton had paid for the mills himself in order to attract settlers to his town.

Mills of course were water-powered, and towns gave a "mill privilege" to the builder so that he would have adequate access to that town resource. Dams and sluiceways had to be built to deliver water to the wheel, and machinery had to be constructed – much of it out of wood, and the metal parts – the "mill irons" – had to be obtained. Mill irons, saws and grinding stones were bought down in Merrimack River towns and generally brought to the Pemigewasset Valley on sleds in winter.

In New Holderness, Nathaniel Thompson was offered land and a mill privilege two years after lots became available in 1767. He took land where the Squam River drops in today's Ashland, built a saw and grist mill, and settled there about 1770 (Hodges 1907: 52). Later, Samuel Livermore, who was attorney general of the province and a proprietor, settled in New

Holderness during the early years of the Revolution. He built a grist mill on Mill Brook and ran it himself in 1776 and 1777, wearing the same dusty coat wherever he went, until he was elected to represent the town in the state assembly. Livermore was a major landowner in New Holderness and in Campton and Plymouth, and later represented New Hampshire in the United States Senate (Colby 1881: 176-177) (Clark 1897: 279-280).

For the settlement of New Chester, each proprietor was assessed money to build saw and grist mills, and two lots were set aside for that purpose:

> . . . whereas John Tolford, Esq. has this Day agreed to Build two Saw mills & two Grist mills . . . (Viz) one grist mill and one Saw mill on the river known by the name of Newfound River and have the one fit for grinding and the other fit for Sawing by the first Day of November next and one grist mill and one Saw mill on the River known by the name of Smiths River within six years from this Date and to keep all the Said mills in good order for ever thereafter . . .
> Voted that the Lots and Land adjoining to Newfound pond River including the Stream and the Lot Stream and falls on Smiths River .
> . . is given and granted to the Said John Tolford his heirs and assigns forever [meeting of February, 1767] (Musgrove 1904: 37-38).

Tolford was one of the proprietors and apparently built the Newfound River mills promptly, because in December, 1768 it was voted that he tend to his grist mill "every first Monday in each month for the year . . ." The Smith River mills lagged, however, and in 1773 the time to complete them was extended for four more years.

One of the most powerful water power sites on the Pemigewasset is at Livermore Falls in Campton – first called Little's Falls, where the river drops 50 feet through a narrow gorge. Moses Little of Newburyport, Massachusetts was one of the original grantees of Campton in 1767, and settled there in 1769. Sometime prior to 1774 he built mills at the falls (shown on the early Holland map of New Hampshire). First was a grist mill, then - of uncertain date - a linseed oil mill (from flax seed), a wool carding and a woven cloth fulling mill.

A neighborhood grew up around Little's Falls, including the home of Moses and his son James, who continued to operate the mills after Moses' death. A bridge crossed the river at the mill dam, connecting the east and west sections of Campton. In 1812, the property was sold to Arthur

Livermore, the son of Samuel Livermore of Holderness, who established his home there, and the falls came to be called Livermore Falls (Campton Historical Society).

The log carriage, driving gear and saw of an up-and-down saw mill. Note that most parts of the mill machinery are made of wood. *D. Heyduk*

Cutting Favor, a proprietor and early settler of New Chester, built his own saw mill on a stream crossing his land, where he sawed lumber to build his frame house and to build four other houses for his sons. The penstock that carried water to the mill ran above the road, so that traffic passed under it (Musgrove 1904: 47) (Morrill et. al. 1976: 2). Many settlers built their own saw and grist mills by damming local streams, and some of those locations became neighborhoods for a time. Today the dams and cellars can still be seen on streams deep in the woods.

## Fords, Ferries and Bridges

The Pemigewasset River could assist those traveling north and south, but it was a serious obstacle to cross when going east and west. Many of its tributaries were rivers in their own right, which also had to be crossed. At first, fords (unobstructed shallow places) were used, but they depended on low water and became dangerous when the river rose. Daniel Kelley, a prosperous resident of New Hampton, drowned in 1813 while trying to cross the Pemigewasset to return home from New Chester. He had been at a militia muster, and it is said that his horse misstepped into deep water at the ford (Musgrove 1904: 106). Farther upstream, a ford where today's Route 104 crosses was so dangerous that it was: "almost impossible to Cross said River with horses unless they are Swimed by side of Conoes . . ." (1799 petition) (Merrill, et. al. 1977: 46). In Campton, a town which was divided by the Pemigewasset, people on the east side of the river attended the church which was built there, while people on the west side attended church in Plymouth (Willey: 1868: 50).

Ferries were operated by private individuals with approval from the legislature. In the 1780s, Sanbornton residents needed to cross the Winnipesaukee River for north-south travel, and did so by Solomon Copps' ferry: "a Good Boat to accommodate Passengers passing and repassing from Gilmantown to sandborntown" (Bouton 1875: 395). They also had to cross the Pemigewasset, and in 1798 petitioned the legislature:

> . . . that Tilton Bennett of said town has attended a ferry over Pemigewasset River between Sanbornton and New-Chester for four years past and has been at great expense to provide and keep in repair suitable boats for said ferry, wherefore your petitioners

*humbly pray your honors would grant said ferry to him.* [signed by
45 Sanbornton residents] (Bouton 1875: 401).

Bennett's toll for his ferry service was two cents per foot passenger, three
cents per horse, ten cents for a chaise and two horses, and twenty cents for
a passenger coach. The Republican toll bridge across the Pemigewasset at
today's Franklin was built by investors in 1800-02. Union Bridge, also
charging a toll, was built between Sanbornton and New Chester in 1808
(Garneau 2002: 338) (Musgrove 1904: 105). Cutting Favor had his own
private ferry to cross the Pemigewasset between his land in New Chester
and his land in New Hampton (Merrill et.al. 1977: 44).

   Two ferries ran between New Hampton and Bridgewater (formerly New
Chester) near the present Bristol Central Bridge site, where a toll bridge
was built in 1823. The dangerous ford at today's Route 104 became the site
of a ferry in 1800. Then, shortly after 1806, a two-span toll bridge was built
by a group of investors, which crossed via an island in the river (now
submerged) (Musgrove 1904: 106-07). About 1820, a bridge first spanned
the Pemigewasset between Holderness and Bridgewater (Ashland 1968).

   There must have been a ford to cross the Pemigewasset at Plymouth,
where both the Province Road from the coast and the College Road from
Wolfeboro met the river. In 1797, a group of investors was incorporated to
build a toll bridge across the Pemigewasset between New Holderness and
Plymouth. That bridge lasted only until 1804, when it was washed away by
a flood. A ferry then replaced the bridge until it could be rebuilt, but the
new bridge was carried away again in 1813 (Speare 1988: 37-45).

   The road west along the Baker Valley and the road to Campton crossed
the Baker River north of Plymouth. According to a 1785 petition, travelers
on these roads crossed at a wide ford which was passable:

> *only a small part of the year, & in cold weather, it is often partly*
> *frozen & partly open, so that to render it difficult to pass. . . . the*
> *Inhabitants . . . who live near the place where said river is generally*
> *crossed have within two years last past, been at great expense in*
> *building a bridge there, but as yet have not been able to finish . . .*

The petitioners asked the legislature that a lottery be allowed to raise 200
Pounds to finish the bridge (Hammond XIII 1884: 228-229).

Entrance to the Union Bridge spanning the Pemigewasset between Sanbornton and New Chester (later Hill). *Evelyn Corliss Auger Collection*

The Pemigewasset Bridge, linking Bristol and New Hampton, painted on a stage curtain. *New Hampton Historical Society*

At Campton, which suffered from its division into two parts by the Pemigewasset, the first bridge was built at the Little's (later Livermore) Falls dam in 1788. That bridge was replaced by another in 1820, built by the owner of the mills, Arthur Livermore. A flood shortly after completion of the bridge carried it away, along with Livermore's dam and mills (Campton Historical Society). The unlucky Livermore had also been an investor in the Plymouth toll bridges which were destroyed in 1804 and 1813. Blair Bridge was built by the Town of Campton in 1829 to cross the Pemigewasset further upstream, with a central pier at mid-river. After being rebuilt many times, it survives today.

**Blair Bridge at Campton, looking north.** *D. Heyduk*

Following the wash-outs of the early century, Plymouth seems to have relied on ferry service across the Pemigewasset until about 1825, when a group of investors built a toll bridge 278 feet long spanning the river. It rested on a stone pier in mid-stream. The bridge was named "Pont Fayette," and called by variations of that name, honoring the Revolutionary War hero Marquis de Lafayette, who was visiting the United

States at that time (Big Haystack Mountain in Franconia Notch was re-named Mount Lafayette in 1824). Despite his earlier losses, Arthur Livermore was one of the investors in the new bridge.

The entrance to Blair Bridge, with a sign: "Five Dollars Fine for Riding or Driving on this Bridge Faster than a Walk." *D. Heyduk*

Bridges deteriorated and needed rebuilding about every fifteen years, aside from periodic damage - or outright destruction - by floods. Towns had substantial outlays for maintenance of roads and bridges, which is why investors often built bridges and collected tolls at a "toll house" located at one end of a bridge.

In addition to the earliest bridges, which have been described here in order to provide a complete catalog from south to north, others were added in the middle and later 1800s, as will appear in Chapters 14 & 15.

Pont Fayette, or LaFayette Bridge, across the Pemigewasset between Holderness and Plymouth is seen here looking south. *Plymouth Historical Society*

## Homesteads

Families put much effort into their homesteads, where they normally worked six days a week. After initially clearing the forest and building a cabin, a frame house and barn were added as quickly as possible. Different types of cleared land were needed: cultivated land for crops; pasture for the essential oxen, cow, horse, and sheep to browse in summer; mowing land to produce at least two cuttings of hay for the animals' winter feed; and an orchard for fruit trees, especially apples for winter storage and for cider. There also was a garden for vegetables and herbs, forest to annually produce twenty cords or more of firewood, and a sugar bush where maples could be tapped to make sugar. The homestead produced much of what the family needed, and a bit of surplus to be traded for things that had to be obtained outside, such as: tools and equipment, sewing supplies, firearms and animal traps, gun powder and shot, pottery and glass, salt, spices, tobacco, tea and rum. Most goods were obtained by trading butter, cheese, maple sugar, animal skins, labor and crop surpluses, rather than by cash payment. Money was scarce, and was needed to pay taxes.

The property owner was taxed on what his farm produced, not on its real estate value. His cultivated land was assessed as one acre for each 25 bushels of corn that it produced, his mowing was calculated as one acre for each ton of "English hay" that he cut, orchard land was counted as one acre for each ten barrels of cider that it yielded, and pasture was measured as four acres for each of his cows. Farms were so standard that these tax categories were used until the 1820s.

## Hill Farm Families and Their Fortunes

The Carters of New Hampton were in many ways like settlers throughout the Pemigewasset Valley. Moses Carter purchased fifty acres from proprietor Jonathan Moulton in 1781 and established a farm on the north slope of Hersey Mountain. He cleared an extensive farm and built a house for his wife Anna and twelve children. Their holdings eventually came to some 175 acres and in the 1810 tax inventory included one acre of tilled land, one acre of orchard, six acres of mowing and twelve acres of pasture. The Carters' livestock that year were one horse, one cow, and four cattle. Moses' land was in the upper drainage of Blake Brook, which he dammed, and built a grist mill and perhaps a saw mill. The access road to the Carter farm became New Hampton's Carter Mountain Road, and by 1786 it was cleared over an eastern spur of Hersey Mountain to Sanbornton. The Carter children attended a nearby one-room school.

Moses' youngest son Levi purchased the original Carter farm from his father in 1811, expanded and improved it, mined clay to fire the bricks for a substantial house, married three times, and raised fifteen children. By the 1830s, town tax records show that the Carter farm included a one acre orchard, one and one half acres of tilled land, nine acres of mowing and thirty-four acres of pasture. In addition to a horse, five cows, two cattle and two oxen, they had seventy sheep. Levi's farm reached 260 acres, but his children grew up and left and in the 1860s he moved to live in New Hampton village. The Carters' more than 80 year connection to their land is reflected today in the name of the road and of the "Carter Valley."

In Sanbornton, on the west slope of Knox Mountain where streams flow down to the Pemigewasset, Edmund Rundlet, together with his wife Hannah, purchased land in 1804 and cleared a farm. They had eight daughters and one son, Josiah, who with his wife Abigail later settled next to his parents' home. A spur road was cut to the Rundlet houses in 1811, but was described as following a "path now trodden." At that time the Rundlet children would have attended a school about a mile down the road along with other children from this new neighborhood, which also had a saw and a grist mill. Edmund expanded his farm up the slope of Knox Mountain in Sanbornton in 1818 and across the town line into New Hampton in 1833. According to Sanbornton Town tax records, by 1831, the Rundlet farm had (in Sanbornton) a ¼ acre orchard, one acre of tillage, four acres of mowing, eight acres of pasture, one horse, two oxen, four cows, three other cattle , and twelve sheep. One of the Rundlet homes was a substantial 32 by 28 foot center chimney house.

From the Rundlet farm a road ran northeast along the town line to two homesteads even higher on the mountain: the Nathaniel Wiggin house and the Jacob Burleigh house. Jacob and Nancy Burleigh had two girls and two boys who walked more than twice as far as the Rundlet children to attend school. Like Edmund Rundlet, Nathaniel Wiggin also owned land across the town line in New Hampton. By 1838 the Rundlets, Burleighs and Nathaniel Wiggin all had departed, selling their farms to neighbors, who grazed sheep, but did not live there. By 1844 the school their children had attended was closed.

Today the Carter, Rundlet, Burleigh and Wiggin hill farms, created with so much labor, are forest once again.

An old New Hampton farm home. *New Hampton Historical Society*

## The Settled Ministers

Grants of new towns, both by the Masonian Proprietors and by the government of New Hampshire, required that a minister be settled and be paid by the town within a few years. With one exception, the grants did not specify that the minister be of any particular denomination. In the 1760s when the grants were made, most settlers were members of the Congregational Church, and town proprietors, and later town selectmen chose to invite Congregational ministers.

In Plymouth, the grant reserved one of the proprietor's shares for a minister, and made that share tax free. With their usual dispatch, the Plymouth proprietors hired Nathan Ward, a Congregational minister, within one year of obtaining the grant. Ward was married with ten children. He arrived in Plymouth in 1766 and soon settled on the lot reserved for him. His salary was to be 36 Pounds for settlement and 50 Pounds, plus 30 cords of wood annually. A log meetinghouse was built by the town in 1768. Even in those early years there was disagreement, however, and fifteen voters refused to pay the tax that supported Rev. Ward. A compromise was reached whereby the dissenters paid the back taxes that they owed, but were relieved from paying tax to support the Congregational Church in the future (Speare 1988: 9, 24).

The 1761 grant of the Town of New Holderness, also made by the Province of New Hampshire, had a different clause than that of Plymouth: ". . . one Share for the first Settled Minister in Comunion with the Church of England as by Law Established-." According to the grant, New Holderness was to be officially a Church of England (Episcopal) town, and it was predominantly settled by Episcopalians, which may help explain its slow growth. Non-Episcopalians would have paid a town tax to support a church they did not attend, and therefore may have chosen to settle elsewhere.

In contrast to Plymouth, New Holderness did not promptly secure a minister. It was not until the later 1780s that Robert Fowle became the settled Episcopal minister there. The town voted in 1788 to pay him: "Two Hundred Dollars yearly as a Sallery in produce at the current price" (*The*

*Town Register* 1908: 55).[4] He married and occupied the parsonage on the minister's lot, which is now part of the property of the Squam Lakes Natural Science Center. It was not until 1797 that the now-historic Episcopal Church was built near today's Holderness School. Robert Fowle remained as minister there for 58 years (Hodges 1907: 67-72).

Some towns, such as Bridgewater, never obtained a settled minister, depending instead on paying itinerant clergymen to preach. Other towns, such as Sanbornton, which found a settled minister, also had churches of other denominations. In 1819, the New Hampshire legislature passed the "Toleration Act," which put all denominations on equal footing. No church would receive town tax support, and all would depend financially upon their members.

---

[4] Money was substantially devalued at that time, and towns were cash-poor. New Holderness also voted to pay a teacher one hundred seventy dollars in produce that year.

## Chapter 6

# Stepping Stones 1761 – 1790

Formative events took place in the three decades following creation of the Pemigewasset Valley's towns: a new county, the Revolutionary War and its chaotic aftermath, people learning about the river, the beginnings of a highway and postal system, and the first United States Census.

In 1773, the provincial government created new counties, and Grafton County, with its western seat at Haverhill and eastern seat at Plymouth, was one. A courthouse was needed at Plymouth, and was built 34 feet square with the required punishment stocks and whipping post, in 1774. It would serve its judicial purpose for almost 50 years (Stearns 1987: 187-189).

The original Grafton County Courthouse at Plymouth. *Plymouth Historical Society*

When the Revolutionary War began suddenly in the spring of 1775, most Pemigewasset Valley towns were less than ten years old and their residents were still clearing land, building homes and cutting roads. Provincial Governor John Wentworth fled New Hampshire that year and a new government was created to continue to administer New Hampshire while it also played its part in the prosecution of the rebellion. Committees of Safety were created in each town to coordinate the revolt. One document that has come down to us is from Matthew Thornton (with whom we are already acquainted), President of the Provincial Congress, dated August 25, 1775, and addressed to the Town of Plymouth. It requests an accounting of the population of the town, including males from 16 to 50 years of age, to be made to the New Hampshire Committee of Safety. It asks for the number of firearms in Plymouth, and the number needed to supply one gun to every person capable of using it. It also requests a report of the quantity of gunpowder in the town and asks the town selectmen and Committee of Safety: "to endeavor to prevent all persons from burning their Powder in shooting at Birds & other Game."

Abel Webster, Town Clerk, answered that the population was 382, that 83 men were between 16 and 50 years old, and that eight men from Plymouth had already joined the army. New Chester reported 26 firearms in the town, 11 more needed, and but two or three pounds of powder (Haight 1941: 15). Pemigewasset Valley towns had responded quickly to the revolt against British rule, and would continue to do so, but with increasing difficulty, during the ensuing eight years of war.

Men were able to mobilize quickly because the British colonial government had organized a militia, with each member required to have a musket, powder, bullets, a gun flint, and other accoutrements. Towns were to store a supply of powder, lead, and flints, and the colonial militia periodically drilled and was inspected (Auger 1976: 59). The new rebellious government of New Hampshire simply put the British militia system to work against its creators. Pemigewasset Valley men fought at Bunker Hill, Bennington, Saratoga, and in other major battles.

All towns - except Peeling, Lincoln and Waterville, which were empty at the time, sent men and supplies. Campton, with only 190 people of all ages in 1775, sent ten men, of whom five died (The Town Register 1908: 73). New Chester provided 34 men out of a total population of 196 (Musgrove 1904: 180). As the war continued, there were repeated requisitions for food to feed the army. In 1781, New Chester supplied 3,165 pounds of beef and

Plymouth sent 7,053 pounds, though one wonders how it was done from the small stock of cattle at that time (Curren 1988: 18) (Speare 1988: 21).

Plymouth's report to the Provincial Congress, 1775

There was hardship in the army, but also at home where women, children and the elderly carried a heavier work load. The government issued paper money in 1775, which at first was valued equally with silver. By 1778, it had devalued so that it took four paper bills to equal one in silver. In 1780, the ratio became one hundred to one, and by 1781 paper money was considered worthless and would not be accepted. As Jonathan Smith noted:

> The State struggled with the problem the best it was able, but could not afford much relief. Things eventually came to such a condition [following the end of the war] . . . that open riots and bloodshed occurred in New Hampshire . . . (Smith 1922: 17).

After the war many young men from Massachusetts and southern New Hampshire came with their families to Pemigewasset Valley towns to settle. A good number of them took up land on the slopes and cleared "hill farms" that became a new feature of the landscape. At the same time, New Hampshire and the new United States were struggling economically, with serious impact on people's lives.

Pemigewasset Valley farmers did not have many sources of cash income, and especially during the 1780s, there was not enough coinage in circulation. This led to people not being able to pay their taxes and debts. The inhabitants of Sanbornton petitioned the legislature in 1785:

> That your Petitioners with others ye Inhabitants of this State, labor under great inconveanency for want of a Currancy or medium of trade Sufficient to transact ye Common business between man and man . . . & we Concive that others in General are Desireous to Discharge all our Debts with ye Strictest Honor, the Payment of which, as also ye Common trading one with another, is Rendered next to Impossable, by Reason of ye Scarcety of money, -and People of all Ranks, & Conditions, are Sue'd & meney Put into Prison all of which tends to Impoverish Individuals & Consequently ye State in General; -we therefore Pray that your Honors would as Soon as Possible make a Sum or Bank of Paper money Sufficient to answer all Debts or Demands in this State or for a medium of trade . . . (Hammond 1884 XIII: 399).

81

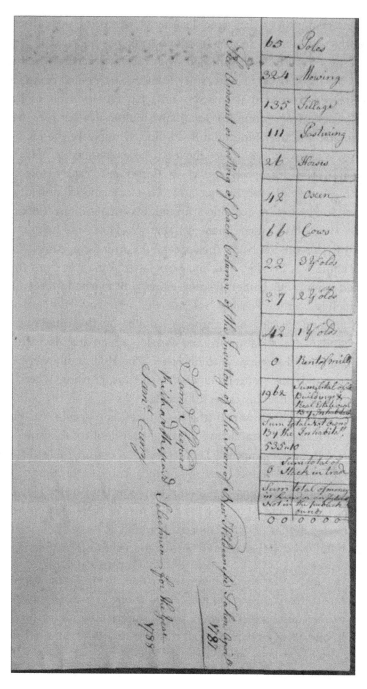

The New Holderness 1787 tax inventory shows 65 voters (males), 26 horses, 42 oxen, 66 cows, and 140 younger cattle. Of 570 acres of cleared land, only 135 acres were plowed.

In New Hampton at that time, Peasley Hoit was the tax collector, but apparently was unable to obtain all the tax payments that were due (Merrill 1977: 22). He then vanished from the town records and was not listed in the 1790 census, but his story from those troubled times can now be told. Deeds record that in 1783 and 1784, Peasley Hoit of Kingston bought 90 acres from proprietor Jonathan Moulton. His land lay mostly on the west side of Carter Mountain Road directly opposite the land bought by Moses Carter in 1781 (see above). These were early days in the settlement of New Hampton, and Moses Carter and Peasley Hoit were the first to buy tracts of land in that area. That coincidence and what later happened to Peasley are explained through his female connections.

Moses' wife Anna, whose maiden name was Hoit, was helping him to establish what would become the successful Carter farm. Anna's mother's maiden name was Peasley, and four years after Anna was born the Hoits had a son whom they named Peasley. Anna Hoit married Moses Carter in 1766 and her brother Peasley Hoit married Margaret Hubbard in 1774. Both Anna and Peasley had thriving families by the time the Carters bought land in New Hampton, and Peasley apparently decided to buy adjoining land and settle next to his sister. The Hoit family were clearing their farm, and the state's financial crisis was growing when Peasley became New Hampton tax collector in 1784.

After Peasley's difficulty with the town taxes, and despite the effort his family was making to establish their home next door to his sister's family, the Hoits left New Hampton. They traveled a considerable distance to settle in Readfield, Maine, near Margaret's younger brother, Dr. John Hubbard. There in the census of 1800 is the record of Peasley Hoit's family of fifteen. Peasley and Margaret lived the rest of their lives in Readfield and are buried in that town's cemetery. It would be better if they could tell their own full story, rather than to piece it together from fragments.

Today we know that the Pemigewasset Valley, with a total watershed of 1,000 square miles, is one of the most flood-prone in New Hampshire. Due to the surrounding steep terrain, runoff occurs rapidly after rain or snowmelt, and: "the river may swell to more than one hundred times its previous discharge level after a storm. Floods typically peak within six hours of a rainstorm's climax" (National Park Service 1996: 8).

Settlers became familiar with what they called "freshets," or floods that occurred in the spring after snowmelt. Low floodplain land such as the Plymouth "meadows" and the lower riverside terraces at New Chester and

Franklin typically were submerged at that time. Of course, records were not kept in the valley prior to the 1760s, so people had only a short acquaintance with the Pemigewasset by the year 1785.

September of that year was rainy, but the weather then turned to Indian Summer until the 20th of October, when very heavy rain driven by a southeast wind fell steadily for three days: a total of nine inches during that time (Perley 2001: 97). The storm was most severe at the coast, but along the Pemigewasset Valley it still caused the highest flood that had been experienced by settlers up to that time.

The first bridge across the Baker River at Wentworth was carried away and at New Chester the Pemigewasset was running about 30 feet above its bed. Historian Richard Musgrove wrote that it was "the greatest freshet ever known on the Pemigewasset." He added that cattle were drowned and: "Simeon Cross, who lived on the intervale in Bridgewater [New Chester at that time], was obliged to move out of his cabin in the night" (1882: 471). In the Merrimack Valley it was recorded as the greatest flood since 1735 (Thomson 1964: M13).

Sudden high water on the Pemigewasset and its tributaries, including the Mad and Beebe rivers in Campton, was common in any year. In 1791, the selectmen of Campton petitioned the legislature for aid, noting that:

> . . . there are a number of rapid streams in said Campton which require expensive bridges. – That by reason of great floods, the town of Campton has sustained considerable losses in the destruction of bridges, and by a necessary removal of roads to a greater distance from the rivers . . . (Hammond 1882 XI: 252).

The selectmen asked for and were granted the ability to tax unimproved land at one penny per acre for two years in order to make the needed repairs. After the major flood of 1785, protection of life and property in the Pemigewasset Valley would continue to be a concern.

Work on roads had produced the beginnings of a highway system in the valley. In 1790 one could go north by road from Sanbornton on the east side of the Pemigewasset through New Hampton and Holderness to Plymouth, or travel to Plymouth on the river's west side from New Chester and through Bridgewater. To cross the river, except at Little's Falls, Campton, one had to use fords, and for that it was best to be on horseback.

From Holderness and Plymouth, one could go north on either side of the river to Campton, and from Campton one could reach Thornton. Beyond Thornton, however, there was no road north to Peeling, Lincoln and Franconia. In 1785, the residents of Campton, Thornton and New Holderness complained to the legislature that they shared a representative with Lincoln and Franconia, but could not reach those northern valley towns by direct road (Hammond XI 1882: 251). In 1790, residents north of Thornton were still petitioning for a road to connect Franconia with the towns of the Pemigewasset Valley to the south (Chapter 4).

There was no mail delivery anywhere in the Pemigewasset Valley until 1781, when the state legislature established postal routes from Portsmouth. One route ran to Plymouth, on to Haverhill, and back to Portsmouth via the Connecticut Valley. A rider on horseback completed the circuit once every two weeks, distributing mail at established stops along his route. The number of routes and riders increased through the 1780s, but there were no post offices in the valley until 1791, when one was established at Plymouth. There, Postmaster Dr. John Rogers handled the mail at his own office (Stearns 1987: 336-339). At that time the mail was carried from Concord via New Chester (now Hill) and Bridgewater to Plymouth and Haverhill, returning back to Concord via Alexandria. The rider was to complete the circuit once a week in summer and once every two weeks in winter. In Franconia, mail was obtained via Haverhill and the Connecticut Valley.

The new United States Constitution established the federal government in 1789, and election of members of the House of Representatives depended upon population, so a census was required. The first U.S. Census was conducted in 1790, to be repeated every ten years. It provided a measurement of progress by Pemigewasset Valley towns in the years since their creation.

After the almost simultaneous founding of ten new towns, the many land surveys, and laborious opening of roads and clearing of farms, a Pemigewasset Valley initially empty of people grew to have a population of 4,660 by 1790. The town fastest to grow was Sanbornton, with almost 1,600 residents, while the slowest to add people was Lincoln, with just 22. Plymouth and New Hampton each had more than 600 inhabitants, while Peeling (Woodstock) appeared not to have any permanent settlers at all, nor did Waterville in its interior valley. Just prior to the 1790 census in

1788, nineteen mile-long New Chester had been divided, creating the new town of Bridgewater north of the Newfound River, while New Chester remained south of that boundary. The census counted 281 residents in the new town and 312 in the old, so the division was about equal in both territory and people.

The twenty-two residents of Lincoln were members of five families who settled in 1782 on land purchased by Nathan Kinsman of Concord. In addition to Nathan, his wife Mercy and their children, there were the families of Nathan and Amos Wheeler and John and Thomas Hatch. Nathan Kinsman's purchase of the land and his family's settlement there gave Mount Kinsman its name (*Upstream*: Summer, 2014).

Other town populations in the 1790 census were: Holderness – 329, Campton – 395, Thornton – 385, and Franconia – 72. The valley towns had all grown since their creation in empty territory, despite hardship, the Revolutionary War, and natural disaster.

The 1790s and early 1800s would see considerable new development and more notable events along the Pemigewasset and "Up in the Notch."

# Chapter 7

# A New Century

The U.S. Census was conducted every ten years from 1790. By 1810, the population of Pemigewasset Valley towns, with the addition of Peeling's 203 newly-settled residents, was 10,276. Sanbornton continued to be the most populous, with 2,884 people, and Lincoln the smallest, with 100.[5] New Hampton had grown to have almost 1,400 residents and Bridgewater to a population of 1,104. Next in order were Plymouth – 937, New Chester – 895, Campton – 873, Holderness – 835, Thornton – 794, and Franconia – 358. Waterville still had not been settled. There had been some boundary changes between towns, which had taken up much of the residents' time in claims and counter-claims, but we will have to leave those details aside.

## Official Positions

When towns matured, as many had by the 1790's, there were many public jobs to be done. These official, but part-time jobs, which are mostly unknown today, offer a window into what concerned people in the years around 1800.

<u>Town Clerks</u> kept the records of the town and handled correspondence.

<u>Constables</u> performed police duties, issued the call to the annual town meeting where men of voting age made decisions for all the residents, and "warned people out of town." The last duty was based on the tradition that towns need not accept just anyone who arrived to live there. New arrivals whom the selectmen deemed to be indigent, were escorted from town by the constable.

<u>Surveyors of Highways</u> kept the roads and bridges in repair, collecting a highway tax in money or labor. Towns were divided into highway districts, each with a surveyor (later known as a Road Agent).

---

[5] This number is high for the time, as Lincoln had 41 residents in 1800 and 32 in 1820.

<u>Surveyors of Wood, Bark and Lumber</u> measured those items prior to sale.

<u>Sealers of Leather</u> did the same for hides which had been tanned into leather. Tanners often filled this position.

<u>Cullers of Staves</u> checked the quality of hoops and staves used to make barrels – the main container of that time.

<u>Sealers of Weights and Measures</u> tested the accuracy of all scales and measuring devices that were used in trade.

<u>Fence Viewers</u> decided on the adequacy of fences and settled disputes between people who shared a fence.

<u>Hog-Reeves</u> protected fields from the depredations of wandering pigs, putting a yoke on a pig or inserting a ring into its nose to keep it from destroying crops. For some reason young men of marriage age were often elected to this office.

<u>Haywards or Field-Drivers</u> protected fields from roaming animals, placing them in the town pound until their owners paid a fee and took them away.

<u>Pound-Keepers</u> managed the town pound and its animals, collecting the fee when owners retrieved them.

<u>Tithingmen</u> maintained people's decorous behavior in church, and in the town and prevented unnecessary travel on the Sabbath.

<u>Deer Keepers and Fish Wardens</u> protected deer, salmon in the Pemigewasset River and shad in the Winnipesaukee. They enforced rules regarding the making of fish weirs.

<u>Overseers of the Poor</u> were entrusted with the care and supervision of poor people who could not support themselves.

<u>Assessors</u> determined the amount of taxable property – animals, produce, mills, ferries and bridges – belonging to each property owner. There usually were several assessors, each in a separate district of the town.

<u>Tax Collectors</u> were to collect taxes based on the assessors' determination. They also collected the annual "poll," or head tax which each man of voting age owed (with some exceptions).

<u>Sextons</u> were officially designated grave diggers.

These positions were filled by auction or by election. In the first case, the person bidding lowest was given the job; in the second case, the officer was compensated by a fee connected to the activity or to the items dealt with (Musgrove 1904: 500-507) (Runnels 1882: 406-420).

*The Farmstead Era*

The list of town officers shows that by the 1790s farming was well established, and needed those services that officials provided. Farms were usually of 100 acres or more in size, based on the original survey lots which their owners had purchased. Villages were beginning to appear, with facilities such as stores and blacksmith shops, that supported the surrounding farmsteads. Just a log cabin and clearing in the early years, a farm now likely consisted of a frame house and barn, outbuildings, tilled fields, extensive pasture and mowing land, orchard and woodlot. There were oxen, cows, probably a horse, and sheep and pigs. Roads, whether local or long-distance, served farmers' need to travel to the nearest village or to carry their products - however modest, to market.

From Sanbornton to Franconia, farmsteads were the economic engines of the valley. Their cheese, butter, hides, cider, maple sugar, and surplus grain were small in quantity, but multiplied by the number of farms, supported stores that sold things the farmers could not produce themselves. Blacksmiths made and repaired farm tools, shod oxen and horses, repaired vehicles and made all types of necessary hardware. The mills that existed around 1800 sawed local lumber and ground local grain, tanned hides of locally-slaughtered animals, carded farmers' wool and fulled (finished) their home-woven cloth. Mill and farm were interdependent. Itinerant shoemakers and tailors, usually from the area, made shoes and clothing for farm families, using the families' own leather and cloth. Asa Edgerly of New Hampton recalled that:

> . . . we all had a special suit of clothes for Sunday, because father kept sheep and had the wool carded, and the girls spun the wool into thread and my mother wove it into cloth and dyed it, and father had a tailoress come there once a year and made the goods into clothing, and father had a neighbor cobbler come there and make the leather obtained from the slaughtering of animals into boots and shoes for the family (Edgerly 1909: 19).

Large families with eight to twelve children continued to be common because farming required much labor. Men and boys did the outdoor work

Blacksmiths did much vital work for farmers. *Plymouth Historical Society*

while women and girls worked indoors, except at planting, harvesting, haying, cider-making and spring sugar-making, when everyone worked together to do as much as possible in the shortest time. Women cooked and preserved the farm's foodstuffs for immediate and long-term use; baked in the farm oven; spun thread, wove woolen and linen cloth and sewed "homespun" clothing; and made butter and cheese for trade. Men tended the fields, orchard and animals; slaughtered and butchered – especially in fall for winter storage; dried, "rippled" (stripped), "retted" (soaked), "broke," and clubbed stalks of flax and combed the fibers to prepare them for spinning; sheared and washed wool; and made and repaired tools and furniture. They also worked on the roads. At times, men, women or children would help a neighbor, for which they would be repaid in equal labor or in goods.

Children reached adulthood and married early, sought farms of their own, and raised the next generation in the same way, through at least the first decades of the 1800s. This accounted for continued population growth, but also led to some further dividing of Pemigewasset Valley towns.

## Town Adjustments

In 1816, the residents of New Holderness secured the approval of the legislature to change the town's name to "Holderness." Across the river in Bridgewater and New Chester, the extent of settlement caused difficulty to some residents in attending town meetings and conducting other town business. The village of Bridgewater on the Newfound River had grown into a center for the surrounding territories of both Bridgewater on the north and New Chester to the south, and in 1819 the people in that district petitioned the legislature to create a new town. The legislature approved, and Bristol was created from the southern portion of Bridgewater and the northern portion of New Chester, totaling about 9,000 acres in all (Child 1886: 176). Bridgewater Village, with its mills at the falls on the Newfound River, became Bristol Village, the seat of the new town.

## Roads, Taverns and a Turnpike

Two roads opened in the early 1800s, and at about the same time. In 1813 the state aided the town of Franconia in improving the rough track that ran through Franconia Notch. Petitioners from several northern towns had pressed the state to give them a route from Franconia, through Lincoln to Thornton and the valley to the south, and this appears to be when that was finally done.

In 1801, farmers of the upper Pemigewasset Valley were agitating for a road that connected the Mad River valley in Thornton with the village of Center Sandwich. Such a road would allow them to carry their produce and drive their animals by a more direct route to the markets of Portland and the New Hampshire coast, returning the same way with goods and supplies that were cheaper there. The Town of Sandwich did little at first, but in 1814, voted enough money to build the Sandwich Notch Road.

The road benefitted businesses in Sandwich at the bottom of the notch where ongoing routes leading east and south were reached. It also opened the 1,400 foot-high notch plateau to farms, a tavern, a mill, and schools (Heyduk 2017: 40-43).

In the 1790s and early 1800s, wheeled vehicles other than ox carts had not reached the Pemigewasset Valley. This was partly due to the condition of roads and absence of bridges, and partly to the nature of travel. Travelers were few and each had a purpose: to deliver the mail, to stock a store, to transport goods or animals to market, to preach on the circuit, or to carry items to and from the mill. These tasks were accomplished by riding a horse, driving an ox cart, or walking while herding animals along the route. Isaac Willey, who grew up in Campton, said that: "Colonel Holmes procured the first chaise [a two-wheel, one horse vehicle] and drove it into town on his return from the General Court [legislature] in Concord in 1811" (Willey 1868: 28). He added that he had not seen a wagon in Campton up until his departure in 1817, and that women commonly rode horses at that time.

People who traveled without an identifiable reason were rare and were suspected of having unsavory motives. Historian Eva Speare wrote that: ". . . nobody except the minister or representative to the legislature traveled ten miles outside the limits of the township unless guilty of a misdemeanor" (Speare 1988: 31). Any question about a person's business was usually resolved when the traveler stopped at a tavern for food, drink or lodging, and was inevitably engaged in conversation.

Because roads were poor and travel slow, travelers often had to seek lodging along their route. At first farmhouses might allow a stopover, but on the more traveled roads taverns, which were licensed to provide food and drink, lodging, and animal feed and shelter, began to appear. Post riders stopped at taverns to leave newspapers and notices and to drop off or pick up mail. People gathered there to learn the news and to order rum, cider, and other alcoholic drinks that the tavern was licensed to serve. One of the most successful tavern locations was at Plymouth village, where the long distance roads met. There, early settler David Webster opened his log house as a tavern, which he expanded as trade increased (Speare 1988: 13-14). In addition to travelers, the tavern served people who stayed in the village for sessions of the Grafton County Court. In 1800, David's son William took over the business and constructed a large frame building with a gambrel roof to become the new Webster Tavern on Plymouth's Main Street (Speare 1988: 38).

Roads, along with bridges, were a great expense to towns, so as with private toll bridges, toll roads were chartered by the legislature to a group of investors to be built and maintained, and tolls charged to users. The only toll road in Pemigewasset Valley towns was the Mayhew Turnpike,

The new gambrel roof Webster Tavern, with part of the old log tavern at left.
*Plymouth Historical Society*

chartered in 1803 to run from the Smith River in New Chester some sixteen miles along the east side of Newfound Lake, to a junction with the Coos Road in Rumney, just west of Plymouth. Tolls were one cent per mile for ten sheep or pigs, two cents for every ten cattle or horses, two cents for each two-wheeled vehicle, and four cents for a four-wheeled vehicle, with like charges for sleighs and sleds. Residents of the town rode free, but those living along the pike helped to maintain it.

The road was later extended south through New Chester. This turnpike shortened a trip from north and west of Plymouth to Boston by many miles, and it was: "common to see in the fall of the year large droves of cattle that fairly choked the turnpikes as they traveled to market" (Musgrove 1904: 103). The road was just as busy in winter, when rollers pulled by oxen were used to pack the surface. Then sleds were used and groups of farmers traveled together to carry their goods to Boston (Ibid). Taverns opened along the Mayhew Turnpike, more farms were cleared, and Bridgewater (later Bristol) Village benefitted too (Haight 1941: 26).

One toll house was at North Main Street in Bristol Village, where Rev. and Mrs. Sleeper were at one time the toll-takers. A story is told that:

> *One day after a storm a traveler, complaining that the road had not been broken out, refused to pay his toll, upon which she* [Mrs. Sleeper] *refused to open the gate. Finally he threw a silver dollar at her feet in the snow. Returning from the house with the change in small pieces she made delivery to him as she had received the dollar* (Wood 1919: 226).

It was in the early 1800s that three long-to-be-remembered events took place in Franconia Notch. First was the discovery of the Old Man of the Mountain in 1805 (Chapter 4). Second was the discovery of the Flume by 93-year-old "Aunt Jess" Guernsey of Lincoln in 1808, while she was exploring for fishing spots. A deep, narrow gorge some 700 feet long, 60-70 feet deep, and only 10 feet wide at its narrowest point, the Flume also had a large boulder lodged in its upper half. Word of her discovery spread, and the "Stone Flume" became another of the novelties for which the Notch would be known. Last, and probably dating after improvement of the Notch road in 1813, was the tale of how Thomas Boise (or Boyce) survived a cold and stormy night in the Notch.

Apparently in the late autumn or winter of the year, and according to historian Sarah Welch, Tom:

> *. . . came up through the Notch with a load of apples, cider and vinegar. He was caught in a blizzard, and his exhausted horse died. It is said he skinned the animal and rolled up in the hide under the edge of a large rock where he was somewhat sheltered from the storm. In the morning a group of men with ox teams came along, breaking out the road, and found his sled and the remains of his horse. They also found him under the rock. The hide had frozen stiff and he was locked inside, but alive. They . . .* [took] *him to the nearest house to be thawed out. When this was accomplished, he was fed and seemed none the worse for his experience* (Welch 1972: 68).

Tom Boise's story was told and retold, and "Boise Rock" became one of the Notch's enduring landmarks.

The "Stone Flume," with its suspended boulder, which remained in place until 1883. *John W. and Anne H. Newton Collection, Museum of the White Mountains, Plymouth State University*

## The Almanack and the Weather

A well-used reference in many Pemigewasset Valley homes for over fifty years was Dudley Leavitt's *Farmer's Almanack*. The *Almanack* was published annually from 1797, in an inexpensive format and bound with string, with a loop for hanging on a nail or peg. It provided Dudley's predictions for major weather events on a monthly basis, based on his astronomical research. The page for each month also carried an illustration, recommendations for farm activities, note of phases of the moon, the tides, and events such as eclipses – with their timing. He listed college vacations, dates on which the courts would be in session, and postage and interest rates. There were articles on miscellaneous subjects, a puzzle, and even poetry. Written specifically for New England, the *Almanack* reached a circulation of 60,000 in the 1840s (Heyduk 2015: 33-39). In many households the *Almanack* and the Bible were the only sources of reading material.

Dudley's astronomical calculations could not anticipate hurricanes and volcanic eruptions, but those events impacted the Pemigewasset Valley in 1815 and 1816. The year 1815 began with steady cold weather and no January thaw, which allowed: "Good sleighing the whole winter" (Runnels 1882: 143). On May 19, three to four inches of snow fell, but the most memorable event was the "Great Gale of September 23." Joshua Lane, the Sanbornton Town Clerk, recorded: "A furious gale or hurricane, and very rainy. Buildings and Timber destroyed" (Ibid). In New Chester and Bridgewater, Richard Musgrove noted: ". . . much damage was done to fruit trees and buildings," and Sidney Perley reported that: "apples were blown from the trees [and] At Sanbornton the loss was estimated at fifteen thousand dollars" (Musgrove 1904: 472) (Perley 2001: 168-69).

Also in 1815, Mount Tambora erupted in Indonesia and sent sulphur and ash into the upper atmosphere, which would make 1816 "the year without a summer." After a warm beginning, the month of June, 1816 brought a hard frost and snow. Then, after a hot interval, there was frost again in early July. August weather was moderate at first, but frost returned on August 21, killing the corn despite bonfires which farmers lit in their fields, and it remained cold through the end of the month. There was snow again on September 11 and hard frosts after the 20th. September also brought the "most severe drought ever known" according to Joshua Lane, with devastating forest fires across northern New England. Then, Musgrove notes: "There was not enough [corn] raised for seed the next year, and provisions of all kinds went to fabulous prices . . . Many had no hay at all the latter part of the winter, and could not obtain any, and many cattle died" (Musgrove 1904: 473). Farmers had a good year in 1817, but some wary people moved west.

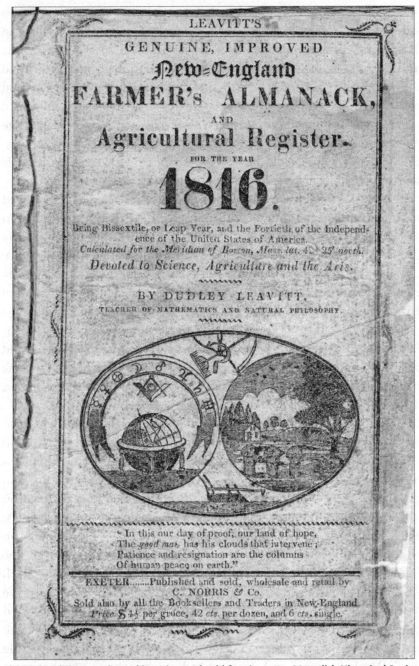

LEAVITT'S

GENUINE, IMPROVED

New=England

FARMER's ALMANACK,

AND

Agricultural Register.

FOR THE YEAR

1816.

Being Bissextile, or Leap Year, and the Fortieth of the Independence of the United States of America.
Calculated for the Meridian of Boston, Mass. lat. 42° 25' north.

Devoted to Science, Agriculture and the Arts.

BY DUDLEY LEAVITT,

TEACHER OF MATHEMATICS AND NATURAL PHILOSOPHY.

"In this our day of proof, our land of hope,
The *good man* has his clouds that intervene ;
Patience and resignation are the columns
Of human peace on earth."

EXETER.......Published and sold, wholesale and retail by
C. NORRIS & Co.
Sold also by all the Booksellers and Traders in New-England.
Price $44 per groce, 42 *cts.* per dozen, and 6 *cts.* single.

The 1816 edition was bound in string and sold for six cents. *Meredith Historical Society*

# Chapter 8

# Agriculture, Education and Industry

In the 1820s, more rapid change began to overtake the farms and villages of the valley. Some was the result of local initiative and some came from far outside the region.

*A New Town and a New Name*

In 1828, after debate of the subject for some years, the New Hampshire legislature created the Town of Franklin from parts of Sanbornton, Northfield, Salisbury and Andover. Franklin was to occupy both banks of the Winnipesaukee and Pemigewasset rivers in the area where those rivers met – the old Native American oxbow territory of ages past. The residents who had petitioned for the new town argued that:

> There have recently been erected on the banks of the Winnipesaukee River; within the limits of the proposed new town, a paper mill and cotton manufactory, both of which are now in full and successful operation. From the great falls in this and other streams in that vicinity and the inexhaustible supply of water, there is reason to believe that very extensive manufacturing establishments and other works requiring waterpower will, at no distant period, be erected . . . (The Granite Monthly 1923: 147).

The new town also included the Republican Bridge over the Pemigewasset River, the potential water power upstream at Eastman Falls, and the birthplace of Daniel Webster. Creation of Franklin, and earlier of Bristol, signaled a new path that some valley towns would take.

In 1836, and without unanimous approval, the town of New Chester was re-named Hill in honor of then governor Isaac Hill.

## The New Town of Waterville

Waterville was not yet a town when Moses Foss cleared land in 1819 along the Mad River, as close as possible to his neighbors in Thornton and Campton, while still being on the large unincorporated upland tract that he had purchased. At that time Moses and his wife Sally had six children, and by 1830 they would have nine. Others joined them there, in the narrow valley at the foot of rocky Welch and Dickey mountains. With those settled families, the new, but mostly empty town was incorporated in 1829. Settlers reached Waterville's interior valley around 1830, when the town's population reached 69 (Goodrich 1916: 13) (Goodrich 1952: 2).

One of the settlers in that deep valley - at 1,500 feet in elevation among surrounding mountains in excess of 4,000 feet - was Nathaniel Greeley. Other homesteaders, including Nathaniel's brother, found conditions difficult and did not stay, but Nathaniel:

> cleared a small area, built a log cabin, then traveled the sixty miles
> to Chatham, over on the Maine line, married Nancy Wyman, and
> brought her back by ox-team. He then cut and burned the trees on
> a hundred acres , . . way up to the ledges. Nancy told . . . how, after
> the fire had swept over the mass of fallen trees, she used to shut
> her two little boys in the cabin while she, day after day, gathered
> and burned such half consumed pieces as she was able to handle.
> They planted an orchard . . . Later, having acquired better land,
> Greeley cleared the meadows by the river, felling and burning, then
> removing stumps by ox-team and lever (Goodrich 1952: 3-4).

Gradually, Nathaniel and Nancy made a farm with a frame house and barn, raising cattle that he drove to market. He cut timber too. As early as 1835, a man with lung trouble spent some weeks with the Greeleys, and liking the experience, returned with his wife the next year. Word of the valley's attractions began to spread and fishermen, too, came to Waterville during the summer. Scenery and country life were beginning to appeal to people in the growing cities. The Greeleys, still in their 30s at that time, became inn-keepers in addition to their farming, and summer hospitality would become Waterville's new growth industry (Ibid: 4).

## The Sheep Boom

International events between 1805 and 1815 set the stage for changes in the Pemigewasset Valley during the 1820s, 30s, and beyond. Problems between the United States and Britain in the early 1800s, led to restrictions on trade, to the War of 1812, and to a scarcity of imported goods. Suddenly, British cloth could not be imported, with the result that textile mills were built quickly throughout New England. At the same time, Napoleon Bonaparte's invasion of Spain in 1809 led the Spanish government to lift its prohibition on the export of its fine wool-producing Merino sheep. William Jarvis of Vermont was able to buy almost 4,000 Merinos and ship them to the U.S., where they were bred with local sheep, producing much improved wool for the new textile mills to use (Vermont Historical Society 2004).

The demand for wool by factories and the high price that they would pay led farmers to raise more sheep and clear more land for pasture. For farmers that also meant building high stone walls to enclose sheep pastures; growing more hay, oats and corn for winter feed; and building more shelter to protect sheep from winter cold and storms. By the 1830s, mills in Northfield, Franklin, Campton, Holderness, Bristol and Rochester were producing blankets, "satinets," "cassimeres," and other woolen goods, and paying local farmers an average of fifty cents per pound for wool (Benton 1837: 109-110).[6]

Sheep were not counted in tax inventories until the 1830s. Before that, virtually every farm had some sheep for the family's clothing, but the arrival of better stock and growth of the valley's textile mills in the 1820s would have prompted farmers to raise more and better sheep. Our first record of the sheep boom is from 1831, when Campton had 2,675 sheep, New Hampton had 2,493, Holderness reported 2,041, Thornton had 1,580, Bridgewater had 1,387, and even small Bristol had 918 (inventories are lacking for other towns). Each sheep produced some three pounds of wool, so that sheep earned Campton's farmers over $4,000 that year.

---

[6] Mills were - Franklin: Sanborn & Herrick; Northfield: Jeremiah Tilton; Campton: M. Cook; Holderness: __; Bristol: Roberts; Rochester: R. Kimball.

**Sheep grazing inside a high stone wall and fence.** *D. Heyduk*

By 1836, when all the Pemigewasset Valley's towns reported, sheep numbered 21,880, which translated into $32,820 in farm income (some $900,000 today) (Ibid: 12-18). There were "sheep towns," such as Sanbornton with 3,892, Campton with 2,730, Franklin with 2,139, and Plymouth with 2,097, and there were "non-sheep towns," like Lincoln with 12 sheep and Waterville with 77. Waterville's human population was just 69, however, so sheep outnumbered residents. In fact, in many towns sheep outnumbered people, and in Campton it was by more than two to one. Even Peeling, with only 292 people, had 325 sheep.

In 1836, there were some 465,000 sheep in New Hampshire, and wool sold for more than 55 cents per pound. The supply of wool was growing rapidly, however, with Midwestern states also raising sheep and shipping wool cheaply to the east coast via the Erie Canal. In 1836, Ohio alone had 1.78 million sheep. Prices for wool dropped to 25 cents per pound by the late 1840s.

Pemigewasset Valley farmers continued to invest in sheep-raising, with Campton having over 4,000 sheep in 1847, Thornton having more than 3,400, and Bridgewater over 2,500 – all more than in 1836. The boom ended in the 1850s, but returned briefly in the early 1860s due to demand for wool by the army during the Civil War. Plymouth farmers, for example, raised only 900 sheep in 1855, but had more than three times that number in 1864. The later 1800s would see a steady decline in sheep-raising, and of agriculture overall.

A carding machine had many toothed rollers to straighten wool fibers. In early carding mills people took their wool home to spin and weave, but in the textile factories of the 1820s and 30s, other machines spun and wove wool into finished cloth. *D. Heyduk*

## Founding Academies

Until the 1820s, education in the valley was confined to the many basic rural and village schools supported by families of the neighborhood, and subject to frequent changes of teacher, of location, and even of the length of the school term. As population grew and more remote uplands were settled, more schools were needed. New Hampton, a smaller than average

town, had six school districts in 1805, which grew to seventeen districts by
1851 (Merrill 1977: 90-91). The character of the common one-room school
is summarized by a description of the role of the teacher, which was:

> . . . at best, a difficult one. When one considers that the average
> class consisted of about twenty students of all ages and varying
> abilities, he must admit that the challenge to the teacher must have
> been a formidable one. Also facing the teacher was the dearth of
> books which, in most cases had to be obtained from the home of the
> student. The Bible, for lack of any other instructional material, was
> often employed as a tool to instruct reading, writing, grammar, and
> arithmetic – or ciphering as it was then called.
>
> Teachers, during this particular period in our country's history,
> were poorly prepared to assume their teaching responsibilities.
> Teacher colleges were non-existent, and many of New Hampton's
> earliest teachers possessed no more formal education than their
> most advanced students (Ibid).

Into this situation stepped some of the valley's more educated residents
in several towns. They could not reform public education, but they could
offer a next step to students who emerged from it, and that next step was
the private academy.

In New Hampton in 1821, nineteen incorporators petitioned the
legislature for creation of the New Hampton Academy. Under the act that
the legislature passed that year, they had: "the power to appoint and
dismiss instructors, prescribe their duties; establish orders and regulations
for the government of the students, direct the management and
application of the funds and generally direct and control all the concerns
of the institution . . ." (Merrill 1977: 115-116). The academy was to be a
seminary, the Preceptor (head of school) was a Dartmouth graduate with
teaching experience, the "new and elegant" building measured 24 X 32 feet
and was of two stories, and tuition for the 'young gentleman and lady'
students was $3.00 per quarter, with board of $1.00 to $1.38 per week. New
Hampton Academy's first term began in September, 1821. Eighty-seven
students of both sexes, thirteen of whom were from Boston, were enrolled.
The academy supported itself with tuition and donations from dedicated
patrons. In 1826, it became the New Hampton Academical and Theological
Institution under support of the Baptist Church. Enrollment grew to 321
students, many from surrounding towns, by 1831.

Today's New Hampton School was the New Hampton Academy and the Academical and Theological Institution in the early 1800s. *D. Heyduk*

In the neighboring town of Sanbornton, the Woodman Sanbornton Academy was incorporated in 1826, its building having been erected the prior year at Sanbornton Square. This was a boarding school, with strict standards and regulations:

> *No person shall be employed as teacher who is not a professor of religion, of exemplary manners, good natural abilities, and literary and scientific acquirements . . .* [Teachers must] *open and close the school with prayer* [and] *have some portion of the sacred Scriptures read each day by the pupils . . . The Teachers must also inculcate the fundamental principles of the Christian religion, and the great and important Christian doctrines . . .*
>
> [Students are] *not allowed to indulge in profane swearing, any species of gambling, or intemperance, and . . . forbidden to associate with any persons of bad morals, or to frequent grog shops or taverns. Each student shall attend public worship on every Sabbath* [and] *no scholar shall be allowed to attend a dancing school while a member of the academy* (Runnels 1882: 120).

Woodman Academy had 109 male and 71 female students in 1840, with a boarding house that provided 'board, washing, wood and light.' The academy declined, as did the Square, with growth of the mill villages of Franklin and Sanbornton Bridge (Tilton) along the Winnipesaukee River. Its last year was 1857.

Woodman Academy is at left, with the Congregational Church at center, and Sanbornton's Town House at right, in Sanbornton Square. *Runnels 1882*

The earliest initiative to create an academy in the Pemigewasset Valley was taken when Col. Samuel Holmes of Campton donated $500 for the establishment of a private school at Plymouth. The legislature granted the charter in 1808, and the new school was named the Holmes Plymouth Academy. There are no records of its early years, but a building was in place and a principal hired in 1825-26. In 1835, Rev. George Punchard raised funds to replace the old building with a new one, and three acres of land were purchased. A handsome new brick two story building was erected, along with two nearby boarding houses – one for students and one for faculty.

As with other academies, the 168 students came about equally from Plymouth and from other towns. A new Principal, Rev. Samuel Reed Hall, was engaged in 1835, along with twelve faculty members. In 1837, Rev. Hall introduced a course of study to train teachers for the public schools, a far-sighted innovation at the time. The academy continued to operate for some years thereafter, but the buildings had a longer life, eventually becoming the site of the Plymouth Normal School in 1871 (One Hundred and Fiftieth Anniversary 1913: 33) (Speare 1988: 45, 70).

The Grafton County Courthouse at left, the Academy dormitory at center, and the Holmes Plymouth Academy building at right. *Plymouth Historical Society*

## The Rise of Industry

Until about the 1820s, simple saw, grist, carding and fulling mills were to be found throughout the Pemigewasset Valley wherever water power was available, and within reach of the farmsteads that supplied them and that they served. After 1830, growing villages with better water power, such as in Franklin, Bristol, Holderness, Plymouth and Campton, added factories that took in raw material, passed it through a series of processes, and created a finished product. The "mill" and the farm began to go their separate ways.

A unique case was the Franconia Iron Works. This industry was based on the discovery of a rich vein of iron ore in the Gale River Valley. A mine was opened and a charcoal-burning furnace built in 1811, which produced 250 to 500 tons of cast iron per year. In 1838, the mine employed ten men and the furnace employed fifty to one hundred on a part-year basis, with some living in a company boarding house. The foundry made various iron items, including cauldrons and wood-burning box stoves. A fire destroyed the foundry buildings in 1884, and the business was not resumed, but the stone blast furnace remains to mark the site (Welch 1972: 46-50).

In villages of the Pemigewasset Valley where small tanneries had previously supplied farmsteads with leather, a factory approach led to the employment of shoemakers who produced finished shoes and boots in the tannery building. It also led to piecework production by which cutting of leather into standard shapes was done by workers in their homes. This was begun in Bristol in the 1830s, and was likewise used in Plymouth, where housewives received cut leather to stitch together for the manufacture of gloves (Haight 1941: 47) (Speare 1988: 69). In Plymouth:

> *Each shop distributed the bundles* [of glove leather] *to its list of women who expertly sewed the seams with a welt between the two parts by using linen thread and three sided needles that were frequently filed to keep the edges sharp. Scores of housewives kept their glove baskets where every spare minute would be snatched to sew a seam. Although the remuneration was almost a pittance, yet these thrifty women found that many dollars accrued from their glove baskets* (Speare 1988: 69).

Plymouth became a center of glove-making after tanner Alvah McQuestern experimented with tanning deer skin. He developed a method to tan, dye and soften deer hide, which then could be sewn into "Plymouth Buck Gloves." The actual process of making gloves, with piecework done in peoples' homes, did not require a large factory, and beginning in the 1830s, there were several businesses operating in

Plymouth Village and in Glove Hollow (Speare 1988: 67-69). One such glove-maker in the Hollow south of the village was Jason Draper, who would later grow his business into a widely-known sporting goods company (McCormack 2017: 15-16).

Another Plymouth industry was pottery-making, begun prior to 1820 along the Baker River, where fine clay was found. Brick-making began in the area, and then potters used the clay to make "Brown Ware" ceramics. As their production grew, they made miniature pieces that could be used to advertise the dishes, bowls, pitchers, vases, bean-pots, and round, hollow "rum rings" that could be made to order (Speare 1988: 65-67).

Elsewhere, from beginnings in the carding, dyeing and fulling mills that had helped farm women to spin and weave their home-made cloth, factories utilized newly-developed machines to complete the entire cloth-making process. In Bristol village in 1830, for example, a new factory had: "a carding machine and picker, a 50-spindle billey, a 100-spindle jinny, a warping mill, twisting machine, five looms, 1,400 filling bobbins and 600 warping bobbins" (Haight 1941: 47). The factory could produce different kinds of cloth, which women could buy, rather than make themselves. Another trend which the factory introduced was employment of women in the textile mills, which would become a means for their obtaining greater economic and social independence.

Some factories provided lodging in factory-owned boarding houses for their employees, who were mostly women from the surrounding rural area. The Bristol Manufacturing Company employed fifty workers in 1839 in its three story factory, with adjacent housing in a two story boarding house (Ibid). Homeowners in a factory village also gained added income by taking in boarders, and village populations grew. In Campton, the Cook carding mill was established on the Mad River, between the upper and lower village in 1826, and in the 1840s spinning and weaving equipment was installed to become the E. Dole & Company textile factory (America's Textile Reporter 1961). There, as in Bristol and Plymouth, piecework was delivered to women who stitched the factory's pants and shirts. As far away as Woodstock, women were sewing Dole Company pants for twelve cents a pair (Sawyer 2013: 37).

Until the late 1840s, Pemigewasset Valley villages and factories were served only by roads, over which all raw material arrived and all products were shipped to market. Freight wagons pulled by teams of horses provided transport of goods, in some cases all the way from Portsmouth and Boston. Moor Russell, who owned a prosperous store in Plymouth, ran freight wagons drawn by six and eight horse teams to and from the coast (Speare 1988: 36-37). As early as 1828, a factory in Franklin which manufactured cotton yarn and twine was supplied with its raw material by freight wagons, as were textile mills that produced "satinet," a popular cotton-wool blend fabric (Runnels 1882: 221).

In growing factory villages other services appeared: more and larger stores; machine, wheelwright, cabinet and furniture shops; newspapers; fire departments; banks; medical and law offices; clock makers, and even jewelers. As the populations of villages grew, the surrounding countryside lost residents. This was most obvious in the census results for extensively rural towns such as Bridgewater, compared to more industrial towns such as Bristol. In 1830, Bridgewater had 784 residents and Bristol 799, but just ten years later in 1840, Bridgewater had 747 people compared to Bristol's 1,153.

Hawley's glove-making establishment in Plymouth's "Glove Hollow." *Plymouth Historical Society*

An 1820s carding mill known as Mad River Mills became the Campton textile factory of E. Dolc & Co. in the 1840s. *Campton Historical Society*

Industrial development in Holderness was in the village, and used the substantial water power of the Squam River. There was a paper mill in 1810, but paper making at that time (as in Franklin in 1828) was more of a made-by-hand operation than the mechanized process that it would later become. There were two woolen mills in 1840, and although there is no description, at least one of them was probably an integrated factory that made cloth from the ample raw wool that sheep boom farmers supplied. The neighborhood, which would later become industry-centered Ashland Village, grew in facilities and services during this time and drew workers from the surrounding rural area.

## The Northern Valley Towns

Thornton continued to be a farming town from the 1820s to the 1840s, taking part in the sheep boom, and growing to a population of over 1,000. In the narrow valleys among the mountains in 1832, Thornton farmers had just 203 acres of cultivated land, but 500 acres of mowing, and 1,194 acres of pasture. Their farms were more dedicated to stock-raising than to crops, with some 1,500 sheep, 200 horses, and 1,100 oxen and cattle that year – almost three stock animals for each resident. Freight wagons and stage coaches to Franconia Notch passed along the main road on the west side of the Pemigewasset, with the attendant roadside taverns, but the old town center with the meetinghouse and cemetery was on the east side.

The logging industry began during this period, probably on a small scale, with saw mills producing lumber for local use, and the first down-river log drives. Large lumber markets were far to the south, and the Pemigewasset and Merrimack rivers offered the only economical means of delivering logs to distant saw mills. Logging was thus focused on spruce, fir and pine, which would float, leaving hardwood trees standing in the forest.

In the 1820s and 30s, Peeling was a farming town, with several farms and a rural community of some fifteen farmsteads in the Mount Cilley area. In 1840, Peeling changed its name to Woodstock, and the second chapter in its development began: commercial logging. In the census of that year four saw mills were recorded, but those were of small scale, devoted to cutting lumber for local construction. During the 1840's, lumberman Nicholas Norcross bought some 100,000 acres, established winter logging camps, cut fir, pine and spruce, and built a dam to impound water. The dam was opened each spring and logs were floated down the Pemigewasset and Merrimack rivers in log drives to his saw mill in Lowell, Massachusetts (LogginginLincoln 2019) (Conrad 1897: 13-14). Logging also took place in Hubbard Brook Valley west of the Pemigewasset, with saw mills at Mirror Lake (Holmes 2016: xi).

Logging did not mean residence, and the Town of Lincoln remained sparsely populated in the early 1800s, growing from 50 people in 1820 to 76 in 1840. There was not even a town meeting in the years between 1815 and 1829 (*Upstream*, Winter 2015). A hotel and a tavern were established on the road to Franconia Notch, to serve freight drivers and a growing number of tourists who were beginning to travel that route.

Settlers Tom and Mary Pollard moved to a farm on the Pemigewasset's East Branch in 1841. At the time of their arrival the farm was no more than a dilapidated log house at the end of the road. They built a frame house and barn and farmed industriously, with Tom also working as a peddler and as the local distributor for *Leavitt's Farmer's Almanack* (Chapter 7). He collected spruce gum in the East Branch forest and sold it to drug stores (*Upstream*, Winter 2012). This pioneering Lincoln family, in the last house on the edge of a vast East Branch wilderness, would become better known in later years.

Pemigewasset Valley towns had grown and diversified in the 1820s, 30s, and 40s. While the large scale changes described here were taking place, other local events were occurring, and they too, are part of the valley's history.

A topographic map of Franconia Notch at center and the Pemigewasset River flowing south out of the Notch to Plymouth. The East and West branches of the Pemigewasset meet at Woodstock, just south of the dark-shaded Notch. *Boston Public Library*

# Chapter 9

# Stories from the Valley

The Pemigewasset Valley was the scene of some noteworthy local occurrences, which were also windows into the times in which they took place.

## The Mount Cilley Settlers and Peddlers of the Valley

Time slowed as one went north in the Pemigewasset Valley from Thornton, and conditions in Woodstock (then Peeling) in the 1820s were similar to the experience of earlier settlers further south. The Mount Cilley area of Woodstock was settled in 1824, some four miles west of the Pemigewasset River in an intermontane valley. People there were isolated at the end of the road, but the community of fifteen or more families had a saw mill for building lumber, a school for their children, and Doctor Sawyer, who was one of the first settlers. There was a small mill which made starch from their potato crop, and family cemeteries were located here and there. Historian Ida Sawyer wrote of this neighborhood:

> It is hard to picture living conditions on Mt. Cilley, but we know the houses were of sawed lumber and were plastered. The cleared land gave food for oxen and cattle, potatoes and hardy vegetables were raised but early and late frosts made corn and beans a gamble.

> Naming the brooks was simple. The story is told that Thomas Smith coming home from work on the burnt piece looked at the shirts they were wearing and said, "these shirts are going to be hard for Mar'm to clean," whereupon the three men washed them in the brook, which of course became Shirt Brook. Crossing a brook on a log footbridge a man dropped his pipe in the water, so Pipe Brook was christened . . . and naturally the brook past the school was Schoolhouse Brook.

*Many a heartache was suffered on the mountain and one of the saddest has never been forgotten. From the Joseph Smith place a son Napoleon B., wanted to get away either to get more schooling or to see what the outside was like. He had his sister, Alma, throw his few supplies out of the window one evening and he left on his great adventure. The next spring his body and knapsack were found not far from a farmstead.*

*The abandonment of the Mt. Cilley farms has been attributed to the reluctance of the town to keep a road in traveling condition, even for ox carts* (Sawyer 2013: 20-21).

The Mount Cilley settlers could support themselves, but their isolation, especially in winter when it was hard to get supplies up the road, made life there difficult. The last farm was abandoned around 1865, and afterward a hermit settled there and lived alone in comfortable solitude. Just cellar holes and family gravestones remain today.

**Gathering Wood, a painting by George Henry Durrie.** *The Shelburne Museum, see Durrie in the bibliography*

Ida Sawyer also described how Woodstock's people welcomed visits of peddlers,

> . . . who brought wares and fellowship into the village. Often the peddler put his horse in some man's barn and found shelter for himself at the farmhouse each time he came through town. Frank and Henry Smith often kept the peddlers. Woodstock recalls a Rogers who often came with a beautiful big horse of which he took such good care; Joe and Milo Morison also came through with shoes and dry goods. George Foss was last to run a regular route from Plymouth up. The picturesque carts with brooms, clothes baskets, galvanized wash tubs and pails on the outside and all sorts of notions within are things of the past (Sawyer 2013: 38).

## Roads and Bridges

Campton is divided into east and west halves by the Pemigewasset River and also divided north to south by the Mad and Beebe rivers, which enter the Pemigewasset from the east, and by Bog Brook and West Branch Brook, which flow from the west. Before state highways and interstate highways were created in the 20th century, towns were responsible for all their roads and bridges. In 1837, Campton pleaded that it was responsible for maintaining ten wooden bridges, including rebuilding their abutments:

> Village bridge over Mad River – 87 feet
> Elliot bridge – 80 feet
> Spencer bridge – 62 feet
> Southmayd – 84 feet
> Near Parsonage – 93 feet
> Near Cooks Mill- 92 feet
> Bog Brook – 115 feet
> West Branch – 112 feet
> Livermore [Falls] – 255 feet
> Blair – 310 feet

Campton tax-payers also had to maintain "two main roads through the whole length of the town, one on each side of the river, plus about 30 miles in length in back parts of the town" (Campton Historical Society). For most Pemigewasset Valley towns, highway expenditure was the largest item in their budget, and Campton was the most impacted in that respect.

*Millerites of the 1840s*

In his autobiography, historian Richard Musgrove of Bristol recalled that in 1843:

> *I stood by my mother's knees and listened to a discussion by her and the Rev. Nathaniel W. Aspinwall, about the Millerite craze that was then sweeping over the country, and about its disastrous effects on the churches in Bristol and the community in general . . . I clearly discerned that something terrible was abroad in the land, and, indeed, that a calamity had visited Bristol.*
>
> *The chief topic of discussion in those days was the immediate coming of Christ and the end of the world. Large numbers of people completely lost their reasoning powers. They not only believed in the end of the world at a time only a few months in advance, but they contended that a belief in this doctrine was essential to salvation when the end should come. Some went so far as to prepare robes in which to ascend to glory* (Musgrove 1921: 7).

William Miller was a Baptist lay preacher in New York State who predicted the second advent of Jesus Christ based on his reading of the prophesies of Daniel. Most clergy dismissed his prediction, but he gave numerous lectures, sent articles to a Baptist Church newspaper, and had a pamphlet printed. Miller's ideas then appeared in a Boston-based church newspaper, which circulated widely in New England.

Miller did not give an exact date for the "second coming," but at a camp meeting in Exeter, NH, Samuel Snow pronounced that it would be July 10, 1844. Another prediction was October 22. In Bristol and surrounding towns, Musgrove related that:

> *The chief effect of this craze was to unfit people for the every-day work of life. Business was neglected, crops were left ungathered in the field, and many were brought to suffer for their improvidence. David Trumbull of Hill . . . had a large field of potatoes that he*

*declined to dig because he should not need them. One day Hezekiah Sargent, a neighbor, asked permission to dig a few. "Yes," said Trumbull, "dig all you wish. I only want a few to last me the short time I shall stay here." Time wore on and Trumbull needed more potatoes . . . and called on Sargent to help him out, when Sargent coolly replied that he did not know as he had any to spare (Ibid).*

This came to be known as the "Great Disappointment," and had after-effects for several years. Some "Millerites" turned to other doctrines, and some became Shakers.

## Henry David Thoreau

Naturalist, philosopher and author Henry David Thoreau (*Walden, The Maine Woods,* etc.) made a trip through the length of the Pemigewasset Valley in September, 1839. As was his custom, Henry kept a journal in which he recorded the trip. His companion was his brother John, and the two had rowed up the Merimack River from Massachusetts, camping along the bank and on islands, to Hooksett, where they stored their boat in a farmer's barn and walked to Concord. The next day, September 6, they took a stagecoach north to Plymouth, stopping at Lane Tavern in Sanbornton Square, where the passengers probably were served a mid-day meal. Thoreau wrote: "The scenery commences on Sanbornton Square, whence the White Mountains are first visible" (Howarth 1982: 211).

In fact, the mountains are not visible at Sanbornton Square, and it is likely that the Thoreaus first saw the mountains after leaving the Square, as their stage climbed Mountain Road to the stagecoach stop at the top, which was the home of Charles and Sarah Emerson. There the horses probably were changed after the long climb, and Henry and John would have seen the Ossipee and White Mountains across the Emerson's pasture, which was at about 1,300 feet elevation (Heyduk 2017: 35-37).

The stage then continued on to Plymouth, where the Thoreaus began walking north along today's Route 3: "on foot to Tilton's Inn, Thornton." Along the way, Henry noted that "In Campton it is decidedly mountainous" (Journal, September 6).

Leaving Thornton the next morning, Henry wrote: "Walked from Thornton through Peeling and Lincoln to Franconia. In Lincoln visited Stone Flume and Basin, and in Franconia the Notch, and saw the Old Man of the Mountain (Journal, September 7). The road at that time was narrow and enclosed by trees, so their views were limited. Thoreau did not mention the Pool, nor Eagle Cliff, but about the Basin near the Pemigewasset's source he later wrote:

> . . . on the head waters of this stream - by the roadside in the town of Lincoln - a mere brook, which may be passed at a stride, falling upon a rock has worn a basin from 30 to 40 feet in diameter – and proportionally deep – and passes out . . . by a deep channel, scarcely more than a foot in width cut directly opposite to its entrance. It has a rounded brim of glassy water smoothness and is filled with cold transparent greenish water (Howarth 1982: 215).

The brothers spent the night in Franconia and the next day: "walked from Franconia to Thomas J. Crawfords," at the top of Crawford Notch (Journal, September 8). They then climbed Mount Washington. Henry wrote about travel:

> The cheapest way to travel, and the way to travel the furthest in the shortest distance, is to go afoot, carrying a dipper, a spoon, and a fish line, some Indian meal, some salt and some sugar. When you come to a brook or pond, you can catch fish and cook them; or you can boil a hasty pudding; or you can buy a loaf of bread at a farmer's house for fourpence, moisten it in the next brook that crosses the road, and dip it into your sugar, - this alone will last you a whole day; . . . I have travelled thus some hundreds of miles without taking any meal in a house . . . (Thoreau: 1849: "Thursday").

Tourism through Franconia Notch was underway at the time of the brothers' visit in 1839. There was lodging at Knights Tavern near the Flume and at the Lafayette House near Echo Lake. There was stagecoach service from Plymouth. A new era was opening in the upper Pemigewasset Valley.

Henry was 22 years old at the time of his Pemigewasset trip.

View of the Ossipee and White Mountains from the Emerson house, Sanbornton.
*D. Heyduk*

*Daniel Webster*

Daniel Webster was the second youngest son of Ebenezer and Abigail Webster, born in 1782 in that part of Salisbury that later became Franklin. The Websters were not prosperous as farmers, but their situation improved when Ebenezer became a tavern-keeper. Daniel was able to attend Phillips Exeter Academy for a time, and graduated from Dartmouth College before beginning the study of law. He opened his first law practice in Boscawen in 1805, and the following year unsuccessfully defended a man accused of a double murder in a trial held at the Grafton County Courthouse in Plymouth (Speare 1988: 44).

Entering politics at the time of the trade embargo and War of 1812, which he opposed - as most New Englanders did, Webster served in the U.S. Congress, first from New Hampshire and later from Massachusetts. As a U.S. senator he was a skilled orator and statesman, and as an attorney, he was successful and prosperous. The courthouse where he pleaded the 1806 murder case later became Plymouth's Young Ladies Library and is today the Museum of the Plymouth Historical Society (Chapter 6). The Webster family farm in Franklin later became the state Orphans' Home (Garneau 2002: 19-21).

*Floods*

After the first major flood of the settlement period in 1785 (Chapter 6), the Pemigewasset surged again many times. Towns which built bridges, such as Campton, and investors who built toll bridges at Plymouth, New Hampton, Sanbornton and Franklin, found that their property was repeatedly destroyed. The Plymouth-Holderness bridge was washed away in 1804 and 1813, and the Livermore Falls bridge in Campton was destroyed in 1820 (Chapter 5). In February of 1824, heavy rain broke up thick ice on the Pemigewasset, and the high water carried ice downstream like a battering ram. According to the *New Hampshire Patriot*:

> *On Thursday last a flood, the most appalling and tremendous ever known in this part of the country, took place. The extreme cold of the preceding week was followed on Tuesday and Wednesday by*

*southerly winds, which increased to a gale, during a greater part of
which time the rain descended in torrents. The ice which covered
the ground prevented the earth from receiving the water, and the
whole rushed into the streams and rivers. In a few hours the thick
ice gave way and swept bridges and everything else in its path into a
mass of undistinguished ruin* (Musgrove 1904: 473-74).

Musgrove added that "immense quantities of logs . . . were carried
downstream. All the bridges north of . . . Boscawen, except Central bridge
at Bristol, and Livermore's bridge at Campton, were carried away, as was
also nearly every bridge on Baker's river" (Ibid). Among the bridges lost
were the Pemigewasset Bridge at New Hampton, Union Bridge at
Sanbornton, and the Republican Bridge at Franklin. Luckily, the LaFayette
Bridge at Plymouth would not be built until the following year.

On the night of the ice flood, the Sumner family of Hill awoke to find
some two feet of water in their house. George, the father, quickly placed
his wife and baby in a carriage, and without taking time to hitch the horse,
pulled it by hand through water, ice and snow to the neighbors (Hill
Historical Society 1991: 30).

The year 1826 saw two floods: an ice flood in March with floating chunks
of ice two feet thick, and an August flood which followed a prolonged
drought. It had been a:

> *"dry summer," with "grass very short, pastures withered, and
> grasshoppers uncommonly plenty, devouring every green thing". . .
> the deluge of August came in "two great freshets": the larger on the
> 28th, "doing immense damage to roads, bridges and mills". . . then
> in the wet weather that followed there was dysentery, which was
> "mortal in many cases, and most severe near Sanbornton Bridge"*
> [Tilton] (Runnels 1882: 145-146, quoting Joshua Lane's journal).

The torrential rain of August caused landslides in the White Mountains,
one of which killed the members of the Willey family in Crawford Notch.

Other, but less severe floods in the Pemigewasset Valley occurred in
1830, 1839, and 1841. In virtually every flood, destruction in the river's main
valley was accompanied by damage to property and livestock along the
Pemigewasset's tributaries, especially the Mad, Beebe, Baker, Newfound
and Smith rivers.

## Chapter 10

# Artists, Traveling Tourists and Hotels

The Thoreau brothers walked to Franconia Notch from Plymouth, but most travelers took the stage. In the Concord stagecoaches of the time there was seating on top, and that was the best place to see the unfolding scenery. Some of the first visitors were landscape painters, who were drawn by the beauty and spectacle of the Notch and by views along the Pemigewasset River's winding course.

By the 1840s and 50s the valley had very different scenery from that of just half a century before. Settlement of the uplands, where farms dotted the slopes, and where sheep pasture was cleared during the boom, had created a pastoral landscape. Farm fields and pastures touched the river banks, and neat farmsteads and villages were to be seen from viewpoints along the valley's many roads, while distant, still-wild mountains and forests offered a striking contrast. This was the case from Franklin to Thornton, and even Woodstock. Beyond those towns lay the wilder Notch and the rough territory of the Pemigewasset's east and west branches. North of the Notch in Franconia and its surrounding towns, a more cleared landscape again appeared.

Main roads and turnpikes ran north-south along the valley, and were the routes used by freight drivers, market-bound farmers, and stage coaches carrying an ever-growing number of travelers. Villages along the route now had post offices and stores, while taverns and inns dotted the roadside in between. Despite long, harsh winters, periodic floods and bad roads, in summer the valley seemed idyllic. Cities to the south were becoming more industrial, crowded and polluted - which their residents especially noticed during the hot and humid months. Respiratory diseases were more common and severe there. For those who could afford it, the Pemigewasset Valley, Franconia Notch and the high plateau to the north offered clean air, fresh farm food, opportunity for exercise, and splendid scenery. Ever greater numbers of people arrived to spend the summer.

The village of Plymouth, with the Pemigewasset River, the LaFayette Bridge, and the Meadows, by Robert Wilkie. The Pemigewasset House is prominent, but the railroad is not shown. *Trustees of the Boston Public Library, Louis Prang & Co. Collection.*

Thomas Cole's "Morning Mist Rising at Plymouth," 1830. *The Brooklyn Museum*

## The Artists

Among early visitors to the valley was Thomas Cole, one of the founders of landscape painting in the United States. On visits in 1827 and 1828, Cole made sketches of scenes, with notes to himself written in pencil on the sketch – about color, distance, vegetation, and features of the landscape. Back in his New York studio, he painted some of the scenes he had sketched, and one is "Morning Mist Rising at Plymouth," dated 1830 (the date the painting was made). Cole emphasized the wildness of landscapes, bringing nature to the fore, and making natural features more dramatic. His painting at Plymouth is therefore difficult to place; it is in either the Pemigewasset or the Baker valley, and the landscape that it depicts was probably not as steep. Cole may also have left signs of civilization out of the finished work.

Another artist who captured local scenes, but some decades later, was Robert Wilkie. Wilkie's sketches became engravings and were issued as prints by Boston's Louis Prang & Company. His view of the village of Plymouth, with the White Mountains beyond, exaggerates the steepness and proximity of ranges to the north. Wilkie, like Cole, preferred nature to civilization, as seen in his depiction of the Pemigewasset House hotel without any sign of the railroad which ran along the river and had its station and rail yard there. Wilkie accurately and dramatically captured Livermore Falls on the Pemigewasset in Campton, but he made the dam there appear more like a ledge and added human figures which were overly large in proportion to the falls.

Many other well-known landscape artists visited and painted, and their work is a much more accurate picture of the pastoral Pemigewasset River and of landscapes in and around Franconia Notch. Part of the reason for accuracy was that landscape art and vividly written guidebooks were drawing tourists to the river valley and mountains. Those tourists were a prime market for paintings and prints that accurately depicted what they had seen. In paintings of the same scene made by multiple artists, and in contemporary photographs, one can see how accurately the landscapes were painted. In fact, one can travel the valley and Notch today and readily recognize the landscapes captured by artists of over 150 years ago.

Robert Wilkie's "Livermore Falls," with a disguised dam and overly-large figures. *Trustees of the Boston Public Library, Louis Prang & Co. Collection*

Winckworth Allan Gay's painting of Welch Mountain seen from the west bank of the Pemigewasset in Campton, with much cleared land. *The Brooklyn Museum*

Most of the landscape paintings of the second half of the 1800s are historically accurate and show the river and land as it was then – with cows standing in pastures and in the river, and farmhouses, and even resort hotels in places now covered with forest. The work of these artists came to be known as "The White Mountain School," and one of the leading painters of that group was Benjamin Champney, who said:

> I feel if I have not accomplished anything great in art, I have at least given pleasure to the inmates of many homes throughout the land, by giving them faithful reproductions of local scenes (Garvin 2006: 10).

Others who painted in the Pemigewasset Valley and Franconia Notch were Asher B. Durand, Charles Wilson Knapp, Edward and Thomas Hill, Samuel Lancaster Gerry, David Johnson, George W. Waters, Alfred Thompson Bricher, Sylvester Phelps Hodgdon, and F. Schuyler Mathews. They traveled the roads and stayed at lodgings convenient to good views, such as Thomas Sanborn's in West Campton, later known as The Stag and Hounds. A short distance from Sanborn's was the well-known "Starr King View" of Franconia Notch from the Pemigewasset Valley, named for the influential guide book author Thomas Starr King. The Profile House in the Notch also was popular with artists, who could paint conveniently close to their lodging, and display their work for tourists.

## Stage Coaches and the First Rails

In the 1820s, main roads could be traveled by horse-drawn vehicles, and stage lines began to operate between the major centers, notably Concord, Plymouth and Littleton, with many stops in villages and at taverns along the route. Beginning in 1822, one could leave Boston at 3 a.m. and reach Plymouth at 9 p.m., and return the next day, with three round trips per week. These stages carried not just passengers, but mail, which helped to subsidize the service (Lyford 1912: 191).

A trip by stage coach was never comfortable, with rough and dusty or muddy dirt roads, and only partial protection from the weather. Stops to change horses, usually every ten to twelve miles, offered relief and a brief chance to eat and drink. The stage from Concord crossed the Winnipesaukee River to Sanbornton and made at least two stops there: at Lane Tavern near Sanbornton Square and at the Emerson farm on

Mountain Road. It then continued into New Hampton, where it could turn to go north through New Hampton village on the east side of the Pemigewasset, or alternately turn toward Bristol and travel up the river's west side. Both routes converged at Plymouth, which was a switching point for travel to the Connecticut Valley, or up the Pemigewasset and through Franconia Notch to Littleton. A stage route also ran from Concord up the west side of the river through Hill to Plymouth.

In the late 1820s, Concord Coaches began to be built by the Abbot-Downing Company of Concord. They featured a leather strap "thoroughbrace" system that suspended a coach above the wheels, giving a rocking, rather than a jolting ride, and were widely adopted by stage companies (Scheiber 2011: 3-4).

In 1829, a four-horse stage provided service between Plymouth and Littleton, giving passengers access to villages along the upper Pemigewasset and to stops in Franconia Notch and Franconia village. It departed from the Webster Tavern on Tuesdays and Saturdays at 1 p.m., after arrival of the stage from Concord, reaching Gibbs Hotel in Franconia at 6 p.m.. On Fridays and Mondays, the stage left Franconia at 4 a.m., reached Plymouth at 10:00, and Concord at 6 p.m. The fare between Plymouth and Franconia was $1.50 (Welch 1972: 74).

George W. Water's painting of "Eagle Cliff from Profile Lake" in Franconia Notch. *The-Athenaeum, PD*

In the 1830s, the first railroads were built, and one ran north from Boston to Lowell to serve the mills there. It was a success for both freight and passengers, and was extended up the Merrimack Valley to Concord in 1842. Pemigewasset Valley factories were dependent on service by horse-drawn freight wagons at that time, and the potential for larger volume and cheaper shipping by rail was considered essential to their business. People in the valley also wanted a railroad connection closer than Concord, and towns were willing to buy stock to finance a railroad if it came to, or through, their town.

The new Boston, Concord and Montreal Railroad (BC&M) received its charter in 1844 and after strenuous fundraising, began to lay rail in 1846. The route was up the Merrimack River to Tilton, with its factories, then along the Winnipesaukee River to busy Laconia and Lakeport, up the west shore of Lake Winnipesaukee to Meredith, and then northwest through New Hampton to Holderness Village (now Ashland), with its mills, across the Pemigewasset to Bridgewater, and up the west bank to Plymouth. From Plymouth, the line would run along the Baker Valley and over a height-of-land to the Connecticut Valley, with a connection to track running north to Canada (Mead 1975: 19-22).

The BC&M was completed to New Hampton by mid-1849, to Holderness Village by December, and to Plymouth in January, 1850 (Ruell 2019: 1). A freight was the first train to arrive at Plymouth, and then a passenger train with officers of the BC&M. Stage coaches met arriving trains at Plymouth and carried passengers and mail to the upper Premigewasset Valley.

Towns on the west side of the lower Pemigewasset also were anxious for rail service. The Northern Railroad was built from Concord to Franklin on the west side of the river, but at Franklin it turned westward instead of continuing upriver to Hill and Bristol. Those interested in a spur line running north secured a charter in 1846 for the Franklin and Bristol Railroad. It took funding of $150,000 to build the road, and once that was in hand, surveying and construction began in 1847. By June of 1848 the line was complete to its terminus at Bristol, and on July 4 the railroad offered residents a free trip to Concord. In early 1849, the Northern Railroad took over the branch line as part of its system (Musgrove 1904: 144-146).

The BC&M and Northern railroads, and one more to be built later, would have a major impact on towns that they served and on valley history in general. Between 1848 and 1850, all of the Pemigewasset Valley towns south of Plymouth obtained rail service.

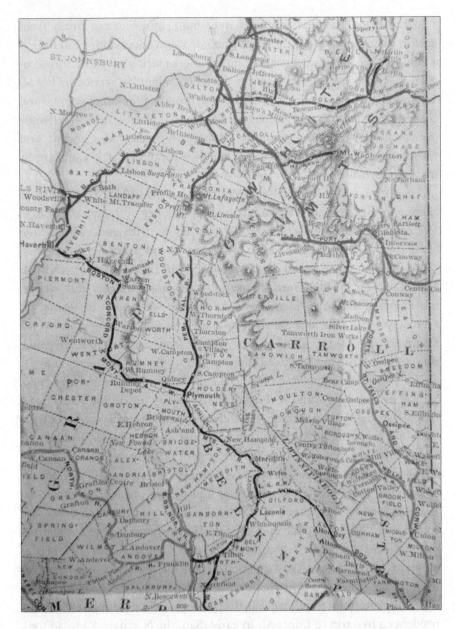

**The BC&M ran from Concord to Northfield, Tilton, Laconia, Meredith, New Hampton, Ashland, Bridgewater and Plymouth. The Northern RR ran from Concord to Franklin, with a branch north to Bristol.** *Author's Collection*

The wood-burning engine "Bristol" on the Northern Railroad. *Bristol Historical Society*

## *Lodging for Every Traveler*

Hardy travelers began visiting the Pemigewasset Valley and Franconia Notch almost as soon as roads and taverns could accommodate them, but sizeable numbers of tourists did not come until stage service and hotels were in place. A busy stopping place was the Webster Tavern in Plymouth, where stage coaches arrived and departed. In 1841, William Webster sold the property to Denison Burnham, who enlarged it as the Pemigewasset House. Other hostelries opened as well, in the village and at the toll house of the LaFayette Bridge. It was common at that time to have a livery stable associated with a hotel, to house travelers' horses or to provide horses and vehicles for those guests who wanted to get around the area (Speare 1988: 76-77).

For travelers going north, lodging and services were available in Campton, Thornton, and Woodstock, and also in Franconia Notch, close to the scenic attractions. In addition to taverns, there were farm and village boarding houses.

The Pemigewasset House, Plymouth, with the BC&M Railroad, which arrived in 1850.
A stage which met the train is seen leaving, probably for the upper Pemigewasset
Valley. *Plymouth Historical Society*

In West Campton, located on the stage route in the scenic Pemigewasset intervale, Thomas Sanborn began a boarding house in 1848. He had owned a hotel in Sanbornton, and his Campton hotel quickly became popular with artists and fresh air seekers. It was expanded several times, and among its conveniences was a post office (Broad 1992).

In the 1840s and 50s, Thornton and Woodstock's tourist attractions were for the most part unidentified, although artists did stop there to capture scenes along the Pemigewasset, as they did in Campton. They may have been accommodated at farmhouses.

On the Notch road in Lincoln, just south of the Flume, was Knight's Tavern, which dated from the early 1800s, and probably served teamsters and drovers who were passing through Franconia Notch. On or near its site, the Flume House was built around 1847, to serve tourists as a lodging and base for visiting the Flume, the Pool and the Basin.

At the north end of the Notch tourist development occurred earlier, with the LaFayette House being built by Stephen and Joseph Gibb around 1835. British visitor Harriet Martineau stayed there on her 1834-36 tour of the U.S., calling it "the solitary dwelling of the pass," and saying: ". . . it had been growing in the woods thirteen weeks before, and yet we were far from being among its first guests (Waterman 1989: 82) (Tolles 1998: 38). The Thoreau brothers may have stayed there on their 1839 walking tour; Henry did not identify their overnight location.

In 1852, the Gibbs sold their hotel to Richard Taft, George Brown and Ira Coffin. The new owners built a new and larger hotel called the Profile House - of 3½ stories and 110 rooms, on the west side of the Notch, and moved the LaFayette House to that site as well. Richard Taft had also purchased the Flume House in 1848, and renovated it in 1853 to have three stories, double piazzas (porches), and accommodation for 200 guests (Tolles 1998: 39, 65). There are no records of how many tourists visited Franconia Notch at that time, but success and enlargement of the hotels suggests that there were thousands. By 1850, one could depart Boston at 7:30 in the morning by train, reach Plymouth by 12:30, have lunch, take the stage to Franconia Notch, and have dinner at the Profile House.

**Thomas J. Sanborn.** *Campton Historical Society*

The *White Mountain Guidebook* of 1858 offers information to travelers going to Franconia Notch from Plymouth:

> *Should* [the traveler] *choose the stage coach, he will enjoy a most delightful ride of twenty-four miles to the* **Flume House**, *tracing the course of the Pemigewasset River. The road in some places is rather rough, but the weariness of the way is amply compensated by the variety of beautiful objects, that are everywhere presented to the view. The river meanders in its winding course, now with placid and quiet current through green meadows, and now in rapid and headlong torrent over its pebbly bed . . .*
> *The little villages of Campton and Thornton are the resort of artists, who spend weeks in the vicinity sketching for future studies. Campton is said to contain more points of fine prospects, than any town in the neighborhood. A quiet little inn upon the roadside looks the abode of comfort. Woodstock and Lincoln are small towns of no particular note. . . . In the late twilight, after a half day's exquisite enjoyment, we climb the hill and soon alight beneath the grateful shelter of the* **Flume House**. *The hotel seems like a "nest among the mountains," as it is relieved by the dark mass, amid which it rests. The* **Profile House** *is in the same region, four miles distant, and passengers who desire, can immediately procede thither* (Eastman 1858: 123).

## Waterville and Greeley's Inn

In Chapter 8, the enterprising Greeleys in the deep valley of Waterville to the east of Campton and Thornton had begun to take in summer boarders during the 1830s. This was prompted by the visit of Ephraim Bull of Concord, Massachusetts, who came for his health and returned the following year with his wife. Bull later became famous as the developer of the Concord Grape. His recollection of the rustic valley at that time was that there were six farms, where people other than the Greeleys lived in log cabins roofed with hemlock bark, and cut firewood to sell in Plymouth for a dollar a cord (Goodrich 1952: 6).

It was some seven miles from Plymouth to Campton on the main road, and another twelve miles along the rough, winding road to Greeley's Inn at Waterville. Nathaniel Goodrich says of the trip from Campton that: "There were a lot of hills. Hauling in the heavy mountain wagons, loaded with people, trunks and supplies was hard on horses and very slow" (Goodrich 1952: 67). Once arrived in the valley, visitors depended on the Greeleys for all their needs, including lodging, meals, sport and entertainment.

In the census of 1850 and 1860, despite the summer hotel business, Nathaniel reported himself as a farmer. His sons Merrill and Henry, however, gave their occupation as "landlords" in 1860. There were also "domestic" workers in the Greeley household in that year, and several men in the town who were "common laborers." It seems that the Greeleys had employees on their farm and in the hotel.

Nathaniel was described by a guest as: ". . . somewhat bent and gnarled. . . . He was very bright and quick at retort and had an immense amount of executive energy that he carried into everything" (Waterman 1989: 201). One of his projects, which was a first in the White Mountains, was the cutting of hiking trails and bridle paths throughout the valley and beyond. During the 1850s, Nathaniel organized workers to plan and clear trails not just to scenic spots in the valley, but to nearby mountain summits (Osceola, Welsh, Tecumseh, and Sandwich Dome), He had a bridle path constructed through the mountains to Crawford Notch (30 miles), another to the villages of Whiteface and Sandwich to the south, and a third from Waterville to Woodstock, which survives as today's Tripoli Road (Ibid: 202).

The guests at Greeley's Inn were fishermen and outdoors people, and Nathaniel made the best possible use of the valley's resources for their enjoyment. It would be some years before mountain hiking became a popular sport throughout the mountains, but Waterville would ever remain one of its centers.

## The Northern Connection

In 1853, travelers could reach Franconia Notch by a second route. The Boston, Concord & Montreal Railroad completed its line from Plymouth to Woodsville on the Connecticut River in that year, and promptly leased the White Mountain Railroad which ran from Woodsville to Littleton. Instead of getting off the train at Plymouth, passengers could take the alternate BC&M rail route west and north of the Notch to Littleton, where a stage then carried them and the mail south to Franconia. According to the BC&M, they could arrive at the Profile House a bit earlier by this route.

Just east of the road from Littleton to Franconia was the town of Bethlehem, with some 950 people at that time, mostly engaged in agriculture and logging. The main east-west road through Bethlehem was also a stage route, which followed the valley of the Ammonoosuc River toward Mount Washington and the Presidential Range. In Bethlehem was the Sinclair Tavern and stage coach stop, which was beginning to see more tourists traveling from Littleton to the White Mountains during the later 1850s, and would grow as a result (Wilson 1999: 30).

The Profile House in Franconia Notch and other tourist hotels all provided both food and lodging for their guests, who often stayed for weeks. The hotels advertised not just their comfortable accommodations, clean air and scenery, but also the quality of their restaurants. They needed fresh milk, butter, cheese, vegetables, and meats, which farms north of Franconia Notch were positioned to provide. Not just farmers, but other people in the area found employment related to the growing summer tourist industry. Thus, the economies of Littleton, Franconia and Bethlehem expanded as the tourist trade grew. The towns north of the Notch became as important to its tourism development as were those to the south, especially since there was no direct rail access to the Notch along the Pemigewasset Valley north of Plymouth.

By 1860, the Pemigewasset Valley and Franconia Notch had seen a great influx of summer visitors, and rapid development of transportation and hospitality. Factories and stores - which were the year-round part of the Pemigewasset Valley's economy, also grew.

# Boston, Concord & Montreal and White Mountains (N. H.) Railroads.

The old, direct, and most convenient route from Boston, New York, and the Southern and Southwestern Cities, to Winnipesaukee Lake, North Conway, White and Franconia Mountains.

The Boston, Concord and Montreal Railway is fifty-nine miles nearer, is cheaper, and more romantic in its scenery, than any other; and requires much less conveyance by stage to visit all points of interest in the mountains.

From Boston, trains leave the Depots of the Boston and Maine Railroad, at 7.30 A.M., and 12 M., and 5 P.M.; Boston and Lowell, 7 and 8 (Express) A.M., and 12 M., and 5 and 6 P.M.

By the first train travellers can leave the cars at Weirs, dine at Centre Harbor, arrive at Conway in the evening, and reach the Mountains, by the Eastern Notch, the next day at noon.

Or can leave the cars at Plymouth (where they have ample time to dine), and reach the Profile House in the Franconia Notch at 6 P.M., by Stage.

Or continue on to Littleton, where Stages will immediately leave for the Franconia Mountains, arriving at Profile House 5.30 P.M., or to Whitefield, the nearest point approached by Railroad to the Mountains, where Stages will at once leave for the Waumbeck House, Jefferson, Twin Mountain House, Carroll, and arriving at the Crawford House, White Mountains Notch, at 7.30 P.M.

Passengers via Boston, leaving in the afternoon, can connect with the train from Boston at 8 A.M., via Lowell, and 7.30 A.M., via Lawrence, and 12 M.

The Norwich line of Steamers, " **City of Boston** " and " **City of New York**," connects with the first train up in the morning, by the route from Norwich, through Worcester to Nashua, and thus makes a direct line from New York to all points in the Mountains.

### From Philadelphia and the South.

Passengers leaving Philadelphia to connect with the Norwich boat in New York can reach the Mountains next day, having a night's rest on board the steamer. This forms the best and most direct route to Baltimore and the Southern cities.

Steamer " **Lady of the Lake**," Captain W. A. SANBORN, during the season of navigation, leaves Weirs for Centre Harbor, Wolfborough, &c., on arrival of each train.

J. A. DODGE, Supt.

The BC&M drew its summer clientele from the whole Northeast. *Eastman's White Mountain Guidebook*

## Chapter 11

# Changes at Mid-Century

The valley's towns came to the mid-1800s with differing prospects for the future. A town's population, the nature of its economy, the impact of new railroads, the enticement of the West, and dislocations caused by the Civil War all were at play in the changing mid-century world.

## The Valley's Shifting Population

All towns in the Pemigewasset Valley had grown in population until 1830, but after that industrial and commercial towns continued to grow, while those which were mostly agricultural began to lose people. Hill's population peaked in 1830, as did Bridgewater's, New Hampton's and Thornton's. Campton had its largest number of people in 1840. Franconia and Woodstock peaked in 1860. The towns that would continue to grow after 1860 were Franklin, Bristol, Ashland and Plymouth.

Sanbornton lost some of its commercial sector to Franklin in 1828 and more to Tilton in 1869, leaving it largely agricultural. Holderness likewise lost its industry and business sector when Ashland became a separate town in 1868. As primarily agricultural towns, both Sanbornton and Holderness lost population thereafter. Those who left the farms moved to nearby or more distant industrial and commercial centers, or moved to more promising agricultural land in New York and points west. Young women, in particular, went to work in the textile mills of Lowell and Lawrence, Massachusetts, and later, in Manchester.

As an illustration of the out-migration, in the 1830s, some six residents of Bristol and Bridgewater moved to Michigan, three to Wisconsin, three to Illinois, and twelve to Ohio - including Jane Bartlett, a school-teacher. Solomon Cavis, who owned a store in Bristol, wrote in a letter in 1832 that: "There are many in this place that have got the western fever." He later wrote that he, too, wanted to go west, but his prosperous store kept him from doing so (Haight 1941: 36).

Regarding the draw of the factories, historian John Haight, Jr. wrote of the "rosey- cheeked farm girls [who] came cheerfully and hopefully from their farms to have their share of life's experiences in company with their fellows, to save their money, to lift a mortgage, or send a brother to college, or provide for their married homes." He noted that two girls who had gone to Lowell wrote home in glowing terms of their life there and begged their younger sister to join them, "even though they worked twelve hours a day and were paid but two dollars a week" (Ibid: 37).

In 1860, Holderness Village had a peg mill, which made small wooden pegs that were used to manufacture shoes. In the census of that year was William Gordon's boarding house, and living there were six women who worked in the peg mill: Mary Smith – 28, Maritha A. Smith – 25, Maria A. Smith – 22, her twin sister Martha, Hannah Brown – 19, and Josephine Brown – 17. Also living there and working in the mill were Walter Libby – 23, and John Hennessy – 40. The village, with its Squam River water power, also had a paper mill, a stocking mill, and shoe-making shops. There was a busy BC&M station, with parcel express service.

## Franklin Factories and Specialties

A local industry began in the 1850s when Herrick Aiken and his son Walter, working in Herrick's Franklin machine shop, improved mechanized knitting equipment. They designed a circular knitting machine that used a "latch needle" to produce a knitted fabric tube (Garneau 2002: 521). The latch needle opened after the start of a stitch and automatically closed to finish it. William Pepper, working in a knitting mill in Franklin at the same time, also developed an improved knitting machine. These men and others then promptly built factories to manufacture knitting machines, latch needles and knitted garments – especially stockings. Franklin, with its Winnipesaukee River water power, became a center of the industry, and Bristol and Holderness villages also took part. Generally, women employees operated the machines, while men maintained them. Men also worked in the factories that manufactured needles, knitting machines, needle-making machines, and other related equipment.

In the 1860 census, thirty Franklin men were recorded as "machinists," while four were titled "needle manufacturer" – factory owners; one was a yarn manufacturer, and others worked in iron foundries and forges – all related to Franklin's factories. The Northern Railroad brought in raw material and carried manufactured goods away.

Walter Aiken, left, invented knitting equipment, and Alvah Sulloway, right, used Aiken's machines in his Sulloway Mills in Franklin, below. *The Granite Monthly*

Franklin also had a paper mill;  grist mill; carriage and sleigh-making; harness-making; carpentry, cabinet, chair-making and cooper shops; a hotel; stores; a depot of the Northern Railroad; a jeweler and watch-maker; a deputy sheriff; mens' and womens' hat-makers; mens' and womens' tailors; boarding houses; blacksmiths; masons; a brick-maker; railroad hands; marble workers; shoemakers; teamsters; store clerks; a photographer;  a barber;  a butcher; and several doctors, lawyers, teachers and ministers. Several people were listed as "palm leaf braiders," a reference to the makers of palm leaf hats – a local specialty which also was shipped out to other markets.

Franklin also had farms, on which over 200 people worked, and which probably supplied food for those who worked in the mills, stores, offices, and shops of the commercial center. Farms in nearby agricultural towns such as Sanbornton and Hill probably did the same. While industrial-commercial villages drew people from farms, those same centers also provided a growing market for farm products. Farmers who could produce milk, butter, cheese, eggs, meat, vegetables, fruits, hay and grain for local markets or for railroad shipment prospered, while those – especially on the hill farms, who could not produce in quantity, began to abandon the old farmstead way of life. Farmsteads which produced to supply their own needs, but little surplus to sell, were at a disadvantage in the new mid-century cash economy.

*Plymouth's Own Model*

Plymouth had a different profile, as indicated by the census of 1860. There were no factories or boarding houses as in Ashland and Franklin. Instead, there was a type of cottage industry in which products came from multiple sources. Several farmers had second occupations: "farmer & painter," "farmer & butcher," and "farmer & potter" were listed, and there undoubtedly were more. Many people worked from their own shops: seamstresses, tailors, coopers, carpenters, painters, stone masons, blacksmiths, brick-makers, potters, wheelwrights, a jeweler, a livery stable owner, a miller, a "tin-man" - who made many useful household items, and a man who was probably a peddler, but was listed as a "traveling merchant." Physicians and lawyers worked from their respective offices, clergymen from their churches, and a "daguerran artist" (photographer) from his studio. The warden of the Plymouth Poor Farm lived and worked there with his family, overseeing seven residents.

Plymouth's largest industry – glove-making, combined tanneries with small shops and piece-work, which was done in residents' homes. The 1860 census recorded four "leather dressers," four "glove makers," three "glove cutters," and four "glove & mitten manufacturers" – the owners of the businesses. There also were eleven shoemakers, but Plymouth did not have factories, nor did it have industrial machinery; in contrast to Franklin, which had thirty machinists, there was only one person with that title in Plymouth in 1860.

The BC&M Railroad employed a number of Plymouth residents, including the superintendent (Joseph Dodge), a foreman, a "Baggage Master," two firemen, a conductor, a locomotive engineer, a station agent, a "Ticket Master," and two section men. Dependent on the railroad were two "expressmen" who handled and delivered packages sent by rail. Two innkeepers (Denison Burnham and Charles Rogers) depended in good part on the railroad, as did two stage coach drivers (Joseph Bixby and Harrison Marden), who provided transportation between Plymouth's station and points north.

Drivers of the Plymouth & Franconia Stage, with Harrison Marden second from right. *Plymouth Historical Society*

There was a substantial group of professionals: four physicians, seven lawyers, three clergymen, and two teachers. Merchants and "merchant-manufacturers" numbered nine, in addition to other businessmen listed above. These people employed the town's small cadre of wage workers: six clerks, thirteen laborers, and some ten "domestics" – who worked as live-in housekeepers, but were not members of the families where they did so. In Plymouth, these wage jobs were apparently the only means for farm people to move to the village to work.

## BOSTON, CONCORD & MONTREAL RAILROAD.

TIME TABLE No. 98, on and after Monday, July 22, 1872.

☞ No train must leave or pass any Station before the time specified below. ☜

| DOWNWARD TRAINS LEAVE | | | | | | | | STATIONS. | UPWARD TRAINS LEAVE | | | | | | |
|---|---|---|---|---|---|---|---|---|---|---|---|---|---|---|---|
| EXTRA ACCOM. TRAIN. A.M. | No. 1 ACCOM. TRAIN. A.M. | No. 2 MAIL TRAIN. A.M. | No. 3 Through Express Freight. A.M. | No. 4 Through Way Freight. A.M. | No. 5 Express TRAIN. P.M. | No. 6 Express. P.M. | No. 12 EXTRA Express A.M. | | No. 13 EXTRA Express P.M. | No. 7 MAIL TRAIN. A.M. | No. 8 ACCOM. TRAIN. P.M. | No. 9 Express Passenger TRAIN. A.M. | No. 10 Through Way Freight. P.M. | No. 11 Through Express Freight. P.M. | EXTRA ACCOM. TRAIN. P.M. |
| | | | | | | | | Wells River | a 3 52 | | a9 50 | | | | |
| | | 10 17 | 3 30 | 3 40 | 45 46 | 11 15 | 11 37 | Woodsville | 2 38 | 3 25 | 9 42 | 4 35 | 1 30 | | A.M. |
| | | 10 33 | 5 55 4 05 4 00 4 10 | | 6 01 | 1 40 | 11 48 | N. Haverhill | 2 27 | 3 09 | 9 26 | 4 10 4 00 | 1 05 | | |
| | | 10 44 | 4 17 4 22 | 4 27 | 6 11 | 1 55 2 58 | 11 55 | Haverhill | 2 20 | 2 58 | 9 15 | 3 44 3 33 | 12 50 | | |
| | | 10 59 | 4 45 4 55 | 4 50 5 00 | 6 25 | 3 18 3 30 | 12 05 | E. Haverhill | 2 10 | 2 44 | 9 03 | 3 15 3 10 | 12 30 | | |
| | | | 5 20 | 5 25 | | | | SUMMIT | | | | 2 55 | 12 05 | | |
| | | 11 27 | 5 40 5 25 | 5 45 5 55 | 6 50 | 4 05 4 15 | 12 25 | Warren | 1 50 | 2 14 | 8 29 | 2 15 1 28 | 11 45 | | |
| | | 11 38 | 6 45 6 50 | 6 15 | 7 00 | 4 30 | 12 33 | Wentworth | 1 42 | 2 03 | 8 19 | 1 08 1 05 | 11 25 | | |
| | | 11 51 | 7 15 7 25 | 6 38 | 7 12 | 4 48 | 12 43 | W Rumney | 1 32 | 1 59 | 8 07 | 12 43 11 25 | 11 05 | | |
| | | 12 00 | 7 40 7 58 | 6 53 | 7 20 | 5 02 | 12 50 | Rumney | 1 25 | 1 41 | 7 58 | 11 10 11 00 | 10 50 | | |
| | | | | | | | | Quincy's | | | | | | | |
| 5 10 | 7 30 | 12 22 1 03 | 8 45 9 30 | 7 28 7 55 | 7 45 | 5 30 5 55 | 1 05 1 30 | Plymouth | 11 10 12 35 | 1 20 12 55 | P.M. 5 55 | 7 35 | 10 20 9 25 | 10 15 10 00 | P.M. 10 55 |
| | | | | | | | | Bridgewater | | | | | | | |
| 5 24 | 7 45 | 1 17 | 9 55 10 05 | 8 20 | | 6 10 | 1 41 | Ashland | 12 22 | 12 41 | 5 40 | 9 00 8 50 | 9 40 | 10 40 | |
| | | | | | | | | FOGG'S | | | | | | | |
| 5 47 | 8 08 8 10 | 1 39 | 10 45 12 20 | 9 00 | | 6 45 | 1 59 | Meredith Vil. | 12 02 12 20 | 5 19 | 8 08 7 50 | 9 00 | 10 17 | | |
| 5 58 | 8 25 | 1 50 1 51 | | | | | 2 10 2 12 | Weirs, Steamboat. | 11 52 | 12 10 | 5 04 | | 8 40 | 10 05 | |
| 6 09 | 8 35 | 2 04 | 1 10 9 40 2 24 10 00 | | 7 25 | 2 24 | Lake Village | 11 46 | 11 58 | 4 50 | A.M. 6 50 P.M. 9 00 | 8 15 7 55 | 9 53 | |
| 6 13 | 8 44 | 2 09 | 2 51 2 40 | 10 12 | 7 40 | 2 29 | Laconia | 11 35 | 11 53 | 4 45 | 8 50 8 40 | 7 45 | 9 48 | |
| 6 27 | 8 57 | 2 23 | 3 03 3 07 | 10 40 | 8 04 | 2 42 | Union Bridge | 11 22 | 11 39 | 4 31 | 8 15 8 10 | 7 30 | 9 35 | |
| 6 36 | 9 07 | 2 32 | 3 20 3 25 | 10 58 | 8 20 | 2 50 | Tilton, | 11 14 | 11 30 | 4 22 | 7 55 7 45 | 7 05 | 9 25 | |
| 6 49 6 53 | 9 21 9 25 | 2 45 2 47 | 3 55 4 10 | 11 24 11 34 | 8 55 9 07 | 2 01 | Northfield | 11 08 | 11 18 | 4 10 4 00 | 7 20 7 10 | 6 40 6 30 | 9 11 9 07 | |
| 7 03 | 9 35 | 2 56 | 4 25 4 30 | 11 54 | | 3 08 | Canterbury | 10 56 | 11 09 | 3 51 | 6 55 6 50 | 6 15 | 8 57 | |
| | | | | | | | | North Concord | | | | | | | |
| 7 22 | 9 58 | 3 15 | 5 05 5 10 | 12 32 | 9 50 | 3 26 | East Concord, | 10 41 | 10 51 | 3 35 | 6 15 6 05 | 5 40 | 8 37 | |
| 7 27 | 10 03 | 3 20 | 5 20 12 42 | | 10 00 | 3 30 | Concord | 10 35 | 10 45 | 3 30 | 5 55 | 5 30 | 8 30 | |

## Bristol and the Northern Railroad

The Northern Railroad was built from Franklin, with a station at Hill, to its terminus at Bristol in 1848, giving towns on the west side of the Pemigewasset the same freight and passenger connection to the outside that Ashland and Plymouth would obtain via the BC&M just a few months later. People of neighboring Bridgewater had a BC&M station (between Ashland and Plymouth) at the northern end of their town, but most of them found the village of Bristol and its direct train service south to be more convenient. Likewise, residents of the rural town of Alexandria on the west used Bristol as their regional center.

Bristol had the substantial water power of the Newfound River to drive its mills, so in 1860 the little village had a paper mill, a stocking factory, a straw board mill, a tannery, and a business that made bedsteads. There was an academy, or high school, where French and German were taught. The village had a druggist, jeweler, mens' and ladies' tailors, several milliners (ladies' hats), a bakery, a two story hotel, a portrait painter, and a dentist. There were "tinmen," a peddler, employees of the railroad, and a driver of the stage coach which provided ongoing service from the station.

A freight train departing Bristol. *Bristol Historical Society*

## The Civil War's Impact

The Civil War began in 1861 and there was an initial call for 75,000 volunteers for three month's service in the army. Hostilities quickly escalated, however, and the Union Army was found wanting. In the summer of 1862, President Lincoln asked for 300,000 more volunteers to sign up for three year's service. That call was promptly met by men of the Pemigewasset Valley, and later calls as well. The exodus of young men to join the army from 1861 to 1865 had an impact on the valley that would outlast the war itself. At the same time, there was a stimulus to industry and agriculture to supply the needs of the army and navy, which bolstered the factory towns and farms.

In response to the call of 1862, the Twelfth Regiment New Hampshire Volunteers was formed by local initiative from Belknap County and the surrounding area. One thousand men promptly signed up, from Sanbornton, New Hampton, Hill, Bristol, Danbury, Alexandria, Hebron, Bridgewater, and other towns. They were supplied with uniforms and weaponry, drilled at Concord, and transported from the Concord train depot to Washington, DC by the end of September. That put them in position to participate in major early battles, including Fredericksburg and Chancellorsville, where Union losses were very high. Disease spread among them, too, in the poor conditions in which they camped and marched. In all, 320 local men of that one regiment died, 139 of them by disease.

New Hampshire's population in 1860 was 326,073, and the state then contributed some 32,500 men to the army: eighteen volunteer infantry regiments, plus cavalry, artillery and sharpshooter units. Ten percent of the state's total population served in the war. Those who survived – and most did despite disease and wounds, had learned about wider possibilities beyond their home towns.

Wartime created demand for many goods in large quantities, and the factories of the valley expanded. Railroads were in place to transport goods rapidly and economically. Farmers found an expanded market for their beef and pork, grains- including oats for horse feed, beans, and wool for uniforms and blankets. Numbers of sheep had declined sharply at the end of the boom in the 1850s, but increased again during the war. Hill had almost 1,600 sheep in 1863, Thornton had over 4,400, and Franconia had over 1,300. In 1864, Bridgewater had almost 2,000 sheep, Holderness over 1,900, Campton almost 3,400, Plymouth almost 2,800, and New Hampton just under 2,200 (inventories for other towns are lacking).

A new woolen mill was built in Bristol in 1864 to make woolen shirts and drawers. The owner, John Musgrove, experimented by making a knit woolen jacket which he named for nearby Mount Cardigan. The "Cardigan Jacket" style quickly became popular (Musgrove 1904: 382).

Sheep on a Plymouth farm. *Plymouth Historical Society*

The end of the war in 1865 not only resulted in a drop in demand, but also brought military surplus items up for sale, which depressed prices. Western farms had expanded output for the war too, and their lower production costs, with cheap rail transportation, gave their products an advantage over those of New England farms.

As farming declined, and manufacturing adjusted to the post-war economy, the Pemigewasset Valley's scenic attractions would give villages and farms an opportunity to expand in a new direction. The valley would see some other developments too.

# Chapter 12

# Visitors

Travel for health reasons lay behind two historic occurrences: a stranger's visit to Hill and two famous friends' arrival in Plymouth.

## A Water Cure at Hill

Mary Baker Patterson, the wife of a dentist in Rumney, suffered from many ills, both physical and emotional. Her husband carried her around their house and brought her meals in bed. At the start of the Civil War Dr. Patterson went south, and was captured and placed in a Confederate prison in 1862. Mary was then taken in by her sister Abigail, who lived in Tilton. Mary's many health and emotional problems did not improve, and Abigail decided to place her in Dr. William Vail's Granite State Health Institute in nearby Hill.

Dr. Vail's institute occupied a substantial two story building in quiet Hill Village, convenient to the railroad station on the west side of the Pemigewasset. The treatment he offered was called a "water cure," and involved using water from a nearby spring, which other people in the village used as well. This was combined with counseling and diet restrictions that required weeks or months to have an effect. The cure cost about $10 per week, which Abigail paid, plus giving Mary spending money. Mary stayed there while saving her spending allowance, and in October was able to go on her own, and in defiance of her sister, to Portland to see a faith healer, "Dr." Phineas Quimby. This was a time in which spiritualism, phrenology, mesmerism and other medical fads were popular.

In comparison with such other treatments, Dr. Vail's water cure was a type of health resort, and probably helpful for certain conditions. Mary later claimed that it did her no good. She divorced Dr. Patterson after an apparent long separation, married Asa Eddy, and as Mary Baker Eddy, developed her own spiritual approach to medicine which she called "Christian Science" (Cather 1993: 38-43) (Hill Historical Society).

This was Dr. Vail's Health Institute in the 1860s, later divided into apartments. *Evelyn Corliss Auger collection*

## The Pemigewasset House and Nathaniel Hawthorne

Plymouth's popular Pemigewasset House Hotel (Chapter 10), over-looking the Pemigewasset River and distant mountains, caught fire in 1862 and was destroyed. The hotel had been conveniently positioned beside the railroad, where passengers could disembark and immediately find food and lodging. The BC&M Railroad therefore decided to erect its own hotel, even grander than the last, and with the station on its lower, trackside level. Built in 1863, the new Pemigewasset House had three stories in front, four stories in back, and a T-shaped floor plan, which allowed the building to face the village, while having the station and diner in a wing at the rear. There were 150 rooms, gas light, and a large dining room in addition to the trackside diner. A cupola observatory on the roof offered views of the Baker and Pemigewasset valleys, and nearby Mount Prospect. Designed in "Italian Revival" style, the Pemigewasset House: "possessed aesthetic attributes that only a few of the grand hotels of the same period or later could boast" (Tolles 1998: 102). Many visitors to the Pemigewasset Valley appreciated Plymouth and its scenery, and the new hotel added substantially to the village's other assets.

Into this scene in May of 1864 came two old friends: author Nathaniel Hawthorne and former U.S. President Franklin Pierce. Hawthorne had been ill, partly due to nursing a sick friend in Philadelphia, and his doctor thought he needed a change of scene and air. When Pierce saw him, he was surprised to find Hawthorne "feeble and diseased" (from a note written by Franklin Pierce). They set out together from Boston for the Pemigewasset country where Pierce hoped that his friend would recover. On May 18 they came to Plymouth by way of Center Harbor, and checked into the Pemigewasset House.

Hawthorne was not able to sign the hotel register, so Pierce signed for both of them. They were given adjoining rooms with a connecting door. Hawthorne retired after 9:00 p.m., "and soon fell into a quiet slumber" (Ibid). Pierce left the connecting door open, since the beds in each room were opposite one another. At 2:00 a.m. Pierce looked in at Hawthorne and thought that he was in a sound sleep. He checked again at 4:00 and found that Hawthorne had died: "He lies upon his side, his position so perfectly natural and easy, his eyes closed, that it is difficult to realize, while looking upon his noble face, that this is death" (Ibid). All care was taken to gently notify Nathaniel's wife Sophia, who also was ill and therefore did not accompany them. In a time when people read avidly, Hawthorne's name was familiar to everyone.

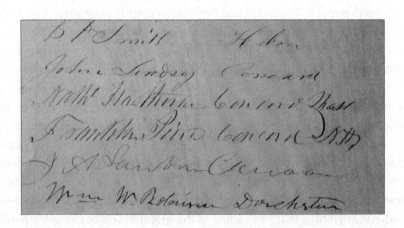

Pierce's entry in the hotel register, May 18, 1864. *Kent Bicknell*

The new Pemigewasset House, front view. *Plymouth Historical Society*

The lobby of the Pemigewasset House, with the BC&M timetable prominently
displayed. *Plymouth Historical Society*

## The Hotel Boom Begins

Limited, but steady-paced summer tourism in Franconia Notch had begun in the mid 1830s with building of the Lafayette House at the Notch's north entrance (Chapter 10). By the late 1840s the Flume House had been built at the Notch's south end, and the new and larger Profile House had replaced the Lafayette House at the north entrance. Both hotels were served by stage coaches from Plymouth and from Littleton, and that is how things remained until the late 1860s, when a sustained tourism boom began.

The three and one half story Profile House was expanded in 1866 to roughly double its size, with 60 added rooms, a dining room capable of seating 500 people, and a billiard hall (Tolles 1998: 66-67). In 1867 a rail line was built from Littleton east toward Mount Washington, passing close to Bethlehem, where passengers could disembark to visit that growing village. In Bethlehem, the Sinclair Tavern had been expanded into the Sinclair House hotel in 1865, to be joined in 1870 by the Mount Agassiz House. In almost every subsequent year, one or more new hotels were built along the village's main Bethlehem Street, and on other streets adjoining it. It was estimated that 4,000 tourists had visited in the 1872 season, staying from a week to three months. By 1874 there were also the Mount Prospect House, White Mountain Boarding House, and several other boarding houses and "cottages" (Town of Bethlehem 1999).

The reasons for Bethlehem's rapid growth were the scenery of surrounding mountains and Franconia Notch to the south; the convenient access by rail; the enthusiasm of villagers, farmers, and business owners for the tourist trade; and a reputation that the town acquired as a health resort. The key health attribute of Bethlehem, aside from its clean, dry air (elevation over 1,400 feet), was its freedom from the pollens that cause hay fever. This reputation became widely known, and hay-fever sufferers from as far away as Chicago traveled to Bethlehem to spend the summer. Unlike the isolated resort hotels of other locations in the mountains, Bethlehem offered a village atmosphere, with stores and sidewalks to stroll. The presence of many hotels, and a large upper class tourist clientele, gave Bethlehem a social atmosphere similar to that of seaside resorts.

A Profile House brochure, Franconia Notch. *John W. & Anne H. Newton Collection, Museum of the White Mountains, Plymouth State University*

The early Flume House, later enlarged, Franconia Notch. *John W. & Anne H. Newton Collection, Museum of the White Mountains, Plymouth State University*

The Sinclair House in Bethlehem. *John W. & Anne H. Newton Collection, Museum of the White Mountains, Plymouth State University*

Frances G. Lee, who visited Bethlehem with her parents as a child, described how they decided to make the long trip from Chicago:

> *My brother George was 7 ½ years older than I, and was from his birth a rather delicate boy. . . . George developed a bad case of hay fever when about 5 ½ years old and Dr. Charlie Adams told my parents that George **must** be moved for the hay fever months to some part of this country free of the disease. He gave them a list of places, Littleton, New Hampshire, and Escanaba, Michigan, being two of those he favored. Mother and Father went up to Escanaba, and didn't like it at all* (Lee 1971: 65-66).

George was taken to Littleton, but still had hay fever there, so the Glessner family decided on Bethlehem, where they would spend each summer for many years, staying at first in a hotel, and later building a summer home which they called "The Rocks." Frances remembered the annual trip:

> *We left Chicago on a sleeping car one morning about 10:00 o'clock and lumbered slowly and noisily to Springfield, Massachusetts. . . . We reached Woodsville-Wells River and there our car was picked*

*up by another engine. . . . Never shall I forget the effect when, stepping off our car in Littleton, I drew the first full breath of good clean country air* (Ibid).

Bethlehem would grow to have thirty hotels and the Glessners would be among the town's leading summer citizens. Many years later, their land would be managed to produce thousands of Christmas trees.

## President Grant's Visit to the Profile House

In August of 1869, at the beginning of his first term as President, Gen. Ulysses S. Grant made a trip to the White Mountains, arriving at Bethlehem by train, and staying at the Sinclair House, where he undoubtedly made quite a stir among the village's summer people. He was then to travel on eleven miles south to the Profile House, which he would reach by coach.

Edmund Cox was one of the Profile House's skilled coach drivers, and at 3:00 p.m. he was sent to Bethlehem with a team of eight prime horses to bring the President and his party down to the Notch. Cox managed his horses judiciously on the way to Bethlehem, because he needed them to perform well on the second half of their twenty-two mile round trip. Shortly before 7:00 p.m. the presidential party were ready to board the coach, and as Aria Cutting Roberts relates:

> *President Grant's trained eye, sweeping over the team with the glance of a connoisseur, at once recognized its excellence. Walking quickly to the driver's seat, he said to Cox: "If you have no objections, I will get up there with you."*
>
> *"It is pretty rough riding up here, General," was Cox's reply. "I can stand it if you can," replied Grant, as he climbed to the high seat. The President was clad in a long linen duster covering as much of his clothing as possible, and he wore a high silk hat and black suit. Sixteen people were in the coach, including Cox* (Roberts 1964).

The Sinclair House telegraph operator sent a notice to the Profile House just as the coach departed at 7:00 p.m. sharp. Cox intended to set a record time for this trip, the last three miles of which was all uphill, and the

President was in for a ride. The opinion among other experienced drivers at the Profile House was that Cox could not arrive in less than two hours. A cannon at Echo Lake, a quarter of a mile from the hotel, was to be fired when the coach passed, to notify those who were waiting. It was heard much earlier than expected, and was thought to be a mistake, but then:

> In what seemed to be an incredibly short time was heard the trampling of the flying steeds . . . and in another moment the party swept around the corner of the hotel into plain view. Ed Cox stood up on the footboard with teeth set, eyes blazing, and every rein drawn tight in his hands. President Grant sat beside him, holding his hat with one hand, and grasping the seat with the other. . . . As they made the circle and drew up in front of the hotel, Cox threw his weight on the brake and stopped at once. He had made the drive in exactly 58 minutes! (Ibid).

President Grant spoke appreciatively of Cox's driving at a reception that evening and at Christmas sent Cox a present of a stage coach whip in a velvet-lined morocco case, with Cox's name engraved on it.

## The Hurricane of 1869 and F. Schuyler Mathews

Just weeks after President Grant's visit to Bethlehem and Franconia Notch, a hurricane struck on October 4, 1869 with what Richard Musgrove of Bristol called:

> . . . the most severe rain storm and freshet since 1826. In a little more than twenty-four hours eight inches of rain fell, and the Pemigewasset and other streams overflowed their banks and great damage was done to crops and other property along the streams. The roads were badly washed and large quantities of timber, lumber and debris passed down the Pemigewasset" (Musgrove 1904: 477).

Moses Runnels in Sanbornton also called it the most severe flood since 1826 (Chapter 9). Water rose quickly at Woodstock, flooding the highway and cutting off access to the bridge. At Plymouth, the intervale was deeply flooded, and a railroad spike was driven into a butternut tree to record the high water mark (Thomson 1964: M38).

Ferdinand Schuyler Mathews, who was a young visitor in Campton at that time, wrote: "The damage to the intervale in '69 was very great 'up river,' many barns & etc. were swept down by the flood, and an enormous amount of debris, including corn, pumpkins, lumber, etc. landed on the meadows all along the line" (Note dated March, 1931, Campton Historical Society). Mathews would later become a well-known professional artist and author, while continuing to be a regular summer visitor to Campton.

An L. Prang & Co. engraving by F. Schuyler Mathews, from "White Mountain Vistas, The Pemigewasset Valley." *John W. & Anne H. Newton Collection, Museum of the White Mountains, Plymouth State University*

*Moses Sweetser in the Valley*

As White Mountain tourism grew, guide books were published to inform visitors about the transportation, hotels, towns and scenic attractions of the area. Guidebook author Moses Sweetser took his task seriously, personally visiting the Pemigewasset Valley and Franconia Notch and gathering information wherever he went. He also assured his readers of his impartiality, writing that "The Publishers placed large resources at the command of the Editor, with the condition that he should receive no special favors from the common carriers and landlords in the mountain region" (Sweetser 1876: Preface).

Outdoor recreation, and in particular - hiking, was just becoming generally popular, and Moses was the first guide book writer to climb many of the mountains, most of which lacked marked trails at that time. In this 1876 guide book he also wrote: "In these days of the advocacy of female suffrage and woman's rights, it needs hardly to be stated that American ladies can accomplish nearly everything which is possible to their sturdier brethren" (Ibid: 35).

The book gave a description of the valley at the time of his visit. Sweetser called Plymouth "one of the most beautiful villages in New Hampshire," and noted that "the professional men necessary to a prosperous shire-town are found here, forming a pleasant circle of society" (Ibid: 278). He reported that eleven firms were producing 130,000 pairs of Plymouth Buck Gloves annually. The beauty of the Plymouth meadows impressed him and he recommended that "beautiful views of the Franconia and Waterville mountains can be obtained over these meadows by driving to the S., along the old Bridgewater Road" (Ibid). A popular excursion was the ascent of Mount Prospect, some 4-5 miles from Plymouth by a "good road," with the reward of an open summit, which was mostly pasture. Sweetser described the expansive view in detail.

He found Ashland to be a "prosperous manufacturing village on Squam River, near its confluence with the Pemigewasset. It turns out annually over $600,000 worth of manufactured goods, including flannels, manilla paper, leather-board, hosiery, lumber, gloves, etc." (Ibid : 363).

For Sweetser, the Pemigewasset Valley "is one of the most beautiful districts among the mountains . . . and both its banks are well populated

157

nearly up to the Flume House" (Ibid: 282). Campton's residents "are nearly all engaged in farming, corn, oats, potatoes and hay being the chief products." Moses found that the town produced 100,000 pounds of maple sugar in 1874, and its forests yielded 500,000 feet of lumber (from saw mills). He also reported that Campton produced "several thousand pairs of pantaloons . . . annually" (E. Dole & Co., Chapter 8) (Ibid: 285).

Sweetser told readers that Thornton "has a deep and fertile soil, prolific in corn and potatoes" (Ibid: 291). He said that Woodstock was principally a logging town, using the river to float logs south, and: "there are three comatose churches in the town, which is not populous enough to support a chapel" (Ibid: 293). Sweetser described hikes in Waterville – Greeley Ponds, Mount Osceola, Mount Tecumseh, and noted that the slide on the south peak of Mount Tripyramid was caused by the hurricane of 1869. He described the view from Sandwich Dome, which included "the white houses of Plymouth" (Ibid: 332).

In Lincoln, Sweetser apparently visited Pollard's boarding house (where that enterprising family worked so hard to make a living – Chapter 8):

*This is the last outpost of civilization on the borders of the vast forest of the Pemigewasset* [East Branch], *and beyond it no road nor trail goes. Mr. Pollard has rooms for about 20 guests, his rates being $1.00 per day. This is a good objective point for sportsmen; but the rude furniture and uncarpeted floors render it less attractive for families"* (Ibid: 276).

The contrast between Pollard's and the Flume and Profile houses could not be more pronounced. Sweetser noted that the Flume House could accommodate 150-300 guests, and was under the same management as the Profile House, which "is one of the best summer hotels in the United States. It accommodates 5-600 guests at $4.50 a day [and] . . . its dining hall is the finest in the mountain region. . . . There are post and telegraph offices, billiard halls and bowling-alleys, bath-rooms, a barber shop, a sales room for pictures and nick-knacks, a livery stable, and other conveniences" (Ibid: 260). He described each of the Notch's scenic attractions in detail that would inform any visitor. For today's historian, Sweetser's book is a rare snapshot of the valley from Plymouth to Franconia at one brief moment in time.

*The Railroads Grow for Summer Folk*

Franconia Notch was undoubtedly the most important tourist attraction in the Pemigewasset Valley, but even in 1878, it had to be reached by stage coach. Bethlehem was a booming summer community, but still did not have rail service directly to the village. Burgeoning hotels had to have all their supplies delivered by freight teams. In 1878-79, the Taft & Greenleaf Company, which owned the Profile and Flume houses, built a narrow gauge railroad from the main BC&M line near Bethlehem, south over 9 ½ miles to their own station at the Profile House. Then, passengers and supplies could take the "Profile and Franconia Notch Railroad" from "Bethlehem Junction" to the Profile station.

In 1881, the Town of Bethlehem built its own narrow gauge railroad from the junction west to the village, with a separate stop for the large Maplewood Hotel. It then became possible for passengers to change from their BC&M train at Bethlehem Junction and ride the narrow gauge into the village, with less fuss and much less dust. People staying at Bethlehem hotels could take the village line out to the Junction, and board the next Profile train to reach that hotel or visit the Notch.

The Pemigewasset Valley north of Plymouth obtained rail service in 1882-83, when the "Pemigewasset Valley Railroad" (PVRR) was built 20 miles from Plymouth to North Woodstock. It was then possible for summer visitors to change trains at Plymouth and take the PVRR for their lodgings at Campton, Thornton or North Woodstock, or go on to the Flume or Profile houses from North Woodstock by stage. The narrowness and scenic nature of Franconia Notch prevented any railroad from running through, although a short extension was built to serve saw mills.

Summer tourism in the upper valley increased, and North Woodstock began its own hotel boom in the 1880s. The PVRR also opened the upper valley to logging on a much greater scale than had previously been possible. Those two very different business activities of the upper Pemigewasset would eventually come into conflict.

The Profile House, and its railroad station with cupola in the trees at bottom. *John W. & Anne H. Newton Collection, Museum of the White Mountains, Plymouth State University*

Passengers disembarking at the Campton rail station. *Campton Historical Society*

*Chapter 13*

# Progress and Decline

In the later 1800s the Pemigewasset Valley developed in industry and tourism, made uneven strides in education, and saw a further decline of farming and of population in predominantly rural towns.

## The Bird's Eye Views

In the 1880s, a new approach to maps known as the "bird's eye view" became popular, featuring a schematic aerial depiction of a village with the major businesses and institutions numbered and listed in the margin. This is useful today as a time-frozen snapshot of the ever-changing industrial and business landscape in which factories and stores often changed ownership or function, and buildings appeared and disappeared.

The Bird's Eye of Ashland shows its substantial industry in 1883, including the making of buck gloves, which had expanded from small shops in Plymouth to larger establishments and better water power along the Squam River:

<u>Ashland Listings</u>
Wilder & Co. Paper Mills
Brethwick & Firth; Carter & Rogers, Woolen Mills
E.F. Bailey, Leather Board Manufacturer
A.E. Harriman, Leather Board Manufacturer
J.S. Draper & Co., Plymouth Buck Glove Manufacturer
Shepard & Fletcher, Millwrights and Machinists
A Grist Mill
H.D. Smith, Glove Dressing Works
Hughes & Huckins; Miss R. Dean, General Merchandise
E.G. Clapp, Stoves and Tin Ware

The Bird's Eye of Ashland, looking east, 1883, shows the Squan River at top, dams which impound it, and the BC&M Railroad with its station. *Boston Public Library*

Ashland, which had separated from Holderness in 1868, also benefitted from the tourist boom focused on Squam Lake, for which the village was the transfer point from rail to horse-drawn transportation, and the business service center for the surrounding area.

Plymouth's bird's eye shows its Lafayette covered bridge over the Pemigewasset River, the large Pemigewasset House hotel and BC&M Railroad station facing the river, its Main Street business district with courthouse, and the river meadows in the foreground. Ten glove works are shown. The rail lines going north and west do not appear, nor does the Baker River, both of which lie to the right of this view.

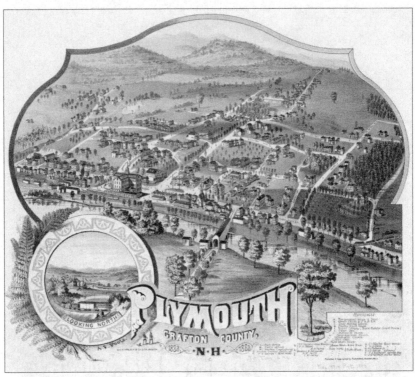

**An 1883 bird's eye looking west, showing the importance of the Pemigewasset shore as a rail corridor and focus of the village.** *Boston Public Library*

Plymouth Listings:
The Grafton County Journal, Newspaper
The Grafton County Democrat, Newspaper
H.S. George; E.P. Huckins; F.H. Rollins, Glove Works
M.A. Ferrin; Emmons & Edmonds, Glove Works
A.W. Avery, C.W. Calley; H.C. Philbrick, Glove Works
J.H. Whitten; H.D. Smith, Glove Works
Little's Hotel
Pemigewasset House
Rose Lawn House
County Court House
Public Library
State Normal School

H.S. George Tannery
F.S. Batchelder, Carriage Shop
J.V. Farnham, Marble Works

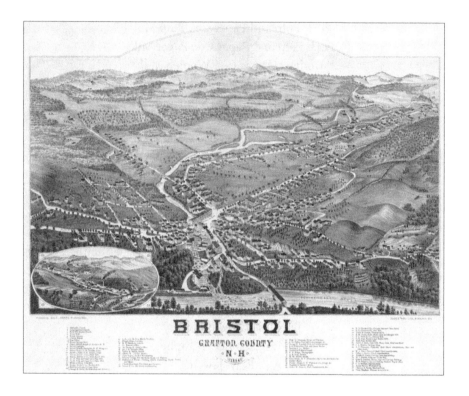

Bristol's 1884 Bird's Eye, looking west, shows the concentration of its industries along the Newfound River, flowing from the upper right to the bottom at center. The Pemigewasset River with its rapids and Central covered bridge are in the foreground, with the steeply falling Newfound River flowing into the Pemigewasset. The tracks of the Northern Railroad are obscured at lower left by the oval inset.

Bristol Listings:
Frank Bingham, Harness Manufacturer
Public Library
Bristol Savings Bank

Depot, Bristol Branch, Northern Railroad
Bristol Weekly Enterprise, R.W. Musgrove
Bristol House
Brown's Hotel
Mason, Perkins & Co., Paper Mill
Mason, Perkins & Co., Straw Board Mill
N.H. Pulp and Paper Co., Pulp Mill
N.H. Pulp and Paper Co., Paper Mill
Dodge & Davis Co., Woolen Mill
Bucklin & Robie; J.A. Haynes, Carriage Shops
George A. Robie, Machine Shop and Foundry
L.D. & C.H. Day, Marble Works
Fling & Chase; K.E. Dearborn, Lawyers
Dr. Fowler; Dr. Calley; Dr. Bishop, Physicians
Quincy A. Ballou; Charles W. Coolidge, Dentists
Cyrus Taylor, General Merchandise
William George, Dry and Fancy Goods and Notions
Dickinson & Horner, Clothing, Books, Shoes
C.A. Pearson; Anson Buxton; Clarence Smith, Blacksmiths
Fred W. Bingham, Stoves & Tinware
C.H. Calley; Arthur W. Prescott, Fruit & Confectionary
J.D. Follansbee, Fish & Oysters
Bucklin & Fowler, Livery
F.H. Brigggs, Photographer
A.B. Pray, Jeweler
H.T. Alexander, Dry Goods & Groceries
C.H. Whitten & Co. Drugs
E.D. Crosby & Co., Croquet Sets & Chair Stock
E.M. Drake, Piano Stools, Saw & Shingle Mill
E.K. Pray, Bobbin Mill
Taylor & Shaw; W.C. Kelley, Grist Mills
A.P. Harriman; M.A. Kent, Plymouth Buck Glove Manufacturers
Calley & Courier, Crutch Manufacturer
M.O. Edgerly, Gun & Sewing Machine Repair

Bristol's businesses perhaps participated more fully in the bird's eye listings than those of Ashland and Plymouth. However that may be, the Bristol catalog is a good portrait of a Pemigewasset Valley village which was dedicated to industrial and commercial development. The listing does not include three saw mill and woodworking establishments, which also were in operation in 1884.

The Pemigewasset River flowing from the north at left is joined by the Winnipesaukee River flowing from top right. The dam shown on the Pemigewasset was proposed, but not yet built in 1884. The Republican covered bridge below the dam linked industrial Franklin at right with the Northern Railroad on the left. *Boston Public Library*

The 1884 Franklin Bird's Eye gives an impressive rendering of the double oxbow, where the Winnipesaukee River flowing from the east twists back upon itself before joining the Pemigewasset flowing from the north. This was a prime fishing spot for thousands of years, and in 1884 is shown as a prime industrial spot as well, due to the strength and reliability of waterpower available there. The Northern Railroad from Concord is shown on the west side of the Pemigewasset, heading north to Hill and onward to Bristol. On the horizon at top left is Hersey Mountain in Sanbornton.

Franklin Listings:

Youngs; Webster House; Franklin House; Winnipesaukee House, hotels
The Merrimack Journal; The Franklin Transcript, newspapers
Franklin National Savings Bank
Skating Rink
Winnipiseogee Paper Co., Paper Mill Nos. 1 & 2
Winnipiseogee Paper Co., Pulp Mill Nos. 1 & 2
Franklin Falls Pulp Company
Aiken's Mills Hosiery, Walter Aiken, Prop.
Knitting Machine Shop
The Franklin Mills, J.J. Wrisley
Sulloways Mills Hosiery, W. Sulloway, Prop.
Clark & Haynes Machine Shop
G.W. Griffin & Co. Saw Company
Sleeper Bros., Sash, Door & Blinds
C.L. Hunt, Photographer
Phelps & Foskett; J. Johnson & Son, Grist Mills
T.O. Calley, Job Printer
Bushey & Eastman; J.W.B. Clement, Carriage Shops
Franklin Needle Works, Knitting Needles
Cate & Ryan Machine Shop
Thomas McConnell, Tannery
Edward P. Taylor, Foundry
R.E. Bean & Co., Manufacturer of "Ready Binders"
David E. Brown, Saw Mill
Judkins Bros., Pattern Job Shop
Kemple & Schyner, Job Dye House
Cummings Bros., Marble Shop
P. Dana, Granite Shop

The Franklin listings show the importance of the knitting industry, with hosiery factories, needle-making, knitting machine-making, pattern-making, and dye establishments. Although not a tourist town, Franklin had four hotels. Paper making from pulp was important, and there were two newspapers and a savings bank. Not listed, but undoubtedly present, would have been boarding houses for the factory workers.

Bird's Eye views show the year-round economies of valley towns which had developed their water power for industry and associated commerce and transportation. Such towns also provided a market for farm produce from surrounding rural areas, along with providing other services for the larger region.

## A Successful Academy

Of the academies founded in the early years of the 19th century (Chapter 8), New Hampton's survived and even thrived over the years. The original Academical and Theological Institution was founded in 1821 as a coeducational school, and remained so, but the boys department and the girls department were in different locations. Enrollment was strong through the 1840s, with 123 men and 150 women enrolled in 1847. The course of study was four years in theology, although only the last two were exclusively for the ministry. A separate classical department prepared students for college. Despite steady enrollment, the school lacked an endowment and began to accumulate debt. An offer to relocate to Vermont was voted on favorably by the controlling Baptist State Convention Board in 1852, and plans for the move were underway, when the school's two literary societies announced that they intended to stay in New Hampton (Merrill 1977: 132-135).

In the end, the head of school and faculty did move to Vermont, taking the old name of the school with them, while the literary societies and their libraries remained in New Hampton. Col. Rufus G. Lewis, a wealthy merchant of New Hampton, offered his support, and also worked to gain the sponsorship of the Free Will Baptist Church. Lewis and others secured a charter from the New Hampshire legislature in 1853 for a new school, to be called the New Hampton Literary and Biblical Institution. The new school occupied the old school's buildings, and like the old, had male and female departments (Ibid: 140-142).

Subjects taught in the male department in 1854 were Latin, Greek and Modern Languages; Mathematics; Natural Sciences; Vocal and Instrumental Music; Elocution; and Penmanship. Female department courses were Mathematics and Intellectual Philosophy; Latin, Italian and French; Drawing; and Wax Fruit. (Ibid: 147-48).

New Hampton and the school felt the impact of the Civil War, as described in *A Small Gore of Land*:

> *During the Civil War there was considerable change in the population of the town. Many of the young men left the area never to return. There was a dramatic decrease in the population after the war, and the [New Hampton] school enrollment suffered to some extent. The reason for these losses was also a result of the generous contributions made by both school and town to the Union cause. There was in addition, however, the cold, inexorable fact that young men were steadily leaving New England for the West, and the Civil War only increased their opportunities* (Merrill 1977: 150).

So many male students were away that in 1864 the graduates were entirely female. The school bell was rung to announce important news, followed by an address and a prayer meeting if the news was bad, or a "levee," during which boys and girls could talk to one another, if the news was good.

Graduates of the girls department tended to go into teaching, and "instruction in all branches of education usually taught in our common schools" was part of the curriculum. During the 1870s the theological department moved out of the school and courses in agriculture, science and business were added. Students boarded in village houses, each of which took either boys or girls (Ibid: 152-54).

Prominent people were invited to give lectures, as when Ralph Waldo Emerson addressed the school, then named simply the New Hampton Literary Institution, in July of 1875. He came accompanied by his daughter Ellen, who acted as his secretary and who wrote a letter about their trip which tells us a good deal. They took the train to Franklin, and then the Bristol branch line to Bristol village:

> *Mr. McIntyre* [a graduating student] *received us at Bristol at about five o'clock. He had a carryall for us, and we first drove by one of the finest falls I ever saw – indeed two, one on each side of the bridge . . . and then through enchanting scenery under a perfect sky for about five miles to New Hampton . . .*
> *I didn't know what the lecture was to be – had paid no attention to it. I therefore . . . read it diligently till I heard a band of music. I*

sewed it quick [to keep the pages in order], *and had hardly time to get my bonnet on before the procession . . . headed by the Concord, N.H. band, stood at the gate. A marshall with portentous baton took Father, and a humbler one with pink ribbons on a cane took me, and assigned us to our places in the procession, and we marched in unbroken silence with infinite solemnity to the Academy . . .*

*The audience was unusually responsive for a country audience, and a universal scream of delight hailed Miss Fanny Forbes' speech about dress* [apparently a humorous approach] . . .

*The first thing after breakfast* [the next day] *the band of music and Academic Procession appeared at the gate and carried us once more to the Hall where they had regular Commencement Exercises till one o'clock . . . At three o'clock Mr Dyer introduced Mr. Bray with a horse and carryall at the gate ready to take us to Plymouth, and away we started and oh! enjoyed Mr. Bray greatly. Never before have I heard the Yankee dialect in such perfection. "That 'ere clover, blowed out, looks kinder splendid, don't it?" And he said "leetle" and "hoss," and when he told us about having bought his hoss last week his infant grandson at his side turned gaily round and said, "Yes, he pretty nigh cleaned out his wallet."*

*We took the cars* [train] *in Ashland and left them at the Pemigewasset House at Plymouth. There we took tea, went to walk, saw a most lovely sunset, and I went to bed before dark you may be sure. The next forenoon we went strawberrying, and right after* [noon] *dinner took the stage for the Flume House. We had the box seat with the driver. The day was perhaps the most heavenly ever seen - clear July glory - and I being dressed for a sleigh ride was able to forgive the coldness of the wind . . . and Father enjoyed every inch of the way and could not have done praising everything* (from a letter of Ellen Tucker Emerson, dated July, 1875, courtesy of Kent Bicknell).

The school provided educational opportunities for many students from the local area, with New Hampton, Bristol, Sanbornton and Holderness well represented. In the 1890s, in addition to traditional courses in the classics, sciences, and English, a commercial course included telegraphy (telegraph operation, especially for freight and express), phonography (short-hand transcription), typewriting, commercial law, book-keeping, banking, and wholesale merchandising. There were school facilities where students could actually practice these business activities. Music, art and athletics were offered, there was a student orchestra, and students had access to New Hampton's Gordon-Nash Public Library. However, the old rule of separation of the sexes was still in force:

> *The members of the two departments are strictly prohibited from associating together, by way of walks, calls, rides, etc., except by special permission of the Faculty, and from holding protracted conversation* (Catalogue, 1897).

Daily attendance at prayer service in the school chapel was required, as was attendance at Sunday public religious services. Students were to avoid "use of intoxicating drinks, profane and indecent language, playing at cards or dice, or any other game of chance" and to "abstain from the use of tobacco, in all its forms, on the premises of the Institution, and from smoking on the street and in places of public resort" (Ibid). Under the heading of "Freedom from Temptation," the advantages of New Hampton Village in the 1890's are described:

> *It is true that a person may be vicious anywhere, but some places are freer from temptation than others. And it has frequently been remarked that New Hampton village is more favorable in this respect than any other place where there is a school of this grade.*
> *There is no saloon, no billiard hall, no place where intoxicating liquors can be obtained by students, no place of public resort where temptation to idleness and vice are presented to pupils. There are no manufactories, there is no foreign population . . . and yet the village is provided with all the accommodations of a thrifty and populous community* (Ibid).

There were supervised dormitories and separate dining facilities for men and women, and the catalogue states that: "Good hard wood can be obtained at about $4.00 per cord" (Ibid).

New Hampton's main street in the 1890s, with the school at left. *1897 Catalogue*

An apparent outdoor class in surveying, 1890s. *New Hampton Historical Society*

## The Plymouth Normal School

Industry progressed along the lower Pemigewasset, while tourism grew in the river's upper reaches. Many one-room schools in the valley's wide rural landscape did not advance apace. In fact, as farming declined in the face of Western competition, rural towns had less tax revenue to support schools. Teachers of those schools often were not adequately prepared, and the salaries offered by revenue-poor towns did not entice more qualified teachers to accept positions there. The problem was systemic, and needed a multifaceted solution, but one step was to increase the number of well-qualified teachers. The New Hampton Literary Institute addressed this problem on the pre-college level and many graduates went directly into teaching after graduation. The New Hampshire legislature passed a law in 1870 to establish a Normal (teacher-training) School to prepare young people for the teaching profession, and towns were invited to submit proposals to be the site of the new institution.

The Town of Plymouth purchased the former Plymouth Holmes Academy building and dormitory, and donated them. The BC&M Railroad donated, and citizens did too. The local school district offered to help support a model school where its children would be taught. Plymouth became the site of the Normal School, and classes began in 1871 (Speare 1988: 100).

Candidates for admission had to pass an entrance examination in arithmetic, geography, and grammar. Students paid their room and board and the state paid faculty members and provided books and supplies. Students committed to teach school in New Hampshire after graduation or compensate the state for the value of their education. Eighty students were enrolled in the first class.

There were two courses. The first course included arithmetic, geography, US history, English grammar, book-keeping, reading, spelling, penmanship, drawing, botany, and physiology. The second, more advanced course covered algebra, physical geography, physiology, botany, natural philosophy, book-keeping, drawing, and rhetoric. Students also chose two other subjects from a list that included geometry, chemistry, astronomy, geology, zoology, political economy, intellectual or moral philosophy, and "evidences of Christianity." In addition to classroom study, students practiced teaching in the Model School attended by

Plymouth children. There also was instruction in gymnastics and military drill (from the Catalogue of 1871).

At the beginning, all this was packed into one year. Graduates, who did not average more than twenty-five per year over the school's first thirty years, were in demand and usually had their choice of offers from school districts around the state.

A view of Plymouth from the south, with the Pemigewasset River at right, the railroad and highway. *John W. and Anne H. Newton Collection, Museum of the White Mountains, Plymouth State University*

Plymouth Normal School did not solve the problems of underfunding and inconsistent year to year instruction in small rural schools. For that a more sweeping change in the rural economy was needed.

*Plymouth Normal School—1871*

**The Holmes Plymouth Academy building was expanded and remodeled for Plymouth Normal School in the 1870s.** *Plymouth Historical Society*

## Decline of the Valley's Farms

Rapid industrialization and growth in villages such as Bristol was matched by steady contraction of the farm economy outside the villages. Bristol village grew by drawing people from the surrounding countryside, as indicated in an 1865 letter written by Susan Musgrove: "Tenements are impossible to hire . . . There never was so much business done in Bristol as now. It is estimated that there are two hundred more in the village now than a year ago. And yet they want to come but cannot, for they cannot find a place to live" (Haight 1941: 59). The remaining Bristol farmers had 151 fewer cattle and 547 fewer sheep in 1880 than they had in 1860.

Neighboring, mostly-agricultural Bridgewater shows the same decline. Bridgewater farms had 877 cattle in 1850, but only 480 in 1880, and the number of sheep dropped from 2,213 to just 693 in the same interval. Historian John Haight wrote: "With the use of ice-cooling on freight trains, meat packing had changed from a seasonal to a continuous industry now centered in the West where tremendous herds were raised on the ranges" (Ibid: 42). After the Civil War, Western wool and Southern cotton reduced farmers' ability to profitably raise sheep. Wheat, corn and oats were produced in great quantity and cheaply with agricultural machinery on Western farms and shipped east by rail to sell for less than the grain grown on New England's farms.

Haight writes of the farmers of the valley:

> *Not only the buoyancy, but it seemed that even the spark of life, had fled from their hills. Their main markets were closed to them and they were now forced to specialize on their apple orchards and to turn to dairy farming. Many grew only enough foodstuffs for themselves or their families, and were forced to depend on what work, as day laborers, they were able to find to supply them with the cash . . . for the products they could not grow on their farms* (1941: 43).

Some farmers opened their homes as boarding houses for summer tourists, and earned a substantial seasonal income, but that depended on proximity to railroad stations and main roads. The overall decline and abandonment of farms continued.

## Moses Runnels and Sanbornton History

It was in the years 1881 and 1882 that Rev. Moses Thurston Runnels, the Congregational minister of Sanbornton, published his two volume history of that town. His history and genealogy is remarkably complete, and includes the history of Franklin up to the time of its separation as a separate town in 1828, and the history of Tilton until its division from Sanbornton in 1869. Those two divisions left Sanbornton a primarily agricultural town.

Moses Runnels was born in Vermont in 1830, raised in Jaffrey, NH, and educated at Dartmouth. He decided early to go into the ministry, serving as president of Dartmouth's Theological Society in his second semester there, and training at the Theological Institute of Connecticut after his Dartmouth graduation. He was ordained in Jaffrey in 1856, and then worked for the American Sunday School Union in Wisconsin, Texas and Kansas, traveling thousands of miles on horseback (Blanshard 1982: 2-4).

From 1860 to 1865 he was Congregational minister at Orford, NH, and he next came to lead Sanbornton's Congregational Church. The church was at Sanbornton Square, the old administrative center of town, and he settled his family in the parsonage that he called "Sunshine Cottage," across from the Lane Tavern. He lived and worked there until 1886, seeing the decline of agriculture and loss of population, which must have affected his church. In a letter written in 1869, Runnels stated that his parishioners: "are almost wholly composed of farmers . . . There are no 'rich men' like those we find in the villages on every side of us" (Ibid: 8).

Moses seems to have started early on his historical research, collecting information and genealogical data from the many contacts made in his ministry and as a member of the Superintending School Committee, overseeing the town's sixteen scattered rural school districts. He apparently spent progressively more time on history, and took time off from church work to bring his two historical volumes to publication. In the books, which he published at his own expense except for subscriptions, he wrote of the "decay" of Sanbornton Square. At about the same time, he offered his resignation to the Church Committee, but they gave him six months off instead. In 1886 he resigned to become the minister in East Jaffrey, his childhood home (Ibid: 11-12).

One may wonder if Runnel's history work, which he obviously loved, also made up for a reduction in his pastoral duties, produced by the decline of his town and church. It may be that Runnels' excellent *History of Sanbornton* is itself, in part, a result of the decline besetting rural towns in the years between 1865 and 1882.

The parsonage, Runnels' "Sunshine Cottage," in his *History of Sanbornton*

**A portrait of Moses Runnels from Volume 1 of his *History of Sanbornton***

A revealing postscript to the account of Moses Runnels is that in 1884, while he was on leave, his friends in Sanbornton and neighboring towns held a benefit to help defray his debt from self-financing publication of the two volume history. Items were donated and sold, a skit was performed, and the Laconia band played a free concert for all those assembled. From the Town of Hill alone, twenty-five people attended, and $300 was raised overall (*Bristol Enterprise*, January 17, 1884).

## Chapter 14

# Closing the 19th Century

As the new century approached, people in the Pemigewasset Valley had both problems and opportunities. Towns – even those which had industry, were losing tax revenue on rural property that the owners had abandoned, and on which they were no longer paying taxes. It was a problem that individual towns could not adequately address. On the other hand, opportunity was to be found in serving the increasing numbers of tourists who came each summer to the Pemigewasset Valley.

*Farms for Summer Homes*

In New Hampshire in 1890 there were 1,442 vacant farms, according to reports that the State Board of Agriculture requested from all the state's towns. Those reports revealed that Belknap County had 54 empty farms, Merrimack County had 215, and Grafton County towns had 265. The Board of Agriculture decided on a two-pronged approach: advertising New Hampshire's assets - including attractive and successful farms, and publishing a state-wide real estate listing of the properties that needed to be sold. In 1890, the Board issued a booklet, "Secure a Home in New Hampshire, Where Comfort, Health, and Prosperity Abound," playing a role that the fragmented real estate industry could not. The booklet answered the obvious question of why the listed farms were abandoned:

> *The farms to which we are asking the attention of purchasers are those from which the former occupants have gone in recent years and on which there are tenantable buildings. These farms in many instances will average in location and quality of soil with the occupied farms of the same section. Large and comfortable buildings, substantial fences, and permanent improvements make them in every way desirable. They have become vacated in some instances by the death of the former occupant, who left no children to take up and till the ancestral acres. In other instances the*

*children have sought employment in the neighboring city or village while the parents still were able to manage the farm, and have now become engrossed in other business and cannot return. In other cases the owner has accumulated a sufficient property on the farm to invest in a more extensive business than the farm would afford, and the land and the buildings are still there offering equal inducements to the next occupant ...*

*Hundreds of these farms are located upon hills and mountains, and on the borders of lakes and streams, and would make delightful summer homes. Many of them embrace a broad acreage, good, roomy buildings, and can be put in shape for summer use at little cost; and they can be bought for a price less than many a man pays for having his family crowded into a hotel for a single season* (NH Board 1890: 8-9).

The Board of Agriculture issued its booklet annually for more than twenty-five years, changing its title to "New Hampshire Farms for Summer Homes" in recognition of the fact that most farms were purchased by city people who wanted a place in the country for their families. The booklet featured photographs and descriptions of prosperous farms and attractive country homes in the first part - with testimonials by their owners, followed by listings of available farms in the second part. One such listing in New Hampton in the 1913 brochure was for a: "Farm of 120 acres: pasturage, 40; woodland, 50; suitable for cultivation, 30. House of 10 rooms. Barn 40 x 70; also horse barn, carriage house and shed, corn barn. Fenced with wall and wire. Running water to buildings. Railroad station, 1 mile. Rural [mail] route No. 2. Price $4,000. Address, Young & Thyng, Laconia, N.H." A photograph accompanied the listing. Prospective buyers were to contact the owner or broker to make further inquiries.

Descriptions often noted that farms had large orchards of grafted fruit trees. The booklet contained attractive photographs of scenery and a listing of hotels and boarding houses, so its distribution also encouraged tourism. In 1908 the Board of Agriculture reported the result of its campaign to that date: 4,100 farms had been sold for summer homes, some 200,000 people were visiting the state each summer, and 149 new summer hotels had been built. Of course, towns were once again collecting taxes on property that had been in default (NH Board 1908: 27).

A New Hampton farm for sale, 1913. *NH Board of Agriculture*

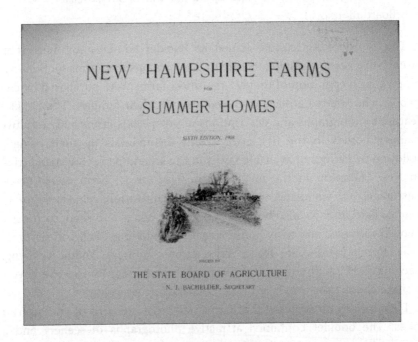

The booklet for 1908

How one purchase was made was described by Frances Lee (Chapter 12), whose parents decided that it would be better to have their own summer house at Bethlehem than to stay in a hotel. They consulted a trusted friend, who advised them to drive by buggy around the countryside:

*So mother and father did just that. They drove past Beech Hill, which has one of the most magnificent views of any place I know and came along to Wallace's. . . . Right in front of the house was a road to the left leading up a steep hill where there was another house of similar construction with more hill beyond it. Mother said, "John, that looks as if there would be a good view on the top of that hill." . . . So he turned the horses to the left and when opposite the old house he tied them to a butternut tree growing beside the wall opposite the house, and he and mother walked on up the hill . . . [and] there sure enough was a beautiful wide view, including Mt. Washington on the right clear around to the Green Mountains in Vermont on the left . . .* [Their friend] *said he thought it was for sale – most everything was – and the arrangements were made . . .* (Lee 1971: 66-67).

The Glessners of Chicago then built their own new house on the property they had purchased, and called it "The Rocks." Their land would later become The Rocks North Country Conservation & Education Center of the Society for the Protection of New Hampshire Forests.

The Glessner house at The Rocks. *NH Board of Agriculture*

*Old Home Week and Day*

At the end of the 19th century, rural valley towns had been losing population for more than 50 years. Bridgewater's residents numbered 667 in 1850, but just 244 in 1900, Hill had dropped from 954 people to 603 in that time, New Hampton's population went from 1,612 to 852, and Thornton's dropped from 1,011 to 552. Governor Frank West Rollins, who was a problem-solver, announced a plan "to have a week in summer set apart to be called Old Home Week, and to make it an annual affair" (Curren 1998). He designated the week of August 28, 1899 and put the Board of Agriculture in charge of coordinating the event in all the state's towns.

Towns were to develop lists of those who had left, who would then be invited to return to their old homes for a week of reunion with family and friends, visits to the scenes of their youth, church services, and a round of festivities – parades, speeches, concerts, athletic events, poetry recitals, picnics, and fireworks. The intent was to interest these visitors, who had prospered in their lives, to perhaps buy an abandoned farm or contribute to the betterment of their old town. Rollins also thought that the event would benefit visitors from cities, as: "The tendency of Old Home Week will be to draw people back to the farms, on the soil, away from the crowded cities, and every man you take away from the city and plant in the country, is a distinct gain to civilization" (Ibid).

The week was to begin with bonfires on mountain and hill tops – "from Coos to the sea," on the night of Saturday, August 26. No count was made, but it was estimated that there were hundreds of fires. In that first year Bristol held an Old Home Day on the shore of Newfound Lake, with music by the Odell Band of Franklin, original poetry and recitations, speeches, and singing of well-known songs. There were swimming races and a baseball game. Baseball was played, too, at Bridgewater's Old Home Day, together with a dinner, "literary exercises," and "phonograph selections" (NH Board 1901: 206, 241).

Other towns began to hold observances in 1900. The Holderness program included the Mount Livermore [Hotel] Orchestra, a banjo and tambourine duet, a whistling solo, and violin, cornet, and piano solos. New Hampton's celebration featured distribution of "maps of the town, showing all the roads and houses with the names of those who had lived in

# WEDNESDAY, AUGUST 24.

The observance of Old Home Day will begin with a parade which will start from Blair's station upon the arrival of the 8.20 A. M. train, headed by Keniston Band of Plymouth.

## 9 A. M.

Music, . . . . . . . Keniston Band

Invocation.

Chorus—"When the Stars are Brightly Shining,"
Children's Class

Address of Welcome, . . F. Schuyler Matthews

Singing—"Home, Sweet Home." . . . By All

Poem by Elbridge Homans, . . . Shirley Wallace

Solo, . . . . . Mrs. Mary Sprague Catlow

Address, . . . . Hon. George A. Littlefield

Solo, . . . . . . . F. O. Bryar

Address, . . . . . Hon. Charles A. Jewell

Music, . . . . . . Keniston Band

Address, . . . . . Hon. George H. Adams

Poem, . . . . Mrs. Martha Merrill Shute

Song—"Where are the Friends of My Youth," A. B. Chase

Addresses. . . by Rev. Quincy Blakely and Others

Letters from absent Sons and Daughters, C. W. Malley

Singing—"Auld Lang Syne," . . . By All

Dinner.

Singing by Prof. Henry Wyatt and others, of old time songs.

Friendly greetings.

## EVENING.

Concert by Keniston Band and other exercises.

Campton's 1904 Old Home Week began with a special Sunday church service followed by this Wednesday program, starting at the train station. *Campton Historical Society* each house in the past." Sanbornton held its observance in the old town hall at Sanbornton Square, and among the guest speakers was Rev. Moses Runnels, the "town historian," who was then living in Newport. Woodstock held an Old Home Sunday in the old meeting house, with three sermons, interspersed with singing of hymns. Then on the following Wednesday, the town's 100th anniversary was celebrated, with Governor Rollins and other dignitaries, cannon firings, and music by White's Silver Band of Meredith. There was a parade of decorated carriages and dinner in the hall of the Pythian Sisterhood, a literary and musical program at Beard's Opera House, and a ball at the Deer Park Hotel (Chapter 15 ) (Ibid: 256, 264, 278, 283-84).

At all Old Home programs there were speakers who had traveled considerable distances to attend, and certainly other former natives who took part as well. As Frank Rollins had anticipated, these visitors later made donations for libraries, public buildings, roads, and other enhancements to their old native towns.

Old Home Day gatherings "in the grove" were popular. *NH Board of Agriculture*

## Pemigewasset Floodwaters

Almost nothing had been done during the 1800s to control flooding of the Pemigewasset River. The exceptions were dams at Woodstock and Livermore Falls on the river's main stem and impoundments on its tributaries which were intended to store water for local mills, or log drives, or for added flow to factories downstream in time of drought. Such dams were quickly overtopped by rivers and streams in times of flood.

The Pemigewasset typically rose with snowmelt in the spring and with heavy summer rain, but there also were unpredictable and more damaging floods. In December of 1878, with snow on the ground and heavy rain, the Pemigewasset quickly rose to destructive power, flooding much higher than in years recently past. The entire Plymouth intervale was inundated. Harry Johnson of Plymouth was told by his father that the "meadows" were flooded almost as high as in 1869, and that in returning from his blacksmith shop on the east side, he was able to row his boat through the Lafayette covered bridge (Thomson 1964: M49).

Richard Musgrove, who published the *Bristol Enterprise* newspaper, and therefore paid attention to weather events, recorded that the late winter and early spring of 1895 had been very dry:

*Previous to April 10, there had been no rain since July, 1894, and wells which never before failed were dry. The water in the lake [Newfound] was the lowest for forty years. . . Mills were short of water and mill owners were alarmed. On Monday, April 10, rain commenced to fall in the morning and continued all day; at night it increased in violence and during two days three inches of rain fell; the streams were bank full and water in the lake was raised three feet. But this was only the beginning. On Friday following the rain began again to fall in torrents, and continued through Saturday and Sunday, seeming to increase in violence as the hours wore away. . . . Monday morning the storm had ceased, but hour after hour the streams continued to rise and a freshet of no ordinary proportions was on. The Pemigewasset was a roaring torrent, flooding fields, overflowing roads, and doing an immense amount of damage. . . .*

*One third of the way between Bristol and Hill the track was under water, in many places the sleepers [ties] stood on end, the rails twisted badly, and the bed of the road gone. Shortly after seven o'clock Monday morning the Ashland toll bridge came down the Pemigewasset; it struck with great force the bank wall at the depot, when its timbers snapped like stubble . . . A large number of bridges in Bristol and vicinity were carried off and the damage to highways and bridges in town was* [high] . . . *The running of trains was suspended for several days, there were no mills, and but little telegraphic communication* (Musgrove 1904: 487).

The Ashland toll bridge that Musgrove mentioned was built about 1870 at the place on the Pemigewasset where the Squam River flows in from the east. It was a wooden covered bridge, built to make a more direct connection between rural Bridgewater and Ashland Village, which many in that section used as their service center. The abutments can still be seen in the Bridgewater town park at Sawhegenit Falls. The bridge was never rebuilt.

Many roads were flooded or washed out, so that it was difficult to travel. The highway from Franklin north to Bristol ran along the Pemigewasset River terrace through Hill at that time, and was badly flooded. Travelers had to go west into the hills in order to make their way north-south.

The swollen Pemigewasset, with Bristol station and the railroad at left and Central Bridge at right, just above the 1895 flood. *Musgrove, History of Bristol*

Less than one year later, on March 1, 1896, the Pemigewasset flooded again, doing less damage to its valley than in 1895, but much more damage south along the Merrimack, especially at Manchester (Ibid: 488).

*Boarding House Attractions*

Efforts to rescue the state's rural economy during the 1890s and into the new century had an impact. People bought farms for summer homes or built their own custom cottages along the Pemigewasset and in the adjoining mountains. Some of them would become enthusiastic participants in the affairs of their summer town. Landscape paintings, photographs of scenic spots, guide books, and railroad advertising promoted summer tourism. Under its crusading publisher Thomas Walker, the *Plymouth Record* newspaper advertised the Pemigewasset Valley and White Mountains. In 1891, Walker sent 25,000 specially illustrated copies of the *Record* to "leading bankers, brokers, merchants, manufacturers, public officers and others" who might visit the region, or invest, or influence other investors to do so (Garvin 1988: 181).

Former governor and problem-solver Frank Rollins issued his own *Tourists' Guide-Book* in which he listed the many farm boarding houses that offered summer visitors fresh air, good food, attentive hosts, and the charms of the countryside (Rollins 1902). In New Hampton, for example, there were eight boarding houses, including Cheswick Cottage, which "sits on an elevation surrounded by mountains. From the piazza [porch] a view of six towns and three counties can be had. Best of vegetables, cream, berries, eggs, and milk. House is connected with long distance and local telephone" (Ibid: 93).

In Sanbornton, one of seven boarding houses was Maplewood Farm, "a 'country home' where all the luxuries of farm life are to be had in abundance. The house is situated on high, dry land, with shade trees, also a piazza 130 feet in length. The drives and walks about here are unsurpassed. The most noted walk is from Maplewood Farm to Lakeside House, called Lovers' Lane, a distance of three quarters of a mile through a pine grove to the lovely Lake Winnisquam" (Ibid: 95). Bridgewater offered four boarding houses and Bristol five.

Campton benefitted from having several stations on the Pemigewasset Valley Railroad, and had seventeen places catering to summer boarders. Sanborn's, which for decades was favored by artists, had grown into The Stag and Hounds, accommodating 80 guests, where "Amusements are plenty, such as golf, tennis, croquet, boating, fishing, a good livery, music, dancing, etc. The artist or botanist, and those seeking rest and pleasure, will find this an attractive resort" (Ibid: 258). While Plymouth had the elegant Pemigewasset House accommodating 250 guests at $2 to $4 per day, it also had seven boarding houses in or near the village, charging $1 to $1.50 per day (Ibid: 286-87).

Farm boarding houses, where children could see the animals and play in country surroundings, were especially attractive to families. Guests stayed for weeks or months, and became attached to their summer retreats. They returned year after year, and often had the same companions, who did likewise.

The Stag and Hounds at Campton. *Campton Historical Society*

## A Picnic in Hill

Guests destined for Hill's Fairview and Maples boarding houses could arrive at the Hill station on the Northern Railroad and be transported with their belongings to their summer lodging. During the course of their stay, excursions would be organized by the boarding house owners to places in the countryside for outings and picnics. Popular destinations were the crests of the western hills, especially Page and Dickerson, where sweeping views east over the Pemigewasset Valley and north to the White Mountains were to be had. In the summer of 1883, the *Bristol Enterprise* reported on one such adventure:

*Father Sol, condescending to show his face last Friday morning, was greeted warmly by the people at The Maples, as well as by all who were anticipating a pleasant day on Dickerson Hill. About ten o'clock three carriages were seen moving along in the direction of the Hill . . . People from The Maples arriving at Fairview, the company was reinforced by a goodly number from that place, and again the procession moved on.*

*The ascent of the hill was not made without a few shrieks from some of the ladies, but they felt that they were more than repaid for the discomfort which they suffered by the view which burst upon them when they gained their destination. The White Mts. were very plainly visible and Mt. Washington, especially, showed at the best advantage. Alighting from the carriages, the ladies opened the door of the old house, which stands on the summit of the hill expecting to find all as silent as the grave . . . when they beheld a bright fire glowing in the ancient stove; the tea kettle singing as if quite at home in the old house, and an impromptu table in one corner, loaded with New Hampshire dainties. The excellent dame who had provided this good cheer, soon appeared and bade them welcome, also giving them to understand that she had come up to get dinner for the men who were out haying on the hill.*

*But the day was too lovely to remain indoors, and the company soon adjourned to the orchard . . . Lunch was served under the trees, and lying back in the tall grass, with the wide stretch of mountains before him, each one enjoyed the good things provided for his comfort. After lunch most of the gentlemen climbed Page Mt., while the ladies sat under the trees, and either talked or sang. So the golden hours passed quickly by, and the procession moved slowly down the hill, but not before many a half regretful glance had been cast, first at the beautiful panorama stretching away into the distance, and then at the orchard, where only the trampled grass under the trees testified that there had been a picnic on the hill.*

190

A Northern Railroad train heading south along the Pemigewasset River. Many summer boarders traveled this route between Franklin and Bristol. *Bristol Historical Society*

Guests enjoying the piazza of Blair's Hotel in Campton. *Campton Historical Society*

*Chapter 15*

# The Changing Upper Valley

The upper Pemigewasset Valley had water-powered mills, logging and tourism before the Pemigewasset Valley Railroad (PVRR) arrived in 1883, but all were boosted by that improvement in transportation.

*Livermore Falls*

Campton had mills at Livermore Falls on the Pemigewasset soon after settlement and a bridge across the river spanning the narrow gorge (Chapter 5). That early bridge used part of the mill dam, and was thus inside the gorge. It was carried away along with the dam by a flood in about 1820, and was replaced by a new bridge of 255 feet in length, built higher in the gorge, at town expense. The wooden bridge was replaced periodically until it was declared unsafe in 1884, but apparently was still used for foot traffic. A berry-picking party is said to have just crossed, when the bridge collapsed behind them, falling 103 feet down into the gorge (Campton Historical Society).

In 1886, the Town of Campton contracted the Berlin (Connecticut) Iron Bridge Company to build a double span, 263 foot wrought iron bridge across the gorge. The Berlin Company's design was a lenticular-shaped "inverted truss" bridge with the roadway on top (Ibid). It used a large natural pillar of rock rising from the gorge as the meeting place of the two spans. Just a short distance from the west side of the gorge was the PVRR track, which had been cut down into bedrock to level the grade where the rails ran beside the river, and by which the pre-fabricated bridge was delivered. The east-west road which crossed over the bridge also crossed this cut before joining the main road from Plymouth, today's Route 3.

Unlike prior wooden bridges with lifespans of fifteen to twenty years, the iron bridge remained in use until 1959, when it was sold for scrap. The bridge truss proved impossible to remove, however, and part is still attached, spanning the west side of Livermore Falls gorge.

The wooden bridge spanning Livermore Falls Gorge appears in this c. 1875 photo of workers at the Dearborn Tannery, located below the falls. *Campton Historical Society, enhanced by Gray & Pape*

The two span lenticular truss iron bridge, viewed from the south. Note the two dams. *Campton Historical Society*

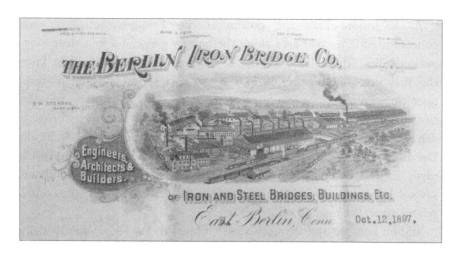

Builders of the Livermore Falls "Pumpkin-seed" Bridge. *Campton Historical Society*

Detail of the truss, showing supports for the roadway that ran on top. *D. Heyduk*

At Livermore Falls the power of the Pemigewasset River was concentrated in a small area along the narrow gorge and in a steep-sided pocket valley, "the hollow," on the east side at the base of the falls. From the first saw and grist mills of the 1700s, a series of water-powered operations took place there. Photographs show a variety of dam configurations, transferring water through penstocks and over wheels, to drive machinery. There was also more passive use of water, as by the Dearborn Tannery, and by a state fish hatchery, both beginning in the 1870s. By 1882, and probably before that, there also were a shingle mill and several houses in the "hollow' below the falls, with more homes and a school up on the road above.

Salmon runs on the Pemigewasset stopped in the 1850s, due to dams below on the Merrimack and to pollution. A Fisheries Commission was organized in 1865, and in 1877, Massachusetts and New Hampshire cooperated in establishing a fish hatchery in the hollow below the falls. Water for the hatchery was piped from a nearby spring. There were no longer any Atlantic Salmon reaching the falls, so Pacific Salmon eggs had to be brought from California. Trout eggs were hatched as well, to stock area streams and ponds. After the salmon eggs hatched, the fry were fed and then released in the Pemigewasset, Baker and Contoocook rivers. Trout stocking was successful, but hatchery-released salmon did not return to the Pemigewasset (Gray & Pape 2015: 31-32).

Next to the tannery, and also using water from the crib dam that had been built there, was Arthur Homans' pulp mill, which used large stone rollers to grind logs into wood pulp. That burned in 1889 after operating just a short time and was replaced by another three story pulp mill owned by the Fibrewood Company. The company used pressed and treated wood pulp to manufacture fibrewood panels, and in 1893, the Eastern Lignoid Casket Company built a mill next door to use fibrewood in making caskets. A flammable substance was used in fibrewood manufacture, and in 1894 caused a fire that destroyed both mills and the Dearborn tannery too (Ibid: 21-25).

That seems to have ended industry in the hollow, though the fish hatchery a short distance downstream continued to operate until the early 1900s. The small group of houses in the hollow continued to be occupied, and a new industry would be built on the west side of the gorge, adjacent to, and using the Pemigewasset Valley Railroad.

Top: Homans' Pulp Mill and houses, 1888. Bottom: Fibrewood (left), Lignoid, and Dearborn buildings, 1893. *Campton Historical Society, enhanced by Gray & Pape*

The Fish Hatchery building, c. 1880. *Campton Historical Society*

Interior of the Fish Hatchery, c. 1880. *Campton Historical Society, enhanced by Gray & Pape*

*The Mad River*

The Mad River flows from mountain slopes surrounding Waterville Valley for some twenty miles through the towns of Thornton and Campton to join the Pemigewasset River. There were numerous dams on the Mad River and its tributary streams in Waterville and Thornton, some used to power saw mills which drew their logs from the surrounding forest, and others used to store water that was released for floating logs downriver (Cheney 1966). Other mills, which produced various goods, were located on the Mad River in Campton.

One of Campton's wooden covered bridges crossed the Mad River between the upper and lower villages, carrying the main north-south road which ran on the east side of the Pemigewasset (today's Route 175). In May of 1867, a four-horse freight team was arriving from Plymouth, heavily loaded with bags of grain and cases of cloth. The weight of the load, including the driver and three men riding on top, collapsed the bridge. The driver and all four horses were killed, but the passengers were able to make it to shore. There was probably some depth of water due to the dam for the Dole & Co. mill just down river.

The Dole Company mill had been operating on Mad River water power since the 1820s, first for carding farmers' wool, and then for manufacturing finished woolen clothing (Chapter 8). Despite the river's fluctuations from low water to flood, the Dole Company expanded its production. Raw wool, first delivered by local farmers and later brought by rail to Campton station, was taken in on the mill's third floor. It was then carded and spun into yarn on the second floor, and passed to weaving and knitting machines, which produced cloth or knit goods. On the first floor were offices, a cutting area, and shipping. In the basement were spin dry machines and dye vats. Heat was supplied by wood for many years, first obtained locally, and then brought by rail (Dole 1991).

The Dole mill produced "satinet," a weave of cotton with wool filling. It also turned out flannel, blankets, suitings and leggings, and was especially well known for its "Campton Pants," made of a heavy fabric that was popular with farmers and lumberjacks for its durability and warmth. The pants were sold by stores around northern New England. Later, more fashionable knit apparel was produced too (Ibid).

Dole was a family business run by several generations. The Doles also operated a grist mill just upriver from the weaving mill. In 1898 they installed electric generating equipment for the factory and also supplied it to subscribers in the village and for street lights.

## E. DOLE & Co., Campton Village, N. H.
### CLOTHING MANUFACTURERS.

From _____ Date _____ No _____

For Mr. _____

Style of Garments _____

Style of Goods. 1st Choice _____ 2d Choice _____

When Wanted _____

**COAT MEASURE.**

Inches.

B.   Round breast under arm _____
C.   Round waist _____
E.   From back seam round elbow to hand _____
A to C.   Length of waist _____
A to D.   Full length of Coat _____
From A round front under arm to A with arm at side _____
Also from E round to E in the same manner _____
From A round under arm to B _____

NOTE.—All measures for Under Coats to be taken over vest with coat off. For Overcoats, to be taken over the under coat. Take measures moderately close, not tight.

**PANTS MEASURE.**

Inches.

H.   Round waist _____
I.   Round hip _____
J.   Round seat _____
K.   Length of inside seam _____
L.   Length of outside seam from top of waistband _____
Size thigh _____
Size knee _____
Size bottom _____
Side or corner pockets _____

**VEST MEASURE.**

Inches.

F.   Round breast _____
G.   Round waist _____
C.   Round hip _____
A to opening on breast B _____
A to C.   Whole length _____
Single or double breast, with or without collar _____

Height _____ Weight _____ Age _____

Stooping shoulders _____
Sloping shoulders _____
Square shoulders _____
Stands erect _____
No. of form on back which best represents customer, No. _____

Size _____ Of Lot _____ Fits satisfactorily with the following exceptions:

Sleeve length _____
Height of collar _____
Size of arm size _____
Size of front _____
Size of back _____
Size over seat _____

[The above acts as a try on and greatly assists in giving satisfactory results if properly filled out.]

(OVER)

Clothing could be ordered by entering one's measurements on this form. *Campton Historical Society*

The Mad River was used to float logs - mostly spruce, down to a crib dam located upstream of the Dole dam, which impounded Campton Pond. Logs were stored in the pond until they were drawn into the McCoy saw mill, which produced standard lengths and widths of lumber. On the river below the Dole factory were saw, shingle, and excelsior (wood shavings used in packing) mills, and a factory that produced sashes, blinds, doors and caskets (Cheney 1966). The Pemigewasset Railroad carried away the finished goods.

## Waterville

Until 1883, when the railroad provided easier travel and freight service to Campton, Waterville was quite isolated. Summer visitors had been coming to Greeley's since the 1830s, but for most of the year, residents did not see outsiders. There apparently were no regular church services. Nathaniel Goodrich quoted from a letter written around 1880 by Mary Briggs about a rare "neighborhood meeting" held at a farmhouse:

> . . . a good many people assembled – I counted twenty besides our party . . . The two Drake babies cooed and jumped about, and the three clocks in the room ticked. Everybody had made an effort to be clean . . . Several of these women cried quietly. Mrs. James Drake told Mrs. Davis that it was the first time her children had ever been to a meeting, and she burst out crying as she spoke. The old women wanted to know if they couldn't buy a book of those hymns – and some of them asked if they couldn't have another meeting before we went away (Goodrich 1952: 6).

The Greeleys had expanded their farm boarding house to hold about sixty guests. Goodrich notes that the facilities were primitive. "There were oil lamps in the public rooms, but when one went to bed he took a candlestick . . . There was no running water in the rooms, of course. I myself remember as late as 1892 the row of privies in the draughty shed connecting the farmhouse with the barn. I'm not sure whether there was a bathtub anywhere" (Ibid: 9).

Even after the railroad whisked people over the seven miles from Plymouth to Campton, it was still twelve miles by mountain road to reach Greeley's. The summer visitors tended to be people of more modest means, including a number of ministers, who sought peace, mountain air, and exercise in place of the expense and the social complications of large resort hotels. In 1883, the Elliotts of Thornton bought the hotel, expanded it, and added a new barn. In 1901 an electric generating plant was installed.

Regular visitors to the valley eventually built cottages around the 3 x 6 mile area, but the quiet ambiance remained. Arthur Goodrich wrote:

> *One feels that he has got into a place different from the usual resorts. Distant views are not to be had, of course, except from the mountain tops, but it does not seem shut in, it is too large, the summits are too far apart for that. There is plenty of sunlight, of air, of woods, of streams and mountains; and the world with its cares and troubles is shut out. Then again it is not fashionable. The class of people who take their summer outings by shifting from a city to a country drawing room do not go to Waterville. Rest, recreation and nature are its chief attractions (Goodrich 1916: 24).*

Summer tourism and cottage life was not the only activity in Waterville. The forest had for decades supplied logs, and that would grow in scope.

Greeley's became Elliott's, and then the Waterville Inn. *John W. & Anne H. Newton Collection, Museum of the White Mountains, Plymouth State University*

## The Pemigewasset Valley Railroad

The Boston, Concord & Montreal railroad ran along the Pemigewasset River south of Plymouth. North of that station was a junction where the BC&M turned west up the Baker Valley, while the Pemigewasset Valley Railroad – built in 1882-83, crossed the Baker River and continued north. The first stop two miles from Plymouth was at Livermore Falls, the second stop at the four mile mark was at Blair's, and the third at eight miles was at Campton Village. Then came Thornton, West Thornton, Woodstock, and at 20 miles from Plymouth - North Woodstock. Other stops were later added, and in 1893 the PVRR was extended one mile east to Lincoln.

The PVRR was operated by the BC&M, which became the Concord & Montreal (C&M) in 1889, and then the Boston & Maine in 1895. In the days of the C&M a tourist booklet was published entitled *Summer Outings in the Old Granite State*, which described the route up the Pemigewasset Valley:

> *The route through the Pemigewasset Valley is in the midst of most attractive scenes . . . Here is a perfect paradise for artists; and this fraternity sends numerous representatives yearly to these localities, the village of Campton and its neighborhoods being especially affected by its itinerants. For the twenty miles that the railroad extends up this valley, or from Plymouth to North Woodstock, successions of grandly rising mountains are continually coming into view, while the minor scenery contains revelations of nature most enticing . . . Within and about Livermore Falls, Blair's, Campton, and the Thornton and Woodstock villages, is the very concentration of natural summer delights, and in their neighborhoods are to be found all the wild and primitive characteristics of the New Hampshire mountain region* (Concord & Montreal Railroad 1890: 52).

## Thornton and Woodstock

The Pemigewasset Valley Railroad ran on the west side of the river in Thornton, and the West Thornton station there gradually drew activity from the east side of the river, where the old town center had been.

Modest tourist boarding houses were located there: Echo Cottage Farm –
10 guests, Green Mountain Farm – 15 guests, Kendall's – 20 guests, and
Maple Grove House – 40 guests. The last was "situated on an elevation of
over 2,000 feet; a thoroughly modern house, recently built and newly
furnished throughout; has broad piazzas, ample play grounds, fine shade
trees, excellent walks and drives; livery connected; plenty of fresh
vegetables, eggs, milk, etc., from the farm. Hunting and fishing. Mails
daily; 5 hours ride from Boston" (Rollins 1902: 288-89).

An important business in the later 1800s was tanning, and Joseph
Campbell established a tannery at Mirror Lake on the west side of the
Pemigewasset, where a road led up into the Hubbard Brook Valley (from
today's Route 3). The tannery, begun in 1855 and employing 20 men, used
hides shipped from Chicago. Campbell related that before the
Pemigewasset Valley Railroad was built, he paid $1.05 per 100 pounds of
hides for transport from Chicago to Boston, and 54 cents more for
transport from Boston to Plymouth. He then had to haul the hides by
horse team from Plymouth to the tannery. After arrival of the railroad, he
paid just 50 cents for each 100 hides delivered to West Thornton (Sawyer
2013: 40-41). In addition to the workers he employed, Campbell also
bought hemlock bark from "barkers," who cut down the trees, peeled off
the bark, and usually left the logs lying unused in the woods. The
Campbell tannery burned in 1888 and was not rebuilt.

Farming in Woodstock did not go much beyond the early farmstead
phase, as at the Mount Cilley settlement (Chapter 9). In the 1880 US
agricultural census, the town had less than fifty farms, which grew
buckwheat, "Indian corn," potatoes, peas and beans. Hay was a major
crop, to be stored to feed the farm's animals and to be sold. Farmers had
chickens, milk cows, and oxen, and some raised hogs. Maple sugar and
apples from extensive orchards supplied the families, with a surplus to sell.
Farm dairies made butter, but not cheese (*Upstream*, Fall, 2008). However,
1880 was on the eve of the railroad's arrival and a resulting boom in
tourism, which probably provided a summer market for vegetables, dairy
products, eggs, and other farm produce needed by hotels that served three
meals a day to all their guests.

Logging and saw mills made up a substantial part of the economy.
Nicholas Norcross, who owned a saw mill in Lowell, Massachusetts, began
logging in Woodstock and Lincoln in the 1840s, and floated pine and
spruce down the Pemigewasset and Merrimack rivers to be made into

lumber at his mill. After that, a local Woodstock entrepreneur, Nathan Weeks, organized the many small logging operators. He rented them oxen, supplied hay, grain and groceries, and bought their lumber (Sawyer 2013: 40).

A log drive on the Pemigewasset at Livermore Falls dam, with drivers posing for the camera. *Campton Historical Society*

Big absentee companies – the New Hampshire Land Company and Publishers Paper Company, owned much Woodstock timber land and sold contracts to local loggers who actually cut the trees and sawed the lumber. In 1907, Woodstock Lumber Company had a dam on the Pemigewasset and a large saw mill, with a boarding house for workers, a company store, and an electric plant at the mill village. The company built a logging railroad up into Thornton Gore on the east side of the Pemigewasset. Logging camps were located along the rail line, to house loggers who cut and limbed the trees, skidded them to landings, and loaded them on flat cars for the trip down to the mill. The PVRR carried finished lumber from mill to market. That mill and most of the community burned in 1913 and the entire operation closed shortly thereafter (Gove 2006: 55-75).

Top: Winter logging at Thornton, camp buildings and logged hillsides. *John W. & Anne H. Newton Collection, Museum of the White Mountains, Plymouth State University.* Bottom: Saw mill workers. *Campton Historical Society*

The Concord & Montreal's summer tourism booklet, effusively written to entice travelers to the Pemigewasset Valley and Franconia Notch. *NH State Library*

Another contractor who did much logging and sawing was George Johnson, who operated on the west side of the Pemigewasset along Woodstock's Moosilauke Brook (West Branch) and in the Lost River area. Johnson gained a reputation for rapacious logging without regard for the after-effects. He built a logging railroad, logging camps and a saw mill to exploit the timber in that steep-sided valley (today's Route 112), and he cut trees from almost vertical slopes (Gove 2006: 41-47). One of his camps was just downstream from Lost River in the years before it was protected as a scenic site. A party of people who were tent camping in that area in September of 1905 met the logging camp boss, and were invited for a visit. Walter James, one of the campers, describes the experience:

> *The cook-house consisted of about half of the main building and contained a large work shelf along the southern end, with barrels and boxes under and over, and a sink at the back corner. The stove, a large range, was directly in front of the door. The rest of the room was occupied by long tables covered with oil cloth, at which the men ate. The remainder of the room was the living room for the men. Along the two sides were the bunks – "double-deckers" – the width of an ordinary mattress, so that each bunk accommodated four men.*
>
> *On Sunday we ate dinner at the lumber camp, and, although I cannot feel that I would wish such kind of food for [a] steady diet, we were all willing to eat our share of the boiled beef and cabbage . . . In addition to the beef and cabbage, the dinner consisted of boiled potatoes, bread and butter, pickles, apple pie, cake, and tea* (English 2005: 98-99).

Johnson's logging railroad connected with the main line of the PVRR, which was operated at the time by the Boston & Maine (B&M). The output of his and other lumbermen's saw mills was an important source of freight income for the B&M, adding considerably to what was earned from tourists during the brief summer season. Of course, the Boston & Maine line also was the way that all logging railroad locomotives, cars, and other equipment and supplies reached the upper Pemigewasset Valley. The large W.D. Veazey saw mill at Mirror Lake in West Thornton had its own connection to the main line.

Arrival of the railroad at North Woodstock in 1883 spurred the building of hotels and boarding houses. The Mountain View House was opened in

1883 at the south end of the village. The Russell House was in the village, and the Fairview House was south along the east side of the Pemigewasset - a country hotel of three and one half stories, with wrap-around piazzas, accommodating 60-100 people (Conrad 1897: 17) (Tolles 1998: 166).

The Deer Park Hotel opened in 1886, just a short drive north of the railroad station. It held 150 guests, and was quickly expanded to accommodate 200, at $3.50 per day or $14 - $21 per week. The hotel's brochure touted its views north into Franconia Notch, east and west to peaks of the White Mountains, and south down the Pemigewasset Valley to Plymouth. Also,

> . . . we have a Deer Park and two beautiful deer. The office, halls and dining room are finished in oak, the parlors in white wood. . . . Steam heat on first and second floors, gas throughout the house. Electric bells,[7] barber shop, bath rooms, a good laundry, billiard and pool tables, bowling alleys, and a good stable, well equipped for mountain travel.
>
> The water supply comes from Loon Mountain, through a three inch iron pipe . . . The piazzas are twelve feet wide and extend entirely around the house. The East, Middle and West Branches join their waters about one hundred and fifty rods below the hotel, forming the Pemigewasset river; these streams are inhabited by beautiful speckled trout in great abundance, making the finest fishing resort in the state.
>
> A good orchestra has been engaged for the season . . . Our rooms are all front ones . . . **The sanitary arrangements are as near perfection as can be obtained, everything discharging into the Pemigewasset river** (the hotel brochure, author's emphasis).

The Deer Park was joined in 1891 by the Alpine Hotel at the north end of North Woodstock Village. Both later had their own golf courses. Other hostelries were the Cascade House, Innette, Parker House, Three Rivers House, and North Woodstock House - all operating in the 1890s.

---

[7] Electric bells were a pre-telephone messaging system in which guests could call for various hotel services from their rooms, by the number of rings that were sounded: bell boy, room service, ice water, etc.

The multi-page brochure of the Deer Park Hotel, printed in color. *NH State Library*

Playing golf at the Deer Park Hotel. *John W. and Anne H. Newton Collection, Museum of the White Mountains, Plymouth State University*

The Alpine Hotel, North Woodstock, and its golf course. *NH State Library*

North Woodstock became a busy village with its combination of lumber and tourism. In 1889 William and Mary Beard came to town and bought the Sunset Farm boarding house to run. In 1897 William built a three story Opera House on North Woodstock's main street. The ground floor was rented for store space: Newman and Lewis' clothing and dry goods; Hardy and Dobson's steam laundry; and Sawyer's bowling alley. The second floor of the Beard Opera House was occupied by the Odd Fellows hall. The opera space had seating for 500, which could be removed for dances. There was a stage and dressing rooms for performers. For the official dedication of the building a masquerade ball was held, and musical and theater performances took place there. On February 20, 1908 a fire destroyed the opera house, the neighboring Fairfield Hotel and livery, and commercial blocks, including the telephone office. New buildings replaced the old, but the opera house was not rebuilt (Russack, *Upstream*, Summer 2008).

## Lincoln and the Henrys

Woodstock had logging and saw mills, but the story of Lincoln as a lumber company town is a different one altogether. It all began when James Everell Henry, who was born in Lyman, NH in 1831, ran a farm and began logging to earn more money. With partners, he bought land and a saw mill in the Zealand Valley and operated kilns that made charcoal. Becoming sole owner in 1882, he built a logging railroad to bring logs out to his mill from land on which his crews had cut all the trees. At Zealand a company town was established for his workers, dependent on logging, charcoal-making and saw mill operations. By the late 1880s the Zealand Valley forest was gone and J.E. looked for more trees to cut. With a partner in about 1890 he bought some 70,000 acres in the huge basin of the Pemigewasset's East Branch in the town of Lincoln, and soon was sole owner. Then in 1892 the equipment, many of his workmen, and his own family were moved from Zealand to Lincoln, where they were to build a complete new company town. His sons had joined the business, called J.E. Henry & Sons, and the town they built was called "Henryville" (Gove 2012: 60-61, 74) (Henry 2016: 16-28).

When the Henrys arrived in August, 1892 there were four houses at the edge of their East Branch forest holdings, one of which was the venerable Pollard boarding house. The women and children were installed in the existing houses as boarders, while men working to build the town lived n tents. Trees were cleared, and six houses, a barn and blacksmith shop, a harness shop and store were quickly put up. The Henrys had to build a one and a half mile connection between their new mill site and the existing Pemigewasset Valley track at Woodstock, while also beginning to build their logging railroad into the East Branch country. By 1894 they had built one of the largest saw mills in New England, obtained Concord & Montreal Railroad ownership of their connecting track, and gotten use of the C&M-operated Pemigewasset Valley line to bring in Henry & Co. equipment and ship out their lumber and pulp logs (Gove 2012: 73-80).

The Henry logging line was officially the East Branch and Lincoln Railroad (EB&L), controlled and maintained by them, while the C&M built a station at Lincoln to handle passengers and freight on its line. Workmen building the EB&L were housed in railroad cars, along with a car for the kitchen and another for the horses. The Henrys earned extra income by running excursion trains along their track, with lunch at one of the logging camps, and they also transported berry-picking parties to gather berries in areas affected by the devastating forest fires that plagued logging operations. The company would eventually build some 51 miles of track to log as much of the East Branch and its tributaries as possible (Gove 2012: 106-07, 128).

Building of the company town continued at the same time. Forty tenement houses without plumbing and three boarding houses had been built by 1900 to house the mill and logging workforce and their families. The village had electricity and in addition to the saw mill, the company operated kilns producing charcoal and a mill to produce wood pulp (Gove 2012: 86-95). In that time, the Town of Lincoln grew from 110 residents in 1890 to 541, and it would reach 1,278 people by 1910 – almost entirely due to Henryville's continued expansion. The population was heavily French Canadian, Maritime Canadian, Irish-American, Polish and Russian. Not all employees in the logging camps spoke English, so the company gave them numbered brass tags for identification at pay time (Henry 2016: 48).

Telephone service arrived in 1901 and a post office in 1902. Also in 1902 the company's new paper mill began production that reached fifty tons of paper daily. In 1903 the company's Lincoln House Hotel was opened. There was a company store, a barn for horses and hay, machine and railroad shops, a grist mill, a warehouse, an engine house for locomotives, a jail, and a hospital supported by employee payroll deduction. Everything was owned by J.E. Henry & Sons and was painted an unvarying yellow with red trim. Henryville was a dry town, but alcohol was available in the "Pig's Ear" neighborhood, west of the Henrys' property line, and therefore outside of their control.[8] Privately-run boarding houses also were available there (Gove 2012: 86-95) (Henry 2016: 40).

The Henrys' Lincoln Hotel was used by the company for business purposes and by the community for functions. It did not have a bar due to the Henrys' no-alcohol policy. Lincoln did not attract tourists. One visitor's assessment of the village was that: "Henryville is a forlorn, treeless lumber village – and we were glad to leave it . . ." (English 2005: 96).

On May 13, 1907 a fire began in the company barn. Flying fragments fell on the store and office building, which burned, and the conflagration spread to the ice house, and tenements on both sides of Main Street. Fire companies from Laconia and Plymouth arrived by train, but only part of the village was saved. The houses of J.E.'s sons John and George were destroyed. Afterward, homeless people slept in the houses that remained, and a building that was to be a YMCA became instead the company store and office. Houses that were destroyed on the railroad side of Main Street were not rebuilt (Henry 2016: 63-66).

---

[8] "Pig's Ear" was slang at that time for a cheap saloon.

The Lincoln Hotel, part of J.E. Henry & Sons. *John W. & Anne H. Newton Collection, Museum of the White Mountains, Plymouth State University*

A view of North Woodstock Village and Franconia Notch from the Mountain View House, *NH Board of Agriculture*

Henryville/Lincoln Village after the fire of 1907. *Upper Pemigewasset Historical Society*

The people of Henryville, later Lincoln Village, appreciated the employment opportunities and the entrepreneurship provided by J.E. Henry & Co. They were hard-working, and enjoyed a sense of community and of common purpose. The village community existed on J.E. Henry's terms, but also on its own. It had a band and a baseball team. The village continued to grow, and its size meant that it had a good school. Beyond Lincoln Village the Town of Lincoln also held the Flume House and the Flume scenic site in Franconia Notch.

*Chapter 16*

# Life at the Turn of the Century

As the 19th century closed and the 20th began, there were continuing patterns in people's lives, such as the annual arrival of summer folk, the big part played by the valley's railroads, and the need for good teachers in rural schools. There were new businesses being established, and unique features of the time which have since passed from the scene.

## The Plymouth Fair

An institution with roots in the 19th century carried forward deservedly into the 20th: the Plymouth Fair. There had been agricultural fairs in New Hampshire and locally in Grafton County for much of the 19th century, and occasionally in Plymouth, but it took the setting-aside of a designated fair ground to give the event permanence. In 1871 land on the north side of the Baker River was leased by the Grafton County Agricultural Society for use as the Plymouth fairground (Stearns 1987: 388-89). In 1896 the Plymouth Fair Association was incorporated to run the annual event. A racetrack and grandstand were there, and buildings for the animals. Advertisements were sold and prize premiums were raised, classes of competitions were decided, and judges selected. Concessions were sold, rules were published and a program was printed.

There were races with substantial prizes, and livestock and poultry competitions for best in breed, with smaller awards. Vegetables, other produce, and flowers were judged, as were dairy products, baked goods, fruit, maple sugar and honey. There were awards for crafts and for various types of paintings: oil, water color, crayon, pastel, and charcoal, and for painting on china, cloth, and umbrella stands. Embroidery and lace work was judged. Some of the rules of the year 1900 fair were:

*Premiums in all competitive departments are open to the world.*
*Entrance fee of one dollar will be charged for each class.*

*Exhibitors have the right to sell their exhibits, but must not deliver them until the close of the fair.*

*All cash premiums awarded are liable to pro rata reduction sufficient to meet any deficiency that may occur in the receipts . . . and other expenses of the fair.*

*Hay and straw will be furnished free to all exhibitors of stock during the three days of the fair.*

*Efficient police will be on duty day and night, but the Association does not hold itself responsible for the safety of articles exhibited.*

**Admission to Park,** *35 cents;* **Children under Fifteen Years,** *20 cents;* **Carriages,** *25 cents.*

*Excursion rates on all trains.*

The fair could be reached by the Boston & Maine Railroad, which sold tickets that included admission, and from places as distant as Berlin - $3.45, and Gorham - $3.30, or as close as Quincy – 50 cents. As the Plymouth Fair took place in September, after the close of tourist season, the railroad could gain passenger income by partnering with the Fair.

There was music by local bands and there were concessions selling souvenirs and food – oyster stew, baked beans, "army style pies," and more. Local merchants, such as Fred Brown's Drug Store and Gould's cooking and heating stoves, had exhibits, too.

The fairgrounds were the Pemigewasset Trotting Park. The Fair was a member of the National Trotting Association and applied its rules to races. There was significant money involved in racing, and consequently, a need to enforce fairness. Under the heading of "Purse Money" the Association advised:

*A sum of money, not less than $500 nor more than $1,000, will be awarded in purses for the fastest Stallion, Geldings, or Mares.* **Should the officers of the Society become satisfied of bargaining between parties to impose a sham race upon the Society and its patrons, they reserve the right to withhold the award.** (author's emphasis)

Top: People entering the main gate of the Plymouth Fair, 1913. Bottom: A concession stand, perhaps with concessionaires, and a Plymouth policeman. *Plymouth Historical Society*

Top: The grandstand and reviewing stand, Plymouth Fair. Bottom: Advertisements in the Fair program. *Plymouth Historical Society*

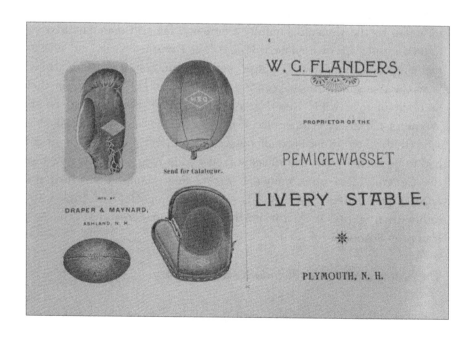

## Fountains for Man and Beast

For many years towns encouraged residents to place water troughs along roads, with a $2.00 – $5.00 per year payment to anyone who did so. The troughs were often hollowed-out logs or masonry basins that were fed by water running from a nearby stream or spring. They were for the convenience of travelers, who could water their horses and also get a drink themselves, as they passed along rural roads. In villages the public water often was more attractively presented in a granite trough, and after 1860, cast iron became available. Foundries, including Concord's H.W. Clapp & Co., began manufacturing iron troughs (Sullivan 2019: 4).

In 1890, Henry Clapp obtained a patent for a cast iron trough that was intended "For Man and Beast." The trough had a large raised bowl from which a horse could drink while in harness, a separate bowl with faucet for people - with a hood to separate their drink from that of the horse, and a water-filled collar at the bottom of the pedestal from which dogs could drink. From the center of the bowl rose a mast, to which a horse could be tied, and which could also contain a street light (Ibid: 13-14).

Henry Clapp became Mayor of Concord and his old company changed its name to the Concord Foundry Company. He still manufactured the fountain under his own name, calling it "The Favorite." Cities and villages, including Hill and New Hampton, bought fountains from both makers from the 1890s into the 20th century. The Town of Hill paid $110 for their fountain in 1931, while New Hampton's "Favorite" was donated by the Women's Christian Temperance Union, cost $145, and was installed in 1900 (Ibid: 76-77) (Kent Bicknell, personal communication). Hill's fountain had to be moved when the village was moved in 1939-40, and is now near the General Store on Commerce Street. New Hampton's, which was apparently donated by the WCTU as an encouragement to drink water rather than spirits, is on the north side of Main Street near the New Hampton School.

## The Young Ladies, and Plymouth Public Library

Before public libraries there were "social," or private libraries, founded by a group of people who wanted to share access to a collection of books.

New Hampton's Clapp "Favorite" fountain does not have a mast, and the dog trough at the bottom of the pedestal is buried. The name is on the hood at back, which protects the fountain's people side. *D. Heyduk*

The library had officers who were empowered to run it, and only those who paid a subscription could borrow the books. In Plymouth in 1873 a group of fourteen young ladies founded such a library, but with the intention of making it accessible to the people of the town. They raised money through fairs, lectures and entertainments, and received donations, one of which in 1876 was a renovated building which had been the original Grafton County Courthouse (photo, Chapter 6). People who wished to borrow books paid an annual membership of one dollar. In recognition of the public good that the Young Ladies Library Association was doing, the Town of Plymouth appropriated money for their library from time to time (Stearns 1987: 328-29).

In 1895 the state legislature passed a law requiring towns to make an annual assessment for a free public library, and to accumulate those funds until such a library could be established. By law, public libraries were to be open at no cost to all the residents of the town, and were to be run by elected trustees. So, in 1896, Plymouth had the Young Ladies Circulating Library with a building, a collection of books, and a librarian, but also the first elected trustees of a public library, which lacked those things. An agreement was reached to merge the two institutions, with the Young Ladies' officers and the new trustees jointly managing the library. The town appropriated funds, and the Young Ladies supplied the building, book collection and librarian. Access was to be open to residents without charge (Ibid: 330-31). Eventually, the library would move to a new building, and in partnership with the Young Ladies Library Association, the old courthouse would become the Museum of the Plymouth Historical Society.

## Frank Woodward and the Town of Hill

The Town of Hill had modest water power from streams which ran from its western hills down to the Pemigewasset River, and it had the Northern Railroad. The village stretched along the main north-south road that ran along the west side of the river, north to Bristol, south to Franklin, and east across the Pemigewasser via the Union (or Belknap) covered bridge to Sanbornton. Like other less-industrialized Pemigewasset Valley towns, it had grist, saw, and other small mills, dedicated local merchants, and town government, churches, and schools. Farms and farm boarding houses were

**The Plymouth Library and librarian when it was housed in the old courthouse.**
*Plymouth Historical Society*

scattered around the countryside, and there was the farmers' Tripeak Grange. The town was served by the *Bristol Enterprise* weekly newspaper published in neighboring Bristol village from 1878 until well into the 20th century, which recorded virtually every event – large or small. Hill had many enterprising residents, but one in particular was responsible for much that happened there: Frank Woodward.

Frank moved to Hill in 1872 and started a small factory which made latch needles for knitting machines used by the large knitting factories in Franklin, Laconia, and other industrial centers. Before long, he sold that business, and began to manufacture a hand-held glass-cutter of his own invention in a new factory: the New England Novelty Works. Employing fifteen workers, he manufactured and sold some one million glass-cutters by 1876. Improvements to the glass-cutter, adding other useful features, and growth of this business then required a larger factory and more employees. A printing plant was added, and in 1912, Frank's electric generating plant served not just his factory, but the village too (Hill Historical Society 1991: 27-29).

To obtain more dependable water power, in 1910, Frank designed a 45-foot high dam to impound Mill (later Needle Shop) Brook, creating a pond one half mile long and thirty feet deep. It was a large dam, which for causes that were disputed, burst early on the night of May 29, 1918. The rushing flood swept down one mile through Hill village, destroying buildings and uprooting trees. Part of the Novelty factory was sheared off and one Hill resident was killed. It was the worst flood in the town's history, overshadowing many serious floods of the Pemigewasset River. Residents were lucky that it occurred after the end of the work day and before they would have gone to sleep (McMillin 1923: 533-36) (Hill Historical Society 1991: 27-29).

Historian Nancy Chaddock of the Hill Historical Society summed up Frank Woodward's many endeavors:

> *He was, throughout his life, buying land, building houses, stables, barns, stores, a community hall and other gathering places, building aqueducts, bridges, and dams, ferries for the Pemi, collecting and selling ice from his ponds, selling coal, hay, and paint. . . . He suffered more than one fire and so recovering from some buildings being burned seemed also to be a regular activity. He also sold property at auctions. He bought and rented homes to folks in town. He also bought woodlots. In addition to making boards and shingles for all the buildings he constructed, Frank used some 40 cords of wood annually in his manufacturing operation . . . He had his own printing operation to advertise his products. He also did a little farming: 13-foot high Egyptian sweet corn is mentioned; also tomatoes weighing 4 ounces each, as well as 500 lb. hogs, his horses, . . . his splendid strawberries , cows, oxen.*

## "Hunter's Day"

The *Bristol Enterprise* reported on an activity that apparently was common in Hill, and perhaps elsewhere in the valley: competitive team hunts in which the object was to shoot as many animals as possible in order to beat a competing team which was doing the same. As one might

An aerial view of old Hill Village along its main street. The Pemigewasset River is at bottom and Union/Belknap Bridge crosses the river at left.
*Evelyn Corliss Auger Collection*

Frank Woodward, c. 1897. *Hill Historical Society*

imagine, Frank Woodward was involved in this activity too – heading one of the teams. As the *Enterprise* described it:

> *Last Saturday, Hunter's Day, was decidedly a pleasant one, and best of all, 32 were engaged in a hunt without accident. Capts. Adams and Woodward's men brought in . . . 285 squirrels, 11 partridges, 1 crow, 1 fox, 2 owls, 1 skunk, 6 blue-jays, 1 muskrat, 2 hedgehogs [porcupines], 10 woodpeckers, and 2 rabbits. Woodward settled the matter with a first-class oyster supper, and challenged the other side for another hunt, that will come off next Saturday* (The Bristol Enterprise, October 16, 1884).

On the following Saturday even more dead animals were brought in, including 381 squirrels, 10 partridges, 20 woodpeckers, 1 hawk, and even a weasel. The event was organized by the Hill Sporting Club.

## The Plymouth Normal School's Growth

By 1900, Plymouth Normal School, which had graduating classes numbering in the 20s during most of the prior decade, began to graduate classes numbering in the 30s, 40s, and even 50s. The school advertised in the program book for Plymouth's Fair that year, the first of James Klock's term as principal, noting that the building was "new and commodious," and that in the Ladies' boarding hall, "Every room [is] light and airy." Minnie Nichols, who enrolled in 1920, recalled:

> *There were only three buildings: a brand new dormitory – Mary Lyon Hall, Rounds Hall with its tower and clock, and the Training School . . . There were about 100 women and no men . . . Sports were mostly intramural but we had a good basketball team which competed with other schools of like nature. We had a glee club which sang three and four part music for women's voices . . . As a state supported institution $5.00 a week covered all expenses except our spending money – class dues, athletic association dues, and membership in the YWCA* (Nichols 1979: 12-13).

The all-female students in laboratory, c. 1900. *School Catalogue*

"A Student's Room," in the c. 1900 *School Catalogue*

## Railroad Events and Tragedies

By the late 1800s and early 1900s the Boston, Concord & Montreal Railroad (BC&M) had become the Concord & Montreal, and then the Boston & Maine, operating on the same tracks through those changes. During that time, the Bristol Branch of the Northern Railroad remained unchanged, and both lines had become essential to the businesses and lives of people in the Pemigewasset Valley. Railroads needed to conduct regular maintenance of their equipment, stations, roadbed, tracks and switches. They needed to carry passengers, the mail, and freight safely and on schedule. Many men were employed to take care of these things on a regular basis, and often were called upon for special effort when the weather or accidents interrupted operations. In a river valley with shoreline tracks and many bridges, damage to the system could be severe.

The Blizzard of 1888 is remembered throughout the Northeast for its severity, and its impact was felt especially in the lower Pemigewasset Valley. Prior to that famous March storm, however, there was another blizzard in January of that winter. The severe January storm brought from 16 to 18 inches of snow, gale force wind, and temperatures of 4 to 10 degrees below zero. Snow was blown into huge drifts against buildings, on roads, and on the railroad. Trains from the south could not reach Concord for three days, nor did Bristol have service over that time. A snow plow wreck on the BC&M between New Hampton and Meredith trapped a passenger train behind the plow train, and the passengers had to walk through deep snow into Meredith, resulting in many cases of frostbite (*Bristol Enterprise* February 2, 1888).

The more famous 1888 blizzard came in the middle of March on a Sunday night, and lasted through Tuesday morning, leaving two feet of snow around New Hampton, Hill and Bristol. The Bristol train did not make its scheduled run on Tuesday, but instead, the engineer and a work gang spent the day opening a way out. Trains and mail from south of Franklin could not get through, and no mail reached Bristol for a week. The New Hampton town meeting was cancelled. Luckily, after snow removal, the rail system north of Franklin and Meredith remained intact (Ibid, March 15, 1888).

On the old BC&M line, which was taken over by the Boston & Maine (B&M) in 1895, one thing did not change – operation of trains by telegraph. There was a dispatcher who was to know the position of all trains on the line by telegraph messages that he received from stations and sent to them. There were two classes of trains: scheduled passenger and freight trains which had the right-of-way as long as they were on time, and "extra freight" trains, which had to stay out of the way of all regularly scheduled traffic. The dispatcher telegraphed instructions to extra freights, which were received at stations, and passed to train crews to tell them what to do. A train leaving a station such as Concord would be given instructions to proceed to another station, where they would receive further instructions regarding their trip. Often an extra freight had to wait on a siding for a scheduled train to pass by before it could continue on its way.

The Plymouth station was an important one. It was in the Pemigewasset House Hotel, which had a diner that served passengers during their train's brief lunchtime stop. One of the most popular items on the menu was chicken pot pie, partly because the diner had the pies hot and ready to serve when a train arrived. Of course, Plymouth was also the station where passengers going upriver transferred to the Pemigewasset Valley line. Trains on the main line originated at Plymouth too.

On August 8, 1895, the B&M "Cannonball" express left Plymouth at 5:35 a.m. on its way to Boston. It was made up of a locomotive, baggage car, smoking car and two passenger coaches. The Pemigewasset Valley along which the track ran was cloaked in morning mist. About one mile south of Plymouth, the Cannonball collided head-on with an extra freight which was headed north. Not only was the freight not supposed to be there, but the fog kept the two trains from seeing each other until they were only some 200 feet apart. The locomotives smashed together with great force, broke up and rolled down the embankment west of the tracks. Seventeen freight cars smashed and derailed, but the passenger cars did not derail, and the 10-12 passengers were not seriously hurt.

The engineer and fireman of the Cannonball jumped before the collision, but they were killed by the wrecked locomotives rolling onto them. The fireman of the freight also jumped, and he too was buried by the wreckage and killed. Other trainmen were injured, but recovered. The inquest that followed, and on which this account is based, revealed that

**Using the telegraph in the Ashland station agent's office, a re-enactment.** *D. Heyduk*

the extra freight was to stop at New Hampton, which they reached before 4:00 a.m., but for some reason, the crew decided to go on, and were fully responsible for the wreck. At the time, telegraph was the only means of instant communication over the rail system, but it still depended on the trainmen's judgement to put instructions into action (Railroad Commissioners 1895: 26-29).

Top: The diner in the Pemigewasset House rail station. Bottom: This appears to be a photo of the August 1895 wreck, with derailed cars of the extra freight. *Plymouth Historical Society*

Another tragic incident involving an extra train took place on January 2, 1902, a cold, icy morning. The B&M Railroad was rebuilding the surface of the Plymouth rail yard, and was getting gravel from a pit just north of the rail bridge over the Pemigewasset at Bridgewater. A side track ran down into the pit from the main line and a locomotive run by engineer Edward Ranno shunted the cars being filled with gravel down into the pit and back up to the main track. The track junction was close to the bridge, and when Ranno brought the gravel cars up out of the pit, he had to back his "extra train" into the bridge in order to clear the switch, before going forward toward Plymouth. In charge of this operation was a conductor based in the pit, with a telegraph to receive orders from the dispatcher.

A regular freight train of 34 cars pulled by two engines, coming from the south, was instructed to wait until 11:05 a.m. before crossing the bridge. The regular freight was running late, and it was past 11:05 when it rounded the curve approaching the bridge, traveling at 25 mph or more. The freight crew suddenly saw a man on the tracks in front of the bridge waving his hands to signal them to stop. They immediately pulled the emergency brake, but it was apparent that their train would not stop before entering the bridge, and the engineer and fireman jumped clear. Inside the bridge on the gravel train, the fireman saw the impending collision and jumped, but engineer Ranno for some reason did not. The locomotives of the freight collided with the locomotive and gravel cars of the extra train, and engineer Ranno either jumped or was thrown 30 feet down onto the ice of the Pemigewasset River. Burning coal from the fireboxes of the locomotives set the wooden bridge on fire and it collapsed onto the ice, with all three locomotives and several freight cars plunging as well.

Engineer Ranno died of his injuries. The inquest determined that the conductor in the gravel pit had sent the gravel train onto the main line, even though it was too late to do so. He then sent a man to stop the regular freight, which he knew was on its way. That man in his haste did not have a flag, and had to wave his hands instead (Railroad Commissioners 1902: 283-286).

From these two wrecks the B&M had four trainmen killed, and lost six locomotives, 35 freight cars, and a 400 foot bridge in the space of just seven years – all along a short stretch of track between Ashland and Plymouth.

Top: The covered, double lattice railroad bridge over the Pemigewasset that burned in January, 1902. *Ashland Historical Society*

Aftermath of the wreck: burned bridge, and fallen locomotives and cars on the frozen Pemigewasset. *Ashland Historical Society*

*Chapter 17*

# Early 20<sup>th</sup> Century Trends and Events

Trends in place in the early 1900s were the continued growth of certain towns in contrast with the slowing of others, the prominence of the railroad in people's lives, industrial development, and growing concern for the valley's natural resources. There also were events in those years which are still remembered today.

## Population, Pulp, Paper and the Pemigewasset

While summer visitors flocked to rural towns, and helped to support farms and services, they did not affect the long-term trend in population. Predominantly rural towns - Sanbornton, Hill, Bridgewater, New Hampton, Holderness, Thornton, Franconia, and Bethlehem, all continued to lose people from 1900 to 1920. Bridgewater's population in 1920 was just 199, and Bethlehem, despite its 30 hotels, lost 395 permanent residents between 1900 and 1920. Bristol, both industrial and rural, reached its peak population of 1,600 in 1900, and then lost 172 people over the next twenty years. Waterville gained people, but probably due to short-term logging operations, and Campton and Woodstock gained modestly.

The towns with industrial villages continued to grow. Franklin's population grew to over 6,300, Plymouth went from under 2,000 people in 1900 to more than 2,350 in 1920, and Lincoln almost tripled in size, reaching 1,473 residents by 1920. Ashland held steady during that period, with some turnover in its various industries.

In Ashland, water power from a 112 foot drop in the Squam River was captured by seven dams, and the uses included a saw mill, a grist mill, an electric generating plant, a fish hatchery, a woolen and a knitting factory, a leather board manufacturer, and three paper mills of the Continental Paper & Bag Company (Ashland Centennial 1968: 30, 79). The B&M

Railroad served these factories, bringing in raw materials and carrying off finished goods. Ashland's paper industry produced newsprint, wrapping paper, toilet and tissue paper, egg cartons and more – all destined for outside markets (Ruell 2019: 23).

The railroad also had heavy passenger traffic in summer, when Ashland station was the transfer point for the many summer visitors to the Squam Lakes and mountains of Holderness. A handsome new building had been constructed by the Concord & Montreal Railroad in 1891, which survives today. In 1901, Ashland was the third busiest station on the Boston & Maine's extensive White Mountain division, with four southbound and four northbound passenger trains stopping daily (Baketel 1901: 125-127). On one Saturday in August of 1903, 300 passengers and 250 pieces of baggage passed through the station (Ruell 2019: 17).

On the Pemigewasset Valley branch between Plymouth and Lincoln, passenger trains ran by day and logs and pulp were transported at night. Livermore Falls, Campton and Lincoln were the focus of overnight log and pulp traffic, and of course the railroad was manned at all times.

The restored 1891 C&M Ashland station. *D. Heyduk*

Track maintenance men, Ashland section. *Plymouth Historical Society*

The Pemigewasset Valley had the native ingredients for one industry in particular: paper-making from wood pulp. Forests which originally yielded logs to be cut for lumber, increasingly were cut to produce pulp wood. The abundant water of the Pemigewasset and its tributaries could be used not just to power machines, but also in the water-intensive pulp and paper-making processes, and to carry away the noxious chemicals, dyes and solids. Rail lines could be pushed into remote mountain valleys to carry pulp wood logs out, and then deliver them to pulp mills. Trains then delivered the processed pulp to paper mills, and carried the finished paper to distant markets.

Franklin had knitting and other industries, but it also had the large Winnipiseogee Paper Company, with its own pulp mill to feed the paper-making factory (Moses 1895: 165, 176). Bristol had the paper mill of Train, Smith & Co., producing six tons of manila paper and newsprint daily, plus the New Hampshire Chemical Pulp Co. and Mason & Berry pulp mills (*The Granite Monthly*, Vol 5: 269). Ashland's paper mills produced a variety of products (above). At Livermore Falls in Campton there were pulp mills in the 1890s (Chapter 15), followed by the large pulp mill of J.E. Henry & Sons, built on the west side of the Pemigewasset in 1901, and operated for many years. The Henry mill was five stories tall, built of brick on a granite first floor, and used a large new timber crib dam to impound the river above the falls. Pulp wood logs were delivered by rail to the mill's siding on the Pemigewasset Valley Railroad and ground by large stone cylinders. The pulp was then dried and shipped by rail to paper mills, including the Henry's own paper mill at Lincoln (Gray & Pape 2015: 26-27).

J.E. Henry & Sons were using their East Branch and Lincoln Railroad to bring timber out of their 70,000 acres of forest to saw mills in the company village of Lincoln. In the later 1890s, cutting trees for pulp became profitable, and the Henrys built their own pulp mills at Lincoln in 1898 - one which produced pulp by grinding, and another "sulphite mill," which used a chemical process. The pulp was shipped by rail to paper mills at Franklin and other locations. Then, in 1901-02 the Henrys built a Lincoln paper mill which consumed 80 cords of spruce per day. The pulp and paper business was more profitable than sawing lumber, so they closed their saw mill in 1908. In 1917 the Henrys sold their entire business to the Parker-Young Company, which continued to make paper, shipping out 80 tons daily by rail (Gove 2012: 95-96, 199-203).

In addition to the Henry pulp mill at Livermore Falls, the pulp and paper boom reached Campton and Waterville in the form of much expanded logging. The mountains at the upper reaches of the Mad River drainage became a focus of logging from the 1890s, and dams were built on the river's upper tributaries to hold a "head" of water to float the logs down to Campton. At Campton, the Winnipiseogee Paper Company built a dam to impound the Mad River and provide a storage point for logs that were driven downstream from Waterville. The operation involved a string of logging camps up on the mountainsides and hundreds of loggers and river drivers. A rail spur was built from the Pemigewasset Valley main line up to Campton Pond, where the logs could be loaded onto flat cars and carried out to mills. The logs were spruce, 12 – 14 feet long, and their passage from Waterville down the rocky river, carried by surging water strategically released from dams upstream, was a spectacle captured by a *Boston Sunday Herald* reporter in 1923:

Top: The Henry & Sons pulp mill at Livermore Falls with its large dam. Bottom:
Paper-making machinery at Lincoln (later date). *John W. and Anne H. Newton
Collection, Museum of the White Mountains, Plymouth State University*

*There was a dull roar and a harsh grinding of great bodies. A wall of logs thousands of them, some as thick through as a huge hog head, came rushing down the river with a sound like thunder rolling close by. Faster and faster they roared along the deep cut while a swarm of men, armed with pike poles, leapt upward on the bank to escape the wood that would have crushed them to death instantly, had they held the places where they had been standing a moment before. At the bend in the river the grinding logs jammed, held for an instant with thousands of their mates piled above them. Swept on by the irresistible force of the raging water behind them, they broke loose and again crashed along tearing away a bridge before them, leaping up on the banks, ripping boulders loose, and wrenching away the bushes until with a final growl the "head" turned another bend and was lost to sight . . . But the water, filled with tossing logs crowded together in a mass that left hardly a chink in the river, continued to come, carrying with it tons and tons of wood from which the bark was being ground off* (Whelton 1923).

Camp 5 at Waterville, housing loggers and horses, but served by roads (which are hiking and ski trails today) rather than a rail line. *John W. and Anne H. Newton Collection, Museum of the White Mountains, Plymouth State University*

Unfortunately for the Pemigewasset River, pulp and paper-making are among the most polluting of industries. Untreated waste water from the mills contained hydrochloric acid, sodium sulfide, bisulfites, chlorine dioxide, and other chemicals. It stained the river brown and filled it with sludge. Sulphur released into the air caused acid rain. Coupled with sewage, and effluent from other industries, it fouled the Pemigewasset and the Merrimack below it.

## The Foster Peg and Bobbin Mill

Wood products continued to be manufactured from the readily available supply in valley forests, and certain kinds of wood were used for particular purposes. Birch was preferred for the small pegs used in shoe manufacture, and could be culled from logging operations around the valley. Thus, in 1897, the Foster family of Massachusetts bought a piece of land in Plymouth on the north side of the Baker River, near where the railroad crosses. A "peg mill" was built and machinery installed that turned birch logs into shoe pegs. A railroad siding allowed for delivery of 2,500 cords of logs annually, and shipment of 300 bushels of shoe pegs each day (Stearns 1987: 360).

The company built housing for workers on the same property, while the Foster brothers who managed the mill built comfortable homes on Plymouth's North Main Street. The very large US shoe industry bought pegs, and so did European shoe manufacturers. By 1904, the Fosters had added the manufacture of bobbins, used in the textile industry, to their plant. Changes in shoe manufacture reduced the use of pegs, and the Foster mill closed around 1920, but the building continued to be used for other purposes and was still known as the "Peg Mill" (Speare 1988: 125-26).

Its location on the floodplain where the Baker River meets the Pemigewasset gave it some renown as a place to measure the height of floods. One reason for this is that the water of the Baker River "backs up" as it hits the flooded Pemigewasset.

## Draper-Maynard Sporting Goods

Jason Draper was a glove-maker, first in Plymouth's Glove Hollow, and after 1878, in a larger plant in Ashland. The company tanned Adirondack deer skins, initially using 1,600 tons of hemlock bark and other treatments

The Peg Mill workers in 1898. *Plymouth Historical Society*

Birch logs piled on the Baker River floodplain at the Peg Mill. *Plymouth Historical Society*

to make their "Plymouth Buck Gloves." Jason partnered with John Maynard and they expanded employment and production steadily. In 1882, they were approached by baseball player Arthur Irwin who asked them to make a padded glove for him to protect his fingers, which had been broken playing ball. Baseball was played bare-handed or with unpadded, fingerless gloves at that time, but Irwin's glove was effective, and quickly became popular with other players. The company also learned that player endorsements boosted sales (McCormack 2017: 30-33).

Finding a larger location in Plymouth, Draper-Maynard built a new plant there in 1900, where they manufactured a range of sporting equipment, including boxing gloves, baseball gloves, footballs and basketballs. They drew on the E. Dole & Co. factory in Campton (Chapter 15) for knitted sportswear, and added custom-tailored uniforms. Yachting shirts and caps, tennis rackets, Indian clubs, baseball bats and hand-stitched balls, hockey sticks, and more were being produced by 1910 with the "D&M" and later, the "Lucky Dog" trademark (Ibid: 47-53).

After a fire burned down the original building in 1911, D&M had a new four story brick building on the site by the next year. Their line expanded further to golf, swimsuits and ski equipment, and in 1922 D&M bought the Peg Mill building to have more production and storage space (Ibid: 63-67).

The company had an ongoing relationship with the Boston Red Sox, and after the Sox won the 1916 World Series, hosted team members at Plymouth and at the Maynard camp on Squam Lake. Babe Ruth and other Red Sox players met Plymouth Normal School girls – who had the morning off, socialized with prominent locals, and tried out D&M equipment (Ibid: 141-147).

E. Dole & Co. made D&M's knitwear, and John Dole mentioned that:

> . . . As a boy I can remember my dad taking a truckload of finished products such as socks, swim suits, and jerseys to Draper & Maynard each day of the week (Dole 1991).

D&M struggled during the Depression of the 1930s, and closed in 1937. The Doles had been producing mostly for D&M, and were hard pressed to continue their business, but they did so, and then transitioned into producing for the military during World War II.

The four story D&M factory on Plymouth's Main Street. *Plymouth Historical Society*

Inside the D&M building where baseball bats and hockey sticks await shipment. *Plymouth Historical Society*

Top: Babe Ruth in fur coat and the Red Soxs greet Plymouth Normal School students. Bottom: Trying out boxing gloves at the Squam camp. *Plymouth Historical Society*

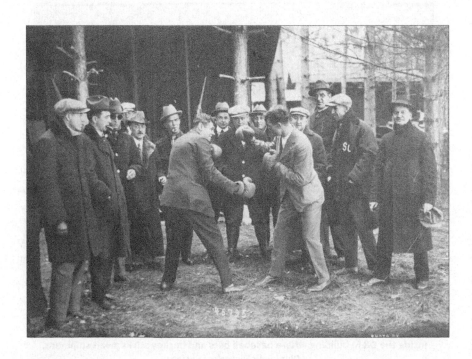

*A Lumber Company Town at Beebe River*

The logger's search for new virgin timber to cut led the Parker-Young Company to buy the entire J.E. Henry & Co business, including land, mills, and Lincoln village in 1917 (above) and also to buy some 22,000 acres in the drainage of the Beebe River in Campton, Sandwich and Waterville that same year. The Beebe River land was completely undeveloped, so Parker-Young's subsidiary Woodstock Lumber Company was given the job of building a large saw mill, a logging railroad up into the mountains, and a complete village for its mill workers.

The saw mill with log storage ponds and all the village buildings were in place within eight months: 19 houses with electricity and plumbing, a boarding house for 200 people, a general store with post office and railroad office, a company office, a garage, and a recreation field. The B&M-operated Pemigewasset Valley railroad ran past the site on the east side of the river, so a station stop was added and a connection made to the company logging line and rail yard. The company's Beebe River Railroad was built some 25 miles up to Whiteface Mountain by 1921, with many trestles, turns, and steep grades. It was used for building, supplying and manning twelve logging camps and for carrying logs down to the mill (Campton Historical Society).

Woodstock Lumber cut mostly spruce, which was used in airplane manufacture and for piano sounding boards, as well as in general construction. Their fire safety practices were lax, however, and led to a large forest fire in 1923. Public outrage, already stoked by loggers' ugly clear cutting and by prior massive White Mountain fires, was focused on Woodstock's Beebe River operations. Luckily, the Beebe River forest still had ample hardwood trees, and in 1925 the Draper Company, which made automatic textile looms, bought the entire Woodstock property (Heyduk 2017: 184-186).

Draper came to Beebe River to make precision wooden bobbins for its looms, and built a bigger mill complex with a new three story brick finishing mill and more housing for its 260 employees. Many of the Woodstock workers in the company village became Draper employees and that relationship and sense of community would last for many years (Draper Corporation 1965).

The original Woodstock saw mill and log storage pond at Beebe River. *Campton Historical Society*

The Draper bobbin mill and company village, clustered around its landscaped pond. *Draper Corporation*

# Chapter 18

# Enjoying and Protecting Northern Lands

While industry, agriculture, and business were being pursued along the lower and middle Pemigewasset Valley, tourists and summer home owners were appreciating the scenery and actively exploring the forest, streams and mountains of the upper valley, Franconia Notch, and nearby Franconia, Bethlehem and Sugar Hill. That activity evolved into concern about protecting the unique natural features of the area.

## Resort Hotel Life

The same railroad that carried logs and pulp also catered to summer visitors. A blow to tourism in the mid-Pemigewasset Valley was a 1909 fire that destroyed the venerable Pemigewasset House in Plymouth. Fire not only eliminated the four story hotel with its elegant restaurant, but also the Boston & Maine Railroad station and its iconic trackside diner. The fire was fanned by a wind that blew sparks onto the meadows across the river, spread to the woods beyond, and destroyed a farm over a mile away from the hotel (Speare 1988: 131). The B&M built a new station with a restaurant, but in a hint of things to come, did not replace the hotel.

Travelers could change at Plymouth for the Pemigewasset Valley line to North Woodstock, with its large Deer Park, Alpine, and Fairview House hotels, plus many cozy boarding houses. The Alpine had the advantage of being at the edge of the village, and offered accommodation for 200 guests, with telephones, a "ladies writing room," a "men's smoking room," dance hall, barber shop, and dining room seating 300.

At North Woodstock a stage met the train to carry travelers into Franconia Notch. They could stay at the Flume House, with easy access to the Flume, Pool, and Basin, until that hotel was destroyed by fire in 1918, and not rebuilt. Charles Greenleaf, who owned both the Profile and Flume Houses, replaced the Flume House with the Flume Tea House, where visitors could get food, drink and souvenirs.

The final destination of the stage from North Woodstock was the Profile House, which was rebuilt in 1905-06 to accommodate 600 guests. It could also be reached by train from Bethlehem to the north, but without the nostalgic and scenic ride on a stage coach through the Notch. The brand new Profile House was four stories high with a shingle exterior highlighted by green shutters. The foyer measured 150 feet long by 60 feet wide, and the dining room was two stories tall, seated 400, and offered views of the surrounding mountains. There also were twenty "cottages," with many bedrooms, connected to the hotel by covered, red-carpeted walkways. The hotel complex, which Greenleaf called an "Alpine Village," had a stable for horseback riding, a 200 car garage, the hotel's own railroad station, boat houses at Echo and Profile lakes, a bath house, and paths winding along the valley to viewpoints such as the Old Man of the Mountain (Tolles 1998: 198-201).

At Echo Lake guests could blow horns provided by the hotel and listen to the echo from the surrounding cliffs. They could take a short path to "Artists Bluff," for the view south down the glacially-carved Notch, or climb Mount Lafayette – the highest point, at over 5,000 feet in elevation. From the Profile House, one could walk to Profile Lake, or take the path along the young Pemigewasset River to the Basin, Pool and Flume. Perhaps most significant was the fact that Charles Greenleaf owned virtually the entire Notch - 6,000 acres, which was preserved for its beauty and the pleasure of the hotel's summer community.

Nearby Bethlehem offered a variety of accommodations in its thirty hotels, the convenience of access by rail, and a village in which guests could stroll and shop. Its Maplewood Hotel, with Maplewood Cottage and Maplewood Hall, accommodated some 600 guests, and had its own railroad station and golf course. The venerable Sinclair House held 300 guests, the Upland Terrace 150-200, three hotels each held 100, and six others each accommodated 75-100. There were a movie theater, four churches, and a variety of stores, including a candy shop selling "White Mountain Cream Kisses" (Bethlehem Board of Trade 1910). Bethlehem also had a newspaper, *The White Mountain Echo*, named for the famous phenomenon to be heard at nearby Echo Lake, and devoted to all aspects of White Mountain tourism.

Top: The New Profile House of 1906, with its dining hall at center. Bottom: The Flume T House, for Flume visitors. *John W. & Anne H. Newton Collection, Museum of the White Mountains, Plymouth State University*

Top: The Maplewood resort complex at Bethlehem.  Bottom: An auto touring party at the Sinclair House, Bethlehem. *John W. and Anne H. Newton Collection, Museum of the White Mountains, Plymouth State University*

Bethlehem had a railroad connection, which made it popular, but the larger area of countryside north of Franconia Notch also attracted summer lodgers, who appreciated the expansive views and the more open surroundings. Sugar Hill was an upland part of the Town of Lisbon which offered several large hotels and smaller boarding houses with views east to Mount Lafayette and the Franconia Range. Sugar Hill hotels were served by the Sugar Hill rail station, from which their coaches carried people back and forth.

The Sunset Hill House opened in 1880 and expanded until it accommodated over 300 guests. It had 1,000 acres and was popular with horseback riders and golfers. Hotel brochures related that:

> *The bowling alley and bachelors' hall contain three alleys of regulation length and width, and fourteen sleeping rooms on second and third floors for the accommodation of young men, at a moderate cost* (hotel brocurure, c. 1900).

Young men often were separated from other guests and accommodated in less commodious quarters. Women did not bowl or play billiards.

> *In the ball-room music for the dance is given by the orchestra maintained here throughout the whole season. In the afternoons the musicians discourse pleasing music in the drawing room; and here too, on wet days the guests listen to favorite concert numbers as they read an interesting book from the very complete hotel library* (hotel brochure, 1919).

The Look-Off Hotel also offered golf for its more than 200 patrons, and in 1904 it was open from June to October. Like most hotels of the time, it had just one set of bath and toilet rooms per floor. It had "gas and electric light and electric bells" in each room, plus telegraph and long distance telephone, a barber shop, laundry, billiards, bowling and tennis. The 1904 hotel brochure advertised that it was:

> *Located high above the level of the sea* [about 1,700 feet] *its dry and elastic air, its cool nights and its perfect drainage are well known and appreciated by thousands of summer visitors. There are no mosquitoes or other troublesome insects. People troubled with hay-fever and asthma find immediate relief in its high elevation and freedom from dust and dampness* (Look-Off Hotel brochure, 1904).

Peckett's-on-Sugar-Hill was opened in 1906-07 as a smaller, more intimate house furnished with antiques. It acquired such a dedicated clientele that it became a club in 1924.

Franconia had the Profile House, the only hotel in the Notch, but it had other hotels too. The Forest Hills Hotel was perched on a hill north of Franconia Village, offering a view southeast into the notch. Afternoon tea was served on the lawn, weather permitting. It was advertised as "ideal for children," and became popular for its opportunities for horseback riding. The hotel maintained a "sporting camp" at Lonesome Lake, above Franconia Notch, reached by hotel guests riding burros, and a bathing pavilion and canoe landing at Profile Lake (Foest Hills brochure).

Pecketts-on-Sugar-Hill was an expanded farmhouse, attentively managed for some 100 guests. *Hotel brochure*

Karl Abbott grew up in Bethlehem in the summers where his father and mother owned the Upland Terrace Hotel. He then owned the Profile House and Forest Hills hotels with his father, and was a life-long hotelier. He wrote that when the Upland Terrace opened for the season, hotel coaches with uniformed porters met the trains. Every bureau in every room had a bouquet of fresh flowers. Regular year-after-year guests always had the same room and the same table in the dining hall. Excursion parties were put in a series of small rooms up under the roof,

> with a bowl and pitcher and slop jar, which we sold for two dollars [a night], American plan, the standard excursion rate. Not a hotel in Bethlehem had rooms with private baths. Uplands had one public bath on each floor and charged 25 cents for use of it. Then [there was] a big room with about twenty beds, which was a dormitory for the young men guests (Abbott, Karl P., 1950: 7-8).

American plan meant that the hotel served three large meals a day. Breakfast was "a choice of steaks, chops, eggs, bacon, sausages, griddle cakes, coffee and fruit."

> People ate their way through the menu. Then they went out and sat in the red and green chairs. The men sat in one group and the women in another. After an hour or so they played croquet or walked . . . down into town to look around the stores. Mid-day dinner was twice as impressive as breakfast. In the afternoons they climbed into the long mountain wagons and drove to Sugar Hill or to see the Old Man of the Mountain (Ibid: 14-15).

The White Mountain Echo's newspaper masthead had a figure blowing one of Echo Lake's tin horns. *John W. & Anne H. Newton Collection, Museum of the White Mountains, Plymouth State University*

The Sunset Hill House at Sugar Hill. *John W. & Anne H. Newton Collection, Museum of the White Mountains, Plymouth State University*

Golfing at the Look-Off Hotel. *Hotel brochure*

*Threats to the Scenery*

Logger George Johnson was cutting a large tract along the Pemigewasset's West Branch (Moosilauke Brook) in Woodstock, which included the Lost River gorge (Chapter 15). People visited this impressive maze of huge rock formations through which the stream had cut a narrow, tortuous path, usually with a guide to get them in and out safely. As with other scenic sites that were included in guidebooks and regarded as part of the state's natural heritage, Lost River was privately owned. Publishers Paper Company held the land and had sold the surrounding timber to Johnson to cut. By 1911, Johnson was logging the area, and Lost River was in danger of being disfigured and becoming inaccessible. The Society for the Protection of New Hampshire Forests (SPNHF) had been founded just ten years before to try to protect some of New Hampshire's vanishing forestland, and stepped in to buy the property and protect it for public access.

Publishers Paper was willing to donate the insignificant 150-odd acres if Johnson and the saw mill with which he had a contract would sell the timber rights. The saw mill owner donated his rights. Thinking that the site was difficult to log in any case, Johnson agreed to sell his share, but at a substantial price. SPNHF raised the money, bought Lost River in 1912, and promptly opened it for public visits (Bruns 1969: 42-43). Then, as Paul Bruns relates:

> *Several years later, in 1916,* [Johnson] *visited the thriving new project at the height of the summer season . . .* [and] *after sitting all day in subdued observation of the throngs paying twenty-five cents admission to the caverns, he turned and said . . . "I never should have sold this place, and I couldn't see it"* (Ibid).

Like Lost River, all the natural wonders of Franconia Notch were privately owned: situated on some 6,000 acres held by Charles Greenleaf's Profile House hotel company. The Notch could be sold and the new owner could do as he pleased with it. Luckily, Greenleaf protected the Old Man of the Mountain and Cannon Cliffs; Echo, Profile and Lonesome lakes; the Basin, Pool and Flume; miles of paths, and acres of surrounding forest - and the public benefitted by having access.

People touring Lost River via its extensive walks and ladders. *Society for the Protection of New Hampshire Forests*

In 1921, Charles Greenleaf offered Karl Abbott the management of the Profile House with an option to buy. Karl, his father and a syndicate bought the hotel and its land, with 29 cottages, a stable, a 200 car garage, a dormitory for most of the 300 employees, and other buildings throughout Franconia Notch. The Abbotts ran the 400 room hotel, where long-term guests rented the cottages, Boston Symphony musicians played every afternoon and evening, 600 people could dine at one time, and the B&M railroad delivered guests to the station (Abbott 1950: 162-69).

Then, on August 2, 1923 a small whisp of smoke was seen coming from the hotel's fourth floor attic. Guests watched as the fire spread, destroying the hotel, cottages, staff dormitory, stable and garage - mostly by spontaneous combustion in the intense heat. Employees worked to save guests' belongings, piling them on the tennis courts, while cash and valuables were saved from the safe. Karl returned from a trip the next day and worked to find lodging for the displaced guests. He paid the staff their full season's wages and helped them to relocate (Ibid: 173-77). Plans were begun to rebuild, but could not be concluded, and the Abbotts contracted a logger to cut timber in the Notch (Bruns 1969: 52).

At that point SPNHF Forester Philip Ayres began to look for a way to make the Notch into a state reservation. Governor John Winant expressed interest, but balked when told that the purchase price would be $400,000. He told Ayres that the state could not contribute more than $200,000, and SPNHF's Executive Committee boldly gave Ayres authority to try to raise the balance. The Storrow family contributed $100,000, Edward Tuck added $10,000, and the Appalachian Mountain Club donated over $7,000 (Ibid: 52-53). In the meantime, SPNHF insisted that the Abbotts cancel their timber contracts while negotiations continued. If negotiations failed, the Notch could be logged.

The New Hampshire Federation of Women's Clubs stepped in to help and began a campaign based on Ayres' estimate that the Notch contained 100,000 trees. A "Buy a Tree" campaign was launched. Conservation organizations and newspapers publicized the effort on a national scale and agreed to accept donations. Philip Ayres wrote articles and SPNHF printed brochures. At a conference of New England Women's Clubs in 1927, Eva Speare of the New Hampshire delegation got the organization's support. The Women's Clubs contributed over $65,000 and school children raised some $1,000 (Jarvis: 114-150). Money to make the Notch a state reservation, half of which was raised via donations, enabled purchase of all 6,000 acres.

On September 15, 1928 a dedication ceremony was held at Profile Lake. The Franconia Notch Forest Reservation was dedicated "as a memorial to the Men and Women of New Hampshire who have served the nation in times of war." There were speeches, band music, a play, and the song "Old Man of the Mountains" by local teacher Frances Ann Johnson.

The state was not prepared to operate the Flume Visitor Center, so SPNHF was given that job for 20 years, paying property taxes to the Town of Franconia, putting $100,000 into property improvements in the Notch, and almost $90,000 into support of the Forestry Commission (Bruns 1969: 54). The state took over the Flume from SPNHF in 1948.

Top: The view south from Artists Bluff over Echo Lake, to the Profile House and the Notch. Bottom: The Old Man of the Mountain – symbol of the Notch campaign. *John W. and Anne H. Newton Collection, Museum of the White Mountains, Plymouth State University*

Top: Sawed or Saved? was SPNHF's campaign slogan. Bottom: The 1928 dedication song. *John W. and Anne H. Newton Collection, Museum of the White Mountains, Plymouth State University*

Other than buying land on its own, the Society for the Protection of New Hampshire Forests worked to get the White Mountain National Forest established in 1911-13. The National Forest would eventually protect Franconia Notch beyond the boundaries of the state forest reservation. At the same time as the Franconia Notch campaign, SPNHF was working on protecting the high slopes of Waterville, where loggers proposed to build a railroad into the Greeley Ponds to cut virgin forest on the surrounding mountains. Some 22,533 acres were at stake. Working with New Hampshire's Congressional delegation over several years, purchase of that land for the National Forest was completed in 1928 (Bruns 1969: 49-51).

The rock formation which made up the Old Man of the Mountain was an alignment of separate ledges which appeared to be a face only when viewed from a particular angle. It was some time before the actual ledges were identified in their precarious location at the south end of Cannon Mountain ridge. In the 1870s it was discovered that the Old Man's forehead had separated from the more solid rock behind it. Decades later in 1906, Rev. Guy Roberts visited the site and became concerned for the stability of the entire formation, but it was not until 1916 that he was able to enlist the help of quarryman Edward Geddes in designing a solution. Geddes installed turnbuckles to secure the forehead from further forward movement, and yearly visits were then made. In 1945 the New Hampshire legislature made the Old Man the state's official emblem, with a Highway Department budget for its maintenance. In this way things continued successfully through the 20th century (Kostecke 1975: 41-48).

Another threat to the Notch's natural environment was proposed construction of Interstate 93 through the narrow glacial valley as a full four-lane highway. Construction approached North Woodstock from the south, and it was apparent that such development would destroy the Notch as a park. Preservation once more became an issue. After being declared a National Landmark by the US Congress in 1973, the Notch gained a reprieve in 1974 when Congress also allowed interstate highways to be two-lane parkways. That solution was adopted, and by the end of the 20th century the scenery and ambiance of Franconia Notch had been protected about as much as human effort could accomplish.

*Chapter 19*

# The Great Floods – and After

The 19th century ended with major Pemigewasset River floods in 1895 and 1896 (Chapter 14). The Pemigewasset had always been prone to flooding, but extensive logging in its upper reaches – along the East Branch, Moosilauke Brook, the Mad River and Beebe River, made the river level fluctuate even more. On the river basin's steep northern slopes forest had fed water into streams more evenly over the summer and slowed and absorbed runoff in the spring and during storms. By the 1890s, bare slopes caused summer flow to slacken more than it had before, forcing the mills downstream at Manchester to close for some time in 1896, even after those mills had been flooded just months before (Hoyt 1990: 325).

In 1903 a new dam was in place across the Pemigewasset at Eastman Falls in Franklin, built to generate electricity. This raised the level of the river for some eight miles above the dam in times of flood, affecting low lying land in Hill and Sanbornton. In January, 1910, two days of rain falling on snow raised river levels dramatically, which broke up the river ice, causing it to be carried down to the new dam. The track of the Northern Railroad's Bristol Branch was flooded several feet deep and ice raked the shorelines. According to the *Bristol Enterprise*:

> *The long* [Union or Belknap] *covered bridge connecting Hill village with Sanbornton was badly damaged, the curved braces running down onto the piers were entirely broken off at each end . . . It is thought that had it not been for the foresight of the Sanbornton selectmen in chaining their end of the bridge . . . with a heavy wire rope to a tree in John Brown's field, their end would have gone down. The selectmen are to repair the bridge as well as possible and allow light travel on it but no heavy teams . . . The ice is piled almost mountain high above and below the bridge.*

**Top: The ice jam at the Union Bridge above Eastman Falls, 1910. Bottom: How the ice
flood impacted the shoreline.** *Evelyn Corliss Auger Collection*

The Sanbornton selectmen's repair of Union Bridge (Chapter 5), lasted until March 22, 1913, when, in "the biggest freshet known in years,"

> . . . the ice went out of the Pemigewasset River carrying with it the old covered bridge connecting . . . Hill and Sanbornton. The water rose to a great height and the big bridge, which was about 300 ft. long, left the piers at about 9:30 a.m. Saturday, and sailed majestically down the river, . . . where it lodged against the ice. . . . The morning train passed safely over the rails and about an hour after, the track and highway was completely submerged, cutting off Hill from the rest of the world. The railroad tracks were carried several rods from the roadbed and telegraph poles were carried off. No trains were run on the branch from Saturday until Tuesday night. . . .
>
> The bridge was burned where it lodged, to prevent further damage, as great fears were felt for the great dam at Franklin . . . many of the older people of Hill have expressed a great deal of sorrow on account of the old bridge, which was built in 1865 . . . (The Bristol Enterprise, March, 1913).

By 1914 a new steel bridge had replaced the old covered one, but although it was higher, the approaches to it still dropped to the floodplain. It was safely above another ice flood in 1915, which submerged some four miles of railroad track and paralyzed rail service for three days. "The highway at the Gulf was about 8 feet under water, and the highway at the Eddy above Hill was about 15 feet under water, making traffic impossible between Bristol and Franklin."[9]

Probably due to the Eastman Falls dam, Hill was flooded by the Pemigewasset again in 1919, 1923, and 1925; in the last case flooding a lumber camp and forcing people to flee in the night.

## The Great Flood of 1927

A tropical storm hit the Pemigewasset Valley on Thursday, November 3 and Friday, November 4, of 1927, dropping from five to ten inches of rain on the steep slopes of the surrounding mountains in the space of 24 hours.

---

[9] Evelyn Auger of Sanbornton provided photos and the Hill Historical Society collected documentation on this sequence of events.

According to the *Plymouth Record* newspaper, streams and rivers rose quickly, reaching the full height of the flood by 6 p.m. Friday. At the bridge between Holderness and Plymouth the Pemigewasset was 30 feet deep – 6 feet over the very top of the gauge.

Along the East Branch at Lincoln the village was not much affected, but no water was reaching the Parker-Young Co. mills, because dams and penstocks were either by-passed or washed out. At one dam the East Branch cut a new channel through the forest, taking a quarter mile of railroad track with it. At Woodstock the West Branch washed out a bridge on Lost River Road and the raging Pemigewasset destroyed a steel railroad bridge.

In Campton four bridges were destroyed: the old West Campton covered bridge across the Pemigewasset, the bridge at Branch Stream, the "Turkey Jim" Bridge on the Pemigewasset, and the Blaisdell Bridge across the Beebe River. "Turkey Jim" Cummings lost not just a bridge, but hundreds of his large flock, which he was about to sell for Thanksgiving.

The Beebe River reached a flood level never before seen – eight feet deep in the new finishing mill of the Draper Corporation and nine to ten feet deep over the railroad track (Chapter 17). Houses and the store in the company town were three to eight feet deep in water, the garage was damaged and the wall of the community center collapsed. In West Campton a road was washed out 20 to 30 feet deep and was being called "another Lost River." At Livermore Falls the high iron bridge was safe, but the Parker-Young Pulp Mill (formerly J.E. Henry) was flooded, with water pouring out of the windows and part of the dam destroyed.

At Plymouth the Baker River was flowing over the railroad track and was one foot deep on the floor of the old Peg Mill. Houses on the intervale in Plymouth and Holderness were deeply flooded and people were rescued by boat. Buildings – including large barns, were washed down river. The Pemigewasset was described as a "mighty yellow flood rushing past at a speed of ten miles per hour" (*The Plymouth Record*, November 12, 1927). For a time all access to Plymouth was cut off. The high water mark was six feet above the spike marking 1869's flood.

The Pemigewasset Valley rail line was severely damaged for over half of its 21 mile length, with track washed out and bridges destroyed. The B&M was damaged system-wide, and the Pemigewasset branch was lower in priority than restoration of the main line (Ibid).

A hydro-electric dam had been built at Ayres Island on the east-west stretch of the Pemigewasset between New Hampton and Bristol in 1922. Water was flowing ten feet above the top of the dam and there was fear downriver that the dam would fail and flood everything in the valley below. It held, and later was built even higher.

At Hill the flood was greater than any other in the town's history. The village was completely cut off for some 24 hours, electricity was cut for a week, and rail service was out for over three days. Sheep which had been grazing on Foster Island in the Pemigewasset were swept away (*The Bristol Enterprise*, November 10, 1927).

**The steel railroad bridge at Woodstock was pushed aside by the 1927 flood.** *Upper Pemigewasset Historical Society*

## The Winter Flood of 1936

Between March 9th and 22nd two heavy rain storms fell on the winter's accumulated ice and snow. The first two-day storm caused rising water and ice, which stopped the B&M's southbound express train just one mile from Plymouth station. Some twenty passengers and the crew had to be rescued in boats manned by the Plymouth Fire Department. As the last person left the passenger car, flood water had risen to the second step.

The Baker River flowed through the highway bridge at left and railroad bridge at right, Plymouth, 1927. *Plymouth Historical Society*

By the time of the flood of 1936, both bridges over the Baker River had been replaced by steel spans, and resisted water surging even higher than in 1927. *Plymouth Historical Society*

North of Plymouth, the Beebe River village was flooded once again, but water did not rise as high as in 1927. The second heavy rainstorm, just one week after the first, brought the greatest flood ever seen from Plymouth south along the Pemigewasset. Especially at the confluence of the Baker and Pemigewasset rivers the water exceeded 1927 levels. It flowed well over the Baker's new steel highway and railroad bridges, and at the Peg Mill it was more than a foot higher than in 1927. The Pemigewasset rose to lap the bottom of the new steel bridge between Holderness and Plymouth, it inundated the intervale and flooded houses there up to the second floor (*The Plymouth Record Citizen*,March 26, 1986). A strange event occurred at the railroad station:

> *The freight cars on the tracks . . . were standing in several feet of water and due to combustion a car of lime caught fire. Members of the Plymouth Fire Department rowed out in boats armed with pails and extinguished the blazes, thus eliminating the danger . . . to the other cars (Ibid).*

Flooding on the Plymouth-Holderness intervale, 1936. *Plymouth Historical Society*

Newspapers were delivered to Holderness by truck and then carried across to Plymouth by boat. Many people were stranded in Plymouth, more than sixty staying in the courthouse after all the hotels had sold out. In Ashland, at the Packard Woolen Mill, water of the Squam River poured fourteen feet high through the dye room, destroying machinery, dye kilns and other equipment.

Further south the Pemigewasset reached the level of the steel bridge between Sanbornton and Hill. Hill Village was completely surrounded by water. There was fear that the Ayres Island Dam at Bristol would not hold; it had held in 1927, but was built even higher in 1930. New Hampton's old covered Pemigewasset Bridge had been replaced at that time by a higher steel structure because the older bridge was below the new dam's height.

At Franklin water surged over the Eastman Falls dam, swept three houses down the river, and flooded low lying parts of the city. More than 100 families needed temporary shelter. The Sulloway Hosiery Mills and Stevens Woolen Mills were badly damaged (Cummings 1936: 14).

River Street in Franklin was flooded in 1936. *Evelyn Corliss Auger Collection*

*The Hurricane of 1938*

There were flood waters again in 1938, but accompanied by the high winds of a hurricane, the likes of which had not visited the Pemigewasset Valley since 1869. Trees in the forest, in woodlots, and along village streets had not been tested by such high wind for 70 years, and the impact was devastating.[10]

It rained for four days beginning September 18, raising rivers and streams, and also soaking the soil holding tree roots. Then on September 21, a hurricane with 80 mile per hour wind made landfall in southern New England. The storm itself was moving at 50 miles per hour, making the impact of its wind closer to 130 mph when it first touched land. The hurricane tracked to the north-west, with its highest wind of some 100 mph hitting central New Hampshire on the storm's east side (Long 2016: 38-47). Historian Eva Speare described the impact:

> *The atmosphere shed a peculiar glare about three o'clock in the afternoon. Then the wind began to blow . . . By six o'clock, limbs began to break off the shade trees while the wind increased to a roar. All night the hurricane raged, damaging houses, barns and forests with terrific velocity.*
>
> *When morning dawned, the havoc was too astonishing. The earth was so soaked that century old elms and maples fell, pulling their roots from the ground. Every street was blocked by its shade trees . . . The forests were a tangle of broken, uprooted and topless logs. Salvage was almost hopeless, because the wood was filled with coarse sand that dulls the saws in the mills. . . . a salt spray covered everything, mingled with finely ground leaves that dried to a crust that demanded scrubbing to remove from walls and windows of the houses.*
>
> *Electric wires were tangled among the fallen poles; telephones were silenced for days.* (Speare 1988: 156-57).

---

[10] Residents will remember Hurricane Irene in 2011, but that storm's damage was more due to rain, than to wind.

Men clear a tree on Route 3 in Plymouth after the hurricane. *Plymouth Historical Society*

More rain fell in the upper Pemigewasset Valley than at Plymouth, and the river quickly rose to flood level. At Woodstock the Fairview covered bridge was carried away. Damage to the Pemigewasset Valley railroad needed to be repaired yet again.

Overall, destruction of the forest was the Pemigewasset Valley's greatest problem. State-wide, 70% of the downed timber was white pine, and sugar maple suffered badly as well. Slopes facing south-east received the strongest gusts, and in those locations much of the forest was down. In the Hubbard Brook Valley in Thornton and Woodstock one such slope lost 82% of its tree cover (Long 2016: 190).

Woodlot owners and maple sugar producers were heavily impacted. There were not enough saw mills to handle the downed trees before insects would damage the wood, so in the 1938-39 winter an effort was made to haul logs out onto frozen ponds, where they would be protected in the water after ice-out. There were 260 such "wet sites" around the state (Ibid: 160). Saw mills could then handle those logs during the following summer.

The price of finished lumber would have plummeted were it not for quick action by the Federal Government in creating the Northeast Timber Salvage Administration, which set a price floor and bought salvaged lumber from woodlot owners at that price. Much of the lumber salvaged from the 1938 hurricane was used in World War II for military construction and for shipping containers.

## Flood Control and Challenges for Hill

Flood damage from the 1936 flood and 1938 hurricane was most severe in the Merrimack Valley, where major industries were affected. Their influence and the general welfare demanded flood control, and the most appropriate site was determined to be the Pemigewasset Valley above Franklin. A flood control dam would be built with a dry bed reservoir behind it. In times of flood the dam would be closed and the reservoir would fill, but according to the design, Hill Village would then be under water. The Army Corps of Engineers would build the dam, and the State Planning and Development Commission would help Hill Village cope with moving to a new location. In Hill, everyone's agreement and participation was needed (Stiles 1942: 11-12) .

The Commission in the person of its director Fred Clark, sketched out a plan for a new village on higher ground above the old one, met with selectmen and townspeople, and got general agreement. The Army engineers determined the value of each resident's current property for the condemnation payment they would receive. Hill created a non-profit corporation to buy the 85 acres of land for their new village, which included both public land and house lots. People who were to move chose their house lots from a map and all paid the same equalized price. Town Meeting gave the selectmen the authority to lay out streets and plan utilities. By 1941 streets and the water system were in place, as were the town hall and school, and some 30 new houses were already occupied. Some houses were moved up from the old village. Both the town and the homeowners had taken on debt, because what they received for their old property did not pay for their new land and buildings, but they were all in about the same position and they had stayed together as a community. Dan Stiles summed it up: "the first thing you must remember as you look at this new village is that it is the work of about fifty families, none of whom were wealthy" (Ibid: 57).

Old Hill Village is seen across the Pemigewasset in this view from Sanbornton. Note that the Hill side of the river is lower than the Sanbornton side. *Evelyn Corliss Auger Collection*

The Franklin Falls flood control dam, looking north-east into Sanbornton. *D. Heyduk*

The Franklin Falls dam was completed in 1943. Along the Pemigewasssset above the dam, parkland was created in the floodplain on the east side of the river, including the millennia-old outlet of Blake Brook in New Hampton, which was the "long carrying place" for portaging canoes around the bend and rapids at Bristol.

Hill Historical Society has placed interpretive markers in the old village to show where buildings stood. By the time the dam was proposed, the Bristol Branch railroad was permanently discontinued due to damage sustained in the 1936 flood. The steel bridge that spanned the Pemigewasset between Hill and Sanbornton, and held through the 1927, 1936, and 1938 floods, was taken down for scrap in the early 1950s. The Republican covered bridge across the Pemigewasset at Franklin survived the 1927 flood, but was deemed inadequate for heavy traffic, and replaced by a steel and masonry bridge in 1931.

The Republican Bridge across the Pemigewasset at Franklin. *Evelyn Corliss Auger Collection*

## Chapter 20

# Beginnings and Endings

About the time that Franconia Notch became a state reservation, Sugar Hill and the Notch began to attract winter ski visitors. Pecketts-on-Sugar-Hill (Chapter 18), offered winter lodging and imaginative recreation for its guests, including bringing them from the Littleton station in sleighs. As their promotional brochure painted the nighttime scene:

> . . . we tucked ourselves snugly under the generous supply of buffalo robes in the big pungs, and were off for the six mile sleigh-ride to Pecketts-on-Sugar-Hill. Up, up, over the Littleton Hills, the lights of the lanterns showing the smooth, white road before us, the high drifts piled on either side of the road, and the shadowy outlines of the forest. Then down along the Gale River valley, by the twinkling lights of a tiny mountain village, we swiftly sped, until, after climbing still higher than before, we drew up before the hospitable inn.

Pecketts offered sleigh outings to scenic spots like Coppermine Camp, Birch Knoll, Bridal Veil Falls, and Franconia Notch, where guests could snowshoe, ski, and sled down hills, eat a hot outdoor picnic or afternoon tea, and perhaps return by torchlight.

> With shouts of glee and merry laughter, we donned our skis and snowshoes. Fascinating secrets of the woodlands were waiting to be revealed. Tiny tracks of partridges . . . and the track of a large bob-cat. Then we were off for adventures on the Red and Blue Trails, but at lunch time were back eager for the goodies which we knew were awaiting us. Did ever anything taste so good to winter picnickers as the broiled steak with fried onions and fried potatoes, griddlecakes, accompanied by thick, hot maple syrup and coffee, all cooked out-of-doors. . . ? (Hotel brochure)

In 1929, daughter Kate Peckett recruited German ski instructors to offer lessons to guests, and to local people as well – one of the first ski schools. Skiing became popular with local boys, who soon were some of the first experts and instructors. She helped found the Franconia Ski Club and raised funds to build the Richard Taft Trail in 1932-33 - the first downhill trail at Cannon Mountain in Franconia Notch (McPhaul 2011: 13-19).

The ski industry developed rapidly in the 1930s. In 1935 the legislature created a commission to build Cannon Mountain's Aerial Tramway. The project attracted much news coverage as Route 3 was re-routed to create the tramway base and parking, and as the up to 115-foot high towers were installed on the mountain. New ski trails were cut at the same time. The tramway opened in June of 1938, and some 100,000 people rode up to the top of Cannon in that first summer (Ibid: 38-40).

The Cannon Aerial Tramway, with Route 3 and parking at bottom.
*Franconia Paper Company*

**At first, there were not many trails.** *Franconia Paper Company*

In the 1930s, the Boston & Maine Railroad began to run "ski trains" up to Plymouth, North Woodstock and Linclon, all of which had recently created trails, and to Littleton, where skiers could go to Pecketts or to Cannon. A Plymouth newspaper account from January, 1934 gives a sense of the scale of this phenomenon:

> *Excellent snow conditions greeted the Boston & Maine Snow Train as it steamed into Plymouth Sunday morning about 11:30 with its fourteen cars drawn by two engines and over six hundred snow fans aboard. . . . The Plymouth Sports Club and the Chamber of Commerce cooperated in welcoming the snow train enthusiasts and in making their visit here as pleasant as possible. Several members of the Sports Club . . . drove to Concord Sunday morning and boarded the train. They distributed circulars on which were printed the various trails and suggestions for spending the day enjoyably.*

*Tickets were sold in advance for the various trucks going to the Golf Course, Mt. Prospect Trail and Tenney Hill. . . . Some of the foremost skiers in the country were here Sunday – some went to Tenney Hill and others remained here in town to try trails recently opened by the Plymouth Sports Club.*

Plymouth Sports Club members were on hand at the golf course to help novices, and they also served a light lunch.

Harry Mellett of the Russell House in North Woodstock wrote that the Appalachian Mountain Club group of 76 that he hosted at his hotel "would not have considered North Woodstock had it not been for the new ski trails; and they were greatly pleased with the Russell Mountain trails." The overnight temperature reached 31 degrees below zero, but the Russell House had installed more heat, and the skiers stayed warm. Mellett wrote, "Of the money received, only $11.75 went out of state, while about $200 was spent in North Woodstock and Plymouth." He thought it good business to encourage winter sports.

Skiers at Plymouth about to depart in trucks for the various ski trails of the area.
*Plymouth Historical Society*

Plymouth added other ski areas in the 1930s: Frontenac, Mount Pero and Huckins Hill. Wendy's Slope opened there in 1940, with Swiss instructor Wendelin Hilty (Davis 2008: 14). The Waterville Inn was open in winter for the first time in 1936 and became a winter sport center from that time on (Bean 1983: 1). By 1941, North Woodstock had trails at Grandview Mountain with a ski tow, Lincoln had the Coolidge Mountain ski slope, Sugar Hill had added the Hamilton slope, and Franconia had the Forest Hill Hotel slope and Scragg Mountain trails, in addition to Cannon Mountain (McPhaul 2011: 70-71).

Ski areas did not expand during the World War II years, but then facilities grew from the late 1940s through the 1960s. The Waterville Inn, which maintained its intimate character, installed two T-bar lifts, and attracted more visitors in winter than in summer. Mary Anne Hyde Saul remembered skiing there in 1962, when it had just "a small base lodge for mocha, lunch and warmth," and "slopes and trails on Snow's Mountain," and where a lift ticket cost $1.50 a day (Saul 2013: 92).

Many small slopes closed in the 1970s, while large areas such as Cannon Mountain, and especially Loon Mountain in Lincoln, and Waterville Valley - which developed as resorts with condominiums, became major ski destinations. Part of their success was due to convenient access from Interstate 93, which reached the upper Pemigewasset Valley in the early 1970s.

At the same time, there were endings. The railroad to the Profile House in Franconia Notch stopped operating in 1921 - even before the hotel burned, and rail service to Bethlehem Village ended in 1925 (Lindsell 2000: 335). That village dwindled as hotels closed, or burned and were not replaced. Contents of the venerable Sinclair House, where President Grant had stayed, were sold at auction in 1976. North Woodstock's elegant Alpine Hotel closed in 1966. The third Pemigewasset House in Plymouth, built in 1913, was torn down in 1958.

In Lincoln, the Parker-Young paper mill became the Marcalus Manufacturing Company mill, and then Franconia Paper Company, before closing down in 1970 (Gove 2012: 258, 272). The Boston & Maine Railroad stopped passenger service from Plymouth to Lincoln in 1953, and ended passenger trains to Plymouth in 1959. B&M went bankrupt in 1970 and the state acquired the track to keep manufacturing alive in Lincoln, but freight service ended in 1973, when wash-outs cut the line (Ibid: 270-273).

Up and down the Pemigewasset Valley, from the 1950s to the 1970s, industries disappeared. In Franklin, the J.P. Stevens textile mill, the last of the city's large industries, closed in 1970. The paper mills of Lincoln, Ashland, and Franklin closed down too. The Beebe River company town where bobbins were made lost its mill in 1968.

In the countryside, old cellar holes and stone walls bear testimony to the many farms, schools, and whole communities that once existed there. Farming and hosting summer visitors had transitioned over two centuries, but those threads came to an end during the late 1900s as well.

In 2003, the "Old Man of the Mountain" – rock ledges which had been ingeniously kept together since 1916 by turnbuckles, and later - epoxy, succumbed to erosion. Charles Greenleaf, who owned the Profile House for many years, had said: "I have always believed that the whole formation would someday all go together," and he was right (Hancock 1984: 41).

A train crew on the Bristol Branch, Northern Railroad. *Bristol Historical Society*

Harold Glover Haying

Bringing in the hay, Plymouth Intervale. *Plymouth Historical Society*

While some things were ending, others were growing. Plymouth Normal School became Plymouth Teachers College in 1939, and with the expansion of its programs - Plymouth State College in 1963. The student population grew from under 300 in 1951, when Dr. Harold Hyde became president, to over 3,000 in 1977, under his administration (Hoyt 1990: 347-49). In 2003, the college became Plymouth State University, and today has over 4,200 students, over half of whom are in graduate study. The university inaugurated the Museum of the White Mountains in 2013, focusing on all time periods and all subjects in that geographic area.

In 1955 the US Forest Service began to research stream flow in the Hubbard Brook Valley in Thornton and Woodstock. The valley is a basin surrounded by mountains on the Pemigewasset River's west side, and includes nine separate watersheds feeding Hubbard Brook. Research then continued to ecological studies of how each watershed responded to different forest uses, and in 1968, the first identification and scientific measurement of acid rain. Hubbard Brook researchers also documented how clear-cutting increases run-off - feeding floods, and how climate change is affecting the forest (Holmes 2016: 11-16, 114-17).

The Squam Lakes Natural Science Center in Holderness was founded in 1966, with a 180 acre former farm as its campus. It opened its exhibits of live wild native animals, all of which were rescued or rehabilitated, in 1969. The center's exhibits and natural science educational programs expanded steadily, reaching more than 70,000 in-person visitors, and others via off-site programs during the 2019 summer season.

In addition to the growth of educational and research activities since mid-century, the valley has seen other changes. From the 1950s to this writing the valley's population has steadily increased. The boarding houses and big hotels of the late 1800s and early 1900s have been replaced by second homes. As industry declined and the valley's natural resources gained protection, the land and the river recovered. Where a pulp mill and massive dam once dominated Livermore Falls, the Pemigewasset River now flows free and children swim at a state park beach. Where loggers once clear-cut thousands of acres and forest fires burned, people enjoy the White Mountain National Forest – managed for multiple uses, including sustainable forestry.

History also is a part of life in the valley today. Historical societies, preservation societies, educational centers, libraries and museums preserve, but also actively expand and share the record of the valley's past. The New Hampshire Division of Historical Resources and other researchers continuously add pieces to the Pemigewasset Valley's story – both prehistoric and historic. Together with historians, artists, photographers, and other chroniclers of prior years, they make it possible for us to steadily expand our understanding of the valley from its glacial beginnings to the present.

Lest we forget - the Pemigewasset flooded during Hurricane Irene in 2011. This sign shows that the high water mark on the intervale south of Plymouth was above the railroad track (at mid-photo). The river is in the background below the hills to the east.
*D. Heyduk*

In spring, 2019, the Pemigewasset exposed an old log crib dam at Livermore Falls.
*D. Heyduk*

# Bibliography

Abbott, Karl P. 1950. *Open for the Season*. Garden City, NY: Doubleday & Co.

*America's Textile Reporter*. 1961. "New Hampshire's Dole Company Is One of America's Oldest." September 7

Ashland Centennial Committee. 1968. *Ashland, New Hampshire Centennial, 1868 – 1968*. Ashland, NH

Auger, Evelyn Corliss. 1976. "The Men Who Fought" in *Revolutionary Sanbornton*, Ralph Sleeper, Ed. Tilton, NH: Sanbornton Bridge Press

Baketel, Leon Burt. 1901. "Ashland: Its Past and Present." *The Granite Monthly*. Vol.30: 123-143

Batchellor, Albert Stillman. 1895. *Town Charters Granted within the Present Limits of New Hampshire Vol XXV*. Concord, NH: Edward N. Pearson, Public Printer

Batchellor, Albert Stillman. 1896. *Township Grants of Lands in New Hampshire Included in the Masonian Patent Vol XXVIII*. Concord, NH: Edward N. Pearson, Public Printer

Bean, Grace Hughes. 1983. *The Town at the end of the road: a history of Waterville Valley*. Canaan, NH: Phoenix Publishing

Benton, C. and S.F. Barry. 1837. *A Statistical View of the Number of Sheep in the Several Towns and Counties in . . . New Hampshire*. Cambridge: Folsom, Wells and Thurston

Bethlehem Board of Trade. 1910. "Bethlehem, New Hampshire."

Blanshard, Roberta Yerkes. 1982. *Moses Thurston Runnels: The Man.* Sanbornton, NH: Sanbornton Historical Society

Boisvert, Richard. 2013. "The First Geologists: Late Pleistocene Settlement of the White Mountains." *The Geology of New Hampshire's White Mountains.* Lyme, NH: Durand Press

Borneman, Walter R. 2006. *The French and Indian War.* New York, NY: Harper-Collins Publishers

Bouton, Nathaniel. 1875. *Documents and Records Relating to Towns in New Hampshire Vol IX.* Concord, NH: Charles C. Pearson, State Printer

Broad, Marjorie E. 1992."The Old Hotels and Inns of Campton" MS. Campton, NH: Campton Historical Society

Broad, Marjorie E. 1998. "Thornton Memories" MS. Campton, NH: Campton Historical Society

Bruns, Paul E. 1969. *A New Hampshire Everlasting and Unfallen.* Concord, NH: Society for the Protection of New Hampshire Forests

Caduto, Michael J. 2003. *A Time Before New Hampshire.* Hanover, NH: University Press of New England

Cather, Willa and Georgine Milmine. 1993. *The Life of Mary Baker Eddy and the History of Christian Science.* Lincoln: University of Nebraska Press

Cheney, Sterle Armstrong. 1966. "Industries along the Mad River from the Early 1860s." *The Plymouth Record*, June 9

Child, Hamilton. 1886. *Gazetteer of Grafton County, N.H. 1709-1886.* Syracuse, NY: The Syracuse Journal Company

Clark, Eleanor J. 1897. "Glimpses of Holderness." *The Granite Monthly* 23: 279-285

Colby, Fred Myron. 1881. "Holderness and the Livermores." *The Granite Monthly* 4: 175-181

Concord & Montreal Railroad. 1890. *Summer Outings in the Old Granite State.* Passenger Department

Conrad, Justus. 1897. "The Town of Woodstock." *The Granite Monthly 23:* 11-23

Cummings, Lew A. 1936. *Flood Waters New Hampshire, 1936.* Manchester, NH: Lew A Cummings Co.

Curren, Thomas S. 1988. *A Bicentennial History of Bridgewater, New Hampshire, 1788-1988.* Bridgewater, NH: Bridgewater Bicentennial Committee

Curren, Thomas S. 1998. *Old Home Day in New Hampshire, 1899 – 1998.* Concord, NH: Inherit New Hampshire

Davis, Jeremy K. 2008. *Lost Ski Areas of the White Mountains.* Charleston, SC: The History Press

Dole, John. 1991. "The History and Development of Dole Mill." Presentation at the Campton Historical Society, April 1

Doner, Lisa. 2013. "Probing the Deep and Mysterious Past of Quincy Bog." *Quincy Bog Notes* 21, no. 1

Draper Corporation. 1965. "Beebe River, Fortieth Anniversary."

Durrie, George Henry. 1859. "Gathering Wood." Oil on canvas 22 ¼ x 30 in. Collection of Shelburne Museum, gift of Mr. and Mrs. Dunbar W. Bostwick 1958 – 3152. Photograph by Andy Dubak

Eastman, Edson C. 1858. *White Mountain Guidebook.* Concord, MA

Edgerly, Asa S. 1909. *He Did It, or The Life of a New England Boy.* San Francisco, CA: H.S. Crocker Company

English, Ben, Jr. and Jane English. 2005. *Our Mountain Trips, Part 1 – 1899 – 1908.* Littleton, NH: Bondcliff Books

Eusden, Dykstra and Woodrow Thompson. 2013. "Forces that Shaped the White Mountains." *The Geology of New Hampshire's White Mountains.* Lyme, NH: Durand Press

Federal Energy Regulatory Commission. 1990. *Livermore Falls Hydroelectric Project.* Washington, DC

Garneau, Albert G. 2002. *Official History of Franklin, New Hampshire.* Concord, NH: Wallace Press Reprographics

Garvin, Donna-Belle, Ed. 2006. *Consuming Views: Art & Tourism in the White Mountains, 1850 – 1900.* Concord, NH: New Hampshire Historical Society

Goodrich, Arthur L. 1916. *The Waterville Valley: A History, Description and Guide.*

Goodrich, Nathaniel L. 1952. *The Waterville Valley: A Story of a Resort in the New Hampshire Mountains.* Lunenburg, VT: The North Country Press

Gove, Bill. 2006. *Logging Railroads along the Pemigewasset River.* Littleton, NH: Bondcliff Books

Gove, Bill. 2012. *J.E. Henry's Logging Railroads.* Littleton, NH: Bondcliff Books

Gray & Pape, Inc. 2015. "Cultural Landscape Report and Environmental Assessment, Livermore Falls, Grafton County, N.H." Providence, RI

Haight, Jr., John McV. 1941. *A History of Bridgewater and Bristol, N.H., 1780-1880.* Bristol, NH: Musgrove Printing House

Hammond, Isaac W. 1882. *Documents Relating to Towns in New Hampshire, Vol XI.* Concord, NH: Parsons B Cogswell, State Printer

Hammond, Isaac W. 1883. *Documents Relating to Towns in New Hampshire, Vol XII.* Concord, NH: Parsons B. Cogswell, State Printer

Hammond, Isaac W. 1884. *Documents Relating to Towns in New Hampshire, Vol XIII.* Concord, NH: Parsons B. Cogswell, State Printer

285

Hancock, Frances Ann Johnson. 1984. *Saving the Great Stone Face: The Chronicle of the Old Man of the Mountain*. Franconia Area Heritage Council

Henry, James Everell, II. 2016. *The Life of James Everell Henry*. Mike Dickerman, Ed. Littleton, NH: Bondcliff Books

Heyduk, Daniel. 2015. *Meredith Chronicles*. Charleston, SC: The History Press

Heyduk, Daniel. 2017. *Stories in the History of New Hampshire's Lakes Region and Pemigewasset Valley*. North Charleston, SC: CreateSpace Independent Publishing

Hill Historical Society. 1991. *Hill Village on the Pemigewasset: Commemorating the 50th Anniversary of the Relocation of the Village of Hill, New Hampshire*. Hill, NH: Hill Historical Society

Hodges, George. 1907. *Holderness: An Account of the Beginnings of a New Hampshire Town*. Cambridge, MA: The Riverside Press

Holmes, Richard T. and Gene E. Likens. 2016. *Hubbard Brook: The Story of a Forest Ecosystem*. New Haven, CT: Yale University Press

Howarth, William. 1982. *Thoreau in the Mountains: Writings by Henry David Thoreau*. New York, NY: Farrar, Straus, Giroux

Hoyt, Joseph Bixby. 1990. *The Baker River Towns*. New York, NY: Vantage Press

Jarvis, Kimberly A. 2007. *Franconia Notch and the Women Who Saved It*. Hanover, NH: University of New Hampshire Press

Kostecke, Diane M., Editor. 1975. *Franconia Notch: An In-Depth Guide*. Concord, NH: Society for the Protection of New Hampshire Forests

Lawson, Russell M. 2015. *The Sea Mark: Captain John Smith's Voyage to New England*. Lebanon, NH: University Press of New England

Lee, Percy Maxim and John G. Lee. 1971. *Family Reunion: An Incomplete Account of the Maxim – Lee Family History*. Privately Printed

Lindsell, Robert M. 2000. *The Rail Lines of Northern New England*. Pepperell, MA: Branch Line Press

LogginginLincoln. 2019. "Woodstock." www.*logginginlincoln.com*. Lincoln, NH: Upper Pemigewasset Historical Society & Rick Russack

Long, Stephen. 2016. *Thirty-Eight: The Hurricane that Transformed New England*. New Haven: Yale University Press

Lyford, James Otis. 1912. *History of the Town of Canterbury, New Hampshire*. Concord, NH: The Rumford Press

March, Arthur F. 1997. *Franconia and Sugar Hill*. Dover, NH: Arcadia Publishing Company

McCormack, Louise S. 2017. *The Draper & Maynard Sporting Goods Company*. CreateSpace Independent Publishing

McMillin, Helen F. 1923. "Making Needles at Hill, The Story of an Indomitable Spirit." *The Granite Monthly* 55: 533-536

McNair, Andrew H. 1949. *The Geologic Story: Franconia Notch and the Flume*. Concord, NH: NH State Planning and Development Commission

McPhaul, Meghan McCarthy. 2011. *A History of Cannon Mountain: Trails, Tales and Skiing Legends*. Charleston, SC: The History Press

Mead, Edgar T. 1975. *The Up-Country Line: Boston, Concord & Montreal RR*. Brattleboro, VT: Stephen Green Press

Merrill, Eliphalet and Phinehas Merrill. 1817. "Franconia." *Gazetteer of the State of New Hampshire*. Exeter, NH: C. Norris & Co.

Merrill, Pauline S., John C. Gowan, and others. 1977. *A Small Gore of Land*. New Hampton, NH: New Hampton Town History Committee

Morrill, Mildred T., Harriette W. Kenney and Lee-Ann Forsyth. 1976. *Hill: The Old and The New*. Hill, NH: Hill Historical Society

Moses, George H. 1895. "New Hampshire's Youngest City: A Sketch of Franklin." *The Granite Monthly*, Vol. 18: 153-179

Musgrove, Richard W. 1904. *History of the Town of Bristol, New Hampshire*. Bristol, NH: R.W. Musgrove

Musgrove, Richard W. 1921. *Autobiography of Capt. Richard W. Musgrove*. Bristol, NH: Mary D. Musgrove

National Park Service. 1996. *Pemigewasset Wild and Scenic River Study*. Boston, MA: New England System Support Office

New Hampshire Board of Agriculture. 1890. "Secure a Home in New Hampshire, where Comfort, Health, and Prosperity Abound." Manchester, NH: John C. Clark, Public Printer

New Hampshire Board of Agriculture. 1901. *Report of the Board of Agriculture*. Manchester, NH: Arthur E Clark, Public Printer

New Hampshire Board of Agriculture. 1908. "New Hampshire Farms for Summer Homes." Concord, NH: The Rumford Printing Company

New Hampshire Dept. of Environmental Services. 2019. "Environmental Fact Sheet: The Pemigewasset River." Concord, NH

Nichols, Minnie S. 1979. *Those Good Old Golden Rule Days*. Center Harbor, NH: Center Harbor Historical Society

*One Hundred and Fiftieth Anniversary of the Granting of the Charter of the Town of Plymouth*. 1913. Plymouth, NH: The General Committee

Perley, Sidney. 2001. *Historic Storms of New England*. Beverly, MA: Commonwealth Editions

Proctor, Mary A. 1930. *The Indians of the Winnipesaukee and Pemigewasset Valleys.* Franklin, NH: Towne & Robie. Also: Amesbury, MA: Powwow River Books

Railroad Commissioners. 1895, *Annual Report.* Concord, NH: State of New Hampshire

Railroad Commissioners. 1902. *Annual Report.* Concord, NH: State of New Hampshire

Roberts, Aria Cutting. 1964. "General Grant's Wildest Ride 95 Years Ago This Week." *The Plymouth Record.* August 29

Rollins, Frank W. 1902. *Tourists' Guide-Book to the State of New Hampshire.* Concord, NH: The Rumford Press

Ruell, David. 2019. "The Railroad in Ashland." MS of Presentation, Ashland Historical Society

Russack, Rick. 2008. "The Beard Opera House." *Upstream*, summer issue. Lincoln, NH: Upper Pemigewasset Historical Society

Saul, Mary Anne Hyde. 2013. *On the Edge: Growing Up in Plymouth, N.H. 1951-1969.* National Writers Union

Sawyer, Ida T. 2013. *Woodstock History.* MS transcribed by Barbara Avery for the Woodstock 250th anniversary

Scheiber, Harry N. 2011. "Coach, Wagon, and Motor-Truck Manufacture, 1813 – 1928: The Abbot-Downing Company of Concord." *Historical New Hampshire 65, 1; 3-29*

Smith, Jonathan. 1922. "How New Hampshire Raised Her Armies for the Revolution." *The Granite Monthly* 54:7-18)

Speare, Eva A. 1988. *Twenty Decades in Plymouth, New Hampshire.* Somersworth, NH: New England History Press and Plymouth Historical Society. Also 1963, Plymouth Bicentennial Commission

Starbuck, David R. 2006. *The Archeology of New Hampshire.* Durham, NH: University Press of New England

Stearns, Ezra S. 1987. *The History of Plymouth, New Hampshire.* Cambridge, MA: University Press (reprint of original 1906 edition)

Stiles, Dan. 1942. *The Story of Hill, New Hampshire.* Concord, NH: The Sugar Ball Press

Sullivan, Larry. 2019. *For the Accomodation of Man and Beast, The Horse Troughs and Drinking Fountains of the Henry W. Clapp Co. and the Concord Foundry Co.* Warner, NH: The Warner Historical Society

Sweetser, Moses F. 1876. *The White Hills: A Handbook for Travellers.* Boston, MA: James R. Osgood and Co.

The Granite Monthly. 1923. "Franklin: A Town, 1828, . . A City 1896." 55: 147-161

Thomson, M.T., W.B. Gannon, M.P. Thomas, G.S. Hayes and others. 1964. *Historical Floods in New England.* Washington, D.C.: U.S. Government Printing Office

Thoreau, Henry David. 1849. *A Week on the Concord and Merrimack Rivers.* Various editions

Tolles, Bryant F. Jr. 1998. *The Grand Resort Hotels of the White Mountains: A Vanishing Architecture.* Boston, MA: David R. Godine

Town of Bethlehem. 1999. *Bethlehem, New Hampshire: A Bicentennial History.* Littleton, NH: Bondcliff Books

*Upstream.* Newsletter of the Upper Pemigewasset Historical Society. Lincoln, NH: www.logginginlincoln.com

*The Town Register. 1908. Augusta, ME: Mitchell-Cony Co., Inc*

Vermont Historical Society. 2004. "An Era of Great Change: William Jarvis and the Great Sheep Craze." Museum and website exhibit.

Waterman, Laura, and Guy Waterman. 1989. *Forest and Crag.* Boston, MA: Appalachian Mountain Club

Welch, Sarah N. 1972. *A History of Franconia New Hampshire*. Littleton, NH: Courier Printing Co.

Whelton, Paul. 1923. "Lumberjacks Wrestle King Spruce on Mad River." *Boston Sunday Hearald*, April 22

White Mountain National Forest. 1997. "Draft Environmental Impact Statement for the Development of Snowmaking Water Impoundments at Waterville Valley Ski Resort." Laconia, NH

Willey, Isaac. 1868. "The Early History of Campton." *The Centennial Celebration of the Town of Campton, N.H.* Concord, NH: A.G. Jones, Printer

Wilson, Gregory C., Ed. 1999. *Bethlehem, New Hampshire: A Bicentennial History*. Littleton, NH: Bondcliff Books

Wood, Frederic J. 1919. *The Turnpikes of New England*. Boston, MA: Marshall Jones & Company

Made in the USA
Middletown, DE
02 November 2024

63293879R00166